ABOUT THE AUTHOR

CHRIS VOSS is one of the preeminent practitioners and professors of negotiating skills in the world. He is the founder and principal of The Black Swan Group, a consulting firm that provides training and advises Fortune 500 companies through complex negotiations. Voss has taught for many business schools, including the University of Southern California's Marshall School of Business, Georgetown University's McDonough School of Business, Harvard University, MIT's Sloan School of Management, and Northwestern University's Kellogg School of Management, among others. He invites you to visit his company's website at www.blackswanltd.com.

TAHL RAZ uncovers big ideas and great stories that ignite change and growth in people and organizations. He is an award-winning journalist and coauthor of the *New York Times* bestseller *Never Eat Alone*. When not researching or writing, he coaches executives, lectures widely on the forces transforming the new world of work, and serves as an editorial consultant for several national firms. He invites readers to e-mail him at tr@tahlraz.com and to visit his website at www.tahlraz.com.

Praise for *Never Split the Difference*

'This book blew my mind. It's a riveting read, full of instantly actionable advice – not just for high-stakes negotiations, but also for handling everyday conflicts at work and at home.'

Adam Grant, Wharton professor and bestselling author of *Originals* and *Give and Take*

'Emphasizes the importance of emotional intelligence without sacrificing deal-making power. From the pen of a former hostage negotiator – someone who couldn't take no for an answer – which makes it fascinating reading. But it's also eminently practical. In these pages, you will find the techniques for getting the deal you want.'

Daniel H. Pink, bestselling author of *To Sell Is Human* and *Drive*

'Negotiation, as someone once said, is "the art of letting someone else have your own way". It's an art well worth learning. And who better to learn from than Chris Voss, whose skills have saved lives and averted disaster?'

Daily Mail

'An easy read filled with anecdotes from Voss's time in the FBI, and by the end you'll be surprised how much you've learned that you can apply right away.'

'Business Books You Should Be Reading This Summer', World Economic Forum blog

'It is thrilling for me to be able to unreservedly recommend this book.'

HR Director

'Fascinating case studies reinforce Voss's vast experience and credentials in the subject matter . . . The writing is snappy and efficient, but also structured in a way that makes the learning process feel natural and fluid.'

Bookbag

NEVER SPLIT THE DIFFERENCE

NEGOTIATING AS IF YOUR LIFE DEPENDED ON IT

CHRIS VOSS
WITH TAHL RAZ

BUSINESS
BOOKS

9 10 8

Random House Business Books
20 Vauxhall Bridge Road
London SW1V 2SA

Random House Business Books is part of the Penguin Random House group of companies
whose addresses can be found at global.penguinrandomhouse.com.

Penguin
Random House
UK

This paperback edition first published by Random House Business Books in 2017
First published by Random House Business Books in 2016

www.penguin.co.uk

A CIP catalogue record for this book is available from the British Library.

ISBN 9781847941497

Printed and bound by Clays Ltd, St Ives plc

Penguin Random House is committed to a sustainable future
for our business, our readers and our planet. This book is made from
Forest Stewardship Council® certified paper.

MIX
Paper from
responsible sources
FSC® C018179

For my mother and father
who showed me unconditional love
and taught me the values of hard work and integrity

CONTENTS

NEVER
SPLIT THE
DIFFERENCE

CHAPTER 1

THE NEW RULES

I was intimidated.

I'd spent more than two decades in the FBI, including fifteen years negotiating hostage situations from New York to the Philippines and the Middle East, and I was on top of my game. At any given time, there are ten thousand FBI agents in the Bureau, but only one lead international kidnapping negotiator. That was me.

But I'd never experienced a hostage situation so tense, so personal.

"We've got your son, Voss. Give us one million dollars or he dies."

Pause. Blink. Mindfully urge the heart rate back to normal.

Sure, I'd been in these types of situations before. Tons of them. Money for lives. But not like this. Not with my son on the line. Not $1 million. And not against people with fancy degrees and a lifetime of negotiating expertise.

You see, the people across the table—my negotiating counterparts—were Harvard Law School negotiating professors.

I'd come up to Harvard to take a short executive negotiating course, to see if I could learn something from the business world's approach.

It was supposed to be quiet and calm, a little professional development for an FBI guy trying to widen his horizons.

But when Robert Mnookin, the director of the Harvard Negotiation Research Project, learned I was on campus, he invited me to his office for a coffee. Just to chat, he said.

I was honored. And scared. Mnookin is an impressive guy whom I'd followed for years: not only is he a Harvard law professor, he's also one of the big shots of the conflict resolution field and the author of *Bargaining with the Devil: When to Negotiate, When to Fight.*[1]

To be honest, it felt unfair that Mnookin wanted me, a former Kansas City beat cop, to debate negotiation with him. But then it got worse. Just after Mnookin and I sat down, the door opened and another Harvard professor walked in. It was Gabriella Blum, a specialist in international negotiations, armed conflict, and counterterrorism, who'd spent eight years as a negotiator for the Israeli National Security Council and the Israel Defense Forces. The tough-as-nails IDF.

On cue, Mnookin's secretary arrived and put a tape recorder on the table. Mnookin and Blum smiled at me.

I'd been tricked.

"We've got your son, Voss. Give us one million dollars or he dies," Mnookin said, smiling. "I'm the kidnapper. What are you going to do?"

I experienced a flash of panic, but that was to be expected. It never changes: even after two decades negotiating for human lives you still feel fear. Even in a role-playing situation.

I calmed myself down. Sure, I was a street cop turned FBI agent playing against real heavyweights. And I wasn't a genius. But I was in this room for a reason. Over the years I had picked up skills, tactics, and a whole approach to human interaction that had not just helped me save lives but, as I recognize now looking back, had also begun to transform my own life. My years of negotiating had infused everything from how I dealt with customer service reps to my parenting style.

"C'mon. Get me the money or I cut your son's throat right now," Mnookin said. Testy.

I gave him a long, slow stare. Then I smiled.

"How am I supposed to do that?"

Mnookin paused. His expression had a touch of amused pity in it, like a dog when the cat it's been chasing turns around and tries to chase it back. It was as if we were playing different games, with different rules.

Mnookin regained his composure and eyed me with arched brows as if to remind me that we were still playing.

"So you're okay with me killing your son, Mr. Voss?"

"I'm sorry, Robert, how do I know he's even alive?" I said, using an apology and his first name, seeding more warmth into the interaction in order to complicate his gambit to bulldoze me. "I really am sorry, but how can I get you any money right now, much less one million dollars, if I don't even know he's alive?"

It was quite a sight to see such a brilliant man flustered by what must have seemed unsophisticated foolishness. On the contrary, though, my move was anything but foolish. I was employing what had become one of the FBI's most potent negotiating tools: the open-ended question.

Today, after some years evolving these tactics for the private sector in my consultancy, The Black Swan Group, we call this tactic calibrated questions: queries that the other side can respond to but that have no fixed answers. It buys you time. It gives your counterpart the illusion of control—they are the one with the answers and power after all—and it does all that without giving them any idea of how constrained they are by it.

Mnookin, predictably, started fumbling because the frame of the conversation had shifted from how I'd respond to the threat of my son's murder to how the professor would deal with the logistical issues involved in getting the money. How he would solve *my* problems. To every threat and demand he made, I continued to ask how I was supposed to pay him and how was I supposed to know that my son was alive.

After we'd been doing that for three minutes, Gabriella Blum interjected.

"Don't let him do that to you," she said to Mnookin.

"Well, *you* try," he said, throwing up his hands.

Blum dove in. She was tougher from her years in the Middle East. But she was still doing the bulldozer angle, and all she got were my same questions.

Mnookin rejoined the session, but he got nowhere either. His face started to get red with frustration. I could tell the irritation was making it hard to think.

"Okay, okay, Bob. That's all," I said, putting him out of his misery.

He nodded. My son would live to see another day.

"Fine," he said. "I suppose the FBI *might* have something to teach us."

I had done more than just hold my own against two of Harvard's distinguished leaders. I had taken on the best of the best and come out on top.

But was it just a fluke? For more than three decades, Harvard had been the world epicenter of negotiating theory and practice. All I knew about the techniques we used at the FBI was that they worked. In the twenty years I spent at the Bureau we'd designed a system that had successfully resolved almost every kidnapping we applied it to. But we didn't have grand theories.

Our techniques were the products of experiential learning; they were developed by agents in the field, negotiating through crisis and sharing stories of what succeeded and what failed. It was an iterative process, not an intellectual one, as we refined the tools we used day after day. And it was urgent. Our tools *had* to work, because if they didn't someone died.

But *why* did they work? That was the question that drew me to Harvard, to that office with Mnookin and Blum. I lacked confidence outside my narrow world. Most of all, I needed to articulate my knowledge and learn how to combine it with theirs—and they clearly had some—so I could understand, systematize, and expand it.

Yes, our techniques clearly worked with mercenaries, drug dealers, terrorists, and brutal killers. But, I wondered, what about with normal humans?

As I'd soon discover in the storied halls of Harvard, our techniques made great sense intellectually, and they worked *everywhere*.

It turned out that our approach to negotiation held the keys to unlock profitable human interactions in every domain and every interaction and every relationship in life.

This book is how it works.

THE SMARTEST DUMB GUY IN THE ROOM

To answer my questions, a year later, in 2006, I talked my way into Harvard Law School's Winter Negotiation Course. The best and brightest compete to get into this class, and it was filled with brilliant Harvard students getting law and business degrees and hotshot students from other top Boston universities like the Massachusetts Institute of Technology and Tufts. The Olympic trials for negotiating. And I was the only outsider.

The first day of the course, all 144 of us piled into a lecture hall for an introduction and then we split into four groups, each led by a negotiation instructor. After we'd had a chat with our instructor—mine was named Sheila Heen, and she's a good buddy to this day—we were partnered off in pairs and sent into mock negotiations. Simple: one of us was selling a product, the other was the buyer, and each had clear limits on the price they could take.

My counterpart was a languid redhead named Andy (a pseudonym), one of those guys who wear their intellectual superiority like they wear their khakis: with relaxed confidence. He and I went into an empty classroom overlooking one of those English-style squares on Harvard's campus, and we each used the tools we had. Andy would throw out an offer and give a rationally airtight explanation for why it was a good one—an inescapable logic trap—and I'd answer with some variation of "How am I supposed to do that?"

We did this a bunch of times until we got to a final figure. When we left, I was happy. I thought I'd done pretty well for a dumb guy.

After we all regrouped in the classroom, Sheila went around the students and asked what price each group had agreed on, and then wrote the result on the board.

Finally, it was my turn.

"Chris, how did you do with Andy?" she asked. "How much did you get?"

I'll never forget Sheila's expression when I told her what Andy had agreed to pay. Her whole face first went red, as if she couldn't breathe, and then out popped a little strangled gasp like a baby bird's hungry cry. Finally, she started to laugh.

Andy squirmed.

"You got literally every dime he had," she said, "and in his brief he was supposed to hold a quarter of it back in reserve for future work."

Andy sank deep in his chair.

The next day the same thing happened with another partner.

I mean, I absolutely destroyed the guy's budget.

It didn't make sense. A lucky one-off was one thing. But this was a pattern. With my old-school, experiential knowledge, I was killing guys who knew every cutting-edge trick you could find in a book.

The thing was, it was the cutting-edge techniques these guys were using that felt dated and old. I felt like I was Roger Federer and I had used a time machine to go back to the 1920s to play in a tennis tournament of distinguished gentlemen who wore white pantsuits and used wood rackets and had part-time training regimens. There I was with my titanium alloy racket and dedicated personal trainer and computer-strategized serve-and-volley plays. The guys I was playing were just as smart—actually, more so—and we were basically playing the same game with the same rules. But I had skills they didn't.

"You're getting famous for your special style, Chris," Sheila said, after I announced my second day's results.

I smiled like the Cheshire cat. Winning was fun.

"Chris, why don't you tell everybody your approach," Sheila said. "It seems like all you do to these Harvard Law School students is say 'No' and stare at them, and they fall apart. Is it really that easy?"

I knew what she meant: While I wasn't actually saying "No," the questions I kept asking sounded like it. They seemed to insinuate that the other side was being dishonest and unfair. And that was enough to make them falter and negotiate with themselves. Answering my calibrated questions demanded deep emotional strengths and tactical psychological insights that the toolbox they'd been given did not contain.

I shrugged.

"I'm just asking questions," I said. "It's a passive-aggressive approach. I just ask the same three or four open-ended questions over and over and over and over. They get worn out answering and give me everything I want."

Andy jumped in his seat as if he'd been stung by a bee.

"Damn!" he said. "*That's* what happened. I had no idea."

By the time I'd finished my winter course at Harvard, I'd actually become friends with some of my fellow students. Even with Andy.

If my time at Harvard showed me anything, it was that we at the FBI had a lot to teach the world about negotiating.

In my short stay I realized that without a deep understanding of human psychology, without the acceptance that we are all crazy, irrational, impulsive, emotionally driven animals, all the raw intelligence and mathematical logic in the world is little help in the fraught, shifting interplay of two people negotiating.

Yes, perhaps we are the only animal that haggles—a monkey does not exchange a portion of his banana for another's nuts—but no matter how we dress up our negotiations in mathematical theories, we are always an animal, always acting and reacting first and foremost from our deeply held but mostly invisible and inchoate fears, needs, perceptions, and desires.

That's not how these folks at Harvard learned it, though. Their theories and techniques all had to do with intellectual power, logic, authoritative acronyms like BATNA and ZOPA, rational notions of value, and a moral concept of what was fair and what was not.

And built on top of this false edifice of rationality was, of course, process. They had a script to follow, a predetermined sequence of actions, offers, and counteroffers designed in a specific order to bring about a particular outcome. It was as if they were dealing with a robot, that if you did a, b, c, and d in a certain fixed order, you would get x. But in the real world negotiation is far too unpredictable and complex for that. You may have to do a then d, and then maybe q.

If I could dominate the country's brightest students with just one of the many emotionally attuned negotiating techniques I had developed and used against terrorists and kidnappers, why not apply them to business? What was the difference between bank robbers who took hostages and CEOs who used hardball tactics to drive down the price of a billion-dollar acquisition?

After all, kidnappers are just businessmen trying to get the best price.

OLD-SCHOOL NEGOTIATION

Hostage taking—and therefore hostage negotiating—has existed since the dawn of recorded time. The Old Testament spins plenty of tales of Israelites and their enemies taking each other's citizens hostage as spoils of war. The Romans, for their part, used to force the princes of vassal states to send their sons to Rome for their education, to ensure the continued loyalty of the princes.

But until the Nixon administration, hostage negotiating as a process was limited to sending in troops and trying to shoot the hostages free. In law enforcement, our approach was pretty much to talk until we figured out how to take them out with a gun. Brute force.

Then a series of hostage disasters forced us to change.

In 1971, thirty-nine hostages were killed when the police tried to resolve the Attica prison riots in upstate New York with guns. Then at the 1972 Olympics in Munich, eleven Israeli athletes and coaches were killed by their Palestinian captors after a botched rescue attempt by the German police.

But the greatest inspiration for institutional change in American law enforcement came on an airport tarmac in Jacksonville, Florida, on October 4, 1971.

The United States was experiencing an epidemic of airline hijackings at the time; there were five in one three-day period in 1970. It was in that charged atmosphere that an unhinged man named George Giffe Jr. hijacked a chartered plane out of Nashville, Tennessee, planning to head to the Bahamas.

By the time the incident was over, Giffe had murdered two hostages—his estranged wife and the pilot—and killed himself to boot.

But this time the blame didn't fall on the hijacker; instead, it fell squarely on the FBI. Two hostages had managed to convince Giffe to let them go on the tarmac in Jacksonville, where they'd stopped to refuel. But the agents had gotten impatient and shot out the engine. And that had pushed Giffe to the nuclear option.

In fact, the blame placed on the FBI was so strong that when the pilot's wife and Giffe's daughter filed a wrongful death suit alleging FBI negligence, the courts agreed.

In the landmark *Downs v. United States* decision of 1975, the U.S. Court of Appeals wrote that "there was a better suited alternative to protecting the hostages' well-being," and said that the FBI had turned "what had been a successful 'waiting game,' during which two persons safely left the plane, into a 'shooting match' that left three persons dead." The court concluded that "a reasonable attempt at negotiations must be made prior to a tactical intervention."

The Downs hijacking case came to epitomize everything *not* to do in a crisis situation, and inspired the development of today's theories, training, and techniques for hostage negotiations.

Soon after the Giffe tragedy, the New York City Police Department (NYPD) became the first police force in the country to put together a dedicated team of specialists to design a process and handle crisis negotiations. The FBI and others followed.

A new era of negotiation had begun.

HEART VS. MIND

In the early 1980s, Cambridge, Massachusetts, was *the* hot spot in the negotiating world, as scholars from different disciplines began interacting and exploring exciting new concepts. The big leap forward came in 1979, when the Harvard Negotiation Project was founded with a mandate to improve the theory, teaching, and practice of negotiation so that people could more effectively handle everything from peace treaties to business mergers.

Two years later, Roger Fisher and William Ury—cofounders of the project—came out with *Getting to Yes*,[2] a groundbreaking treatise on negotiation that totally changed the way practitioners thought about the field.

Fisher and Ury's approach was basically to systematize problem solving so that negotiating parties could reach a mutually beneficial deal—the getting to "Yes" in the title. Their core assumption was that the emotional brain—that animalistic, unreliable, and irrational beast—could be overcome through a more rational, joint problem-solving mindset.

Their system was easy to follow and seductive, with four basic tenets. One, separate the person—the emotion—from the problem; two, don't get wrapped up in the other side's position (*what* they're asking for) but instead focus on their interests (*why* they're asking for it) so that you can find what they really want; three, work cooperatively to generate win-win options; and, four, establish mutually agreed-upon standards for evaluating those possible solutions.

It was a brilliant, rational, and profound synthesis of the most advanced game theory and legal thinking of the day. For years after that book came out, everybody—including the FBI and the NYPD— focused on a problem-solving approach to bargaining interactions. It just seemed so modern and *smart*.

Halfway across the United States, a pair of professors at the University of Chicago was looking at everything from economics to negotiation from a far different angle.

They were the economist Amos Tversky and the psychologist Daniel Kahneman. Together, the two launched the field of behavioral economics—and Kahneman won a Nobel Prize—by showing that man is a very irrational beast.

Feeling, they discovered, is a form of thinking.

As you've seen, when business schools like Harvard's began teaching negotiation in the 1980s, the process was presented as a straightforward economic analysis. It was a period when the world's top academic economists declared that we were all "rational actors." And so it went in negotiation classes: assuming the other side was acting rationally and selfishly in trying to maximize its position, the goal was to figure out how to respond in various scenarios to maximize one's own value.

This mentality baffled Kahneman, who from years in psychology knew that, in his words, "[I]t is self-evident that people are neither fully rational nor completely selfish, and that their tastes are anything but stable."

Through decades of research with Tversky, Kahneman proved that humans all suffer from *Cognitive Bias,* that is, unconscious—and irrational—brain processes that literally distort the way we see the world. Kahneman and Tversky discovered more than 150 of them.

There's the *Framing Effect,* which demonstrates that people respond differently to the same choice depending on how it is framed (people place greater value on moving from 90 percent to 100 percent—high probability to certainty—than from 45 percent to 55 percent, even though they're both ten percentage points). *Prospect Theory* explains why we take unwarranted risks in the face of uncertain losses. And the most famous is *Loss Aversion,* which shows how people are statistically more likely to act to avert a loss than to achieve an equal gain.

Kahneman later codified his research in the 2011 bestseller *Thinking, Fast and Slow.*[3] Man, he wrote, has two systems of thought: System 1, our animal mind, is fast, instinctive, and emotional; System 2 is slow, deliberative, and logical. And System 1 is far more influential. In fact, it guides and steers our rational thoughts.

System 1's inchoate beliefs, feelings, and impressions are the main sources of the explicit beliefs and deliberate choices of System 2. They're the spring that feeds the river. We react emotionally (System 1) to a suggestion or question. Then that System 1 reaction informs and in effect creates the System 2 answer.

Now think about that: under this model, if you know how to

affect your counterpart's System 1 thinking, his inarticulate feelings, by how you frame and deliver your questions and statements, then you can guide his System 2 rationality and therefore modify his responses. That's what happened to Andy at Harvard: by asking, "How am I supposed to do that?" I influenced his System 1 emotional mind into accepting that his offer wasn't good enough; his System 2 then rationalized the situation so that it made sense to give me a better offer.

If you believed Kahneman, conducting negotiations based on System 2 concepts without the tools to read, understand, and manipulate the System 1 emotional underpinning was like trying to make an omelet without first knowing how to crack an egg.

THE FBI GETS EMOTIONAL

As the new hostage negotiating team at the FBI grew and gained more experience in problem-solving skills during the 1980s and '90s, it became clear that our system was lacking a crucial ingredient.

At the time, we were deep into *Getting to Yes*. And as a negotiator, consultant, and teacher with decades of experience, I still agree with many of the powerful bargaining strategies in the book. When it was published, it provided groundbreaking ideas on cooperative problem solving and originated absolutely necessary concepts like entering negotiations with a BATNA: the Best Alternative To a Negotiated Agreement.

It was genius.

But after the fatally disastrous sieges of Randy Weaver's Ruby Ridge farm in Idaho in 1992 and David Koresh's Branch Davidian compound in Waco, Texas, in 1993, there was no denying that most hostage negotiations were anything but rational problem-solving situations.

I mean, have you ever tried to devise a mutually beneficial win-win solution with a guy who thinks he's the messiah?

It was becoming glaringly obvious that *Getting to Yes* didn't work with kidnappers. No matter how many agents read the book with highlighters in hand, it failed to improve how we as hostage negotiators approached deal making.

There was clearly a breakdown between the book's brilliant theory and everyday law enforcement experience. Why was it that everyone had read this bestselling business book and endorsed it as one of the greatest negotiation texts ever written, and yet so few could actually follow it successfully?

Were we morons?

After Ruby Ridge and Waco, a lot of people were asking that question. U.S. deputy attorney general Philip B. Heymann, to be specific, wanted to know why our hostage negotiation techniques were so bad. In October 1993, he issued a report titled "Lessons of Waco: Proposed Changes in Federal Law Enforcement,"[4] which summarized an expert panel's diagnosis of federal law enforcement's inability to handle complex hostage situations.

As a result, in 1994 FBI director Louis Freeh announced the formation of the Critical Incident Response Group (CIRG), a blended division that would combine the Crises Negotiation, Crises Management, Behavioral Sciences, and Hostage Rescue teams and reinvent crisis negotiation.

The only issue was, what techniques were we going to use?

Around this time, two of the most decorated negotiators in FBI history, my colleague Fred Lanceley and my former boss Gary Noesner, were leading a hostage negotiation class in Oakland, California, when they asked their group of thirty-five experienced law enforcement officers a simple question: How many had dealt with a classic bargaining situation where problem solving was the best technique?

Not one hand went up.

Then they asked the complementary question: How many students had negotiated an incident in a dynamic, intense, uncertain environment where the hostage-taker was in emotional crisis and had no clear demands?

Every hand went up.

It was clear: if emotionally driven incidents, not rational bargaining interactions, constituted the bulk of what most police negotiators had to deal with, then our negotiating skills had to laser-focus on the animal, emotional, and irrational.

From that moment onward, our emphasis would have to be not on training in quid pro quo bargaining and problem solving, but on education in the psychological skills needed in crisis intervention situations. Emotions and emotional intelligence would have to be central to effective negotiation, not things to be overcome.

What were needed were simple psychological tactics and strategies that worked in the field to calm people down, establish rapport, gain trust, elicit the verbalization of needs, and persuade the other guy of our empathy. We needed something easy to teach, easy to learn, and easy to execute.

These were cops and agents, after all, and they weren't interested in becoming academics or therapists. What they wanted was to change the behavior of the hostage-taker, whoever they were and whatever they wanted, to shift the emotional environment of the crisis just enough so that we could secure the safety of everyone involved.

In the early years, the FBI experimented with both new and old therapeutic techniques developed by the counseling profession. These counseling skills were aimed at developing positive relationships with people by demonstrating an understanding of what they're going through and how they feel about it.

It all starts with the universally applicable premise that people want to be understood and accepted. Listening is the cheapest, yet most effective concession we can make to get there. By listening intensely, a negotiator demonstrates empathy and shows a sincere desire to better understand what the other side is experiencing.

Psychotherapy research shows that when individuals feel listened to, they tend to listen to themselves more carefully and to openly evaluate and clarify their own thoughts and feelings. In addition, they tend to become less defensive and oppositional and more willing to listen to other points of view, which gets them to the calm and logical place where they can be good *Getting to Yes* problem solvers.

The whole concept, which you'll learn as the centerpiece of this book, is called *Tactical Empathy*. This is listening as a martial art, balancing the subtle behaviors of emotional intelligence and the assertive skills of influence, to gain access to the mind of another person. Contrary to popular opinion, listening is not a passive activity. It is the most active thing you can do.

Once we started developing our new techniques, the negotiating world split into two currents: negotiation as learned at the country's top school continued down the established road of rational problem solving, while, ironically, we meatheads at the FBI began to train our agents in an unproven system based on psychology, counseling, and crisis intervention. While the Ivy League taught math and economics, we became experts in empathy.

And our way worked.

LIFE IS NEGOTIATION

While you might be curious how FBI negotiators get some of the world's toughest bad guys to give up their hostages, you could be excused for wondering what hostage negotiation has to do with your life.

Happily, very few people are ever forced to deal with Islamist terrorists who've kidnapped their loved ones.

But allow me to let you in on a secret: Life is negotiation.

The majority of the interactions we have at work and at home are negotiations that boil down to the expression of a simple, animalistic urge: *I want.*

"I want you to free the hostages," is a very relevant one to this book, of course.

But so is:

"I want you to accept that $1 million contract."

"I want to pay $20,000 for that car."

"I want you to give me a 10 percent raise."

and

"I want you to go to sleep at 9 p.m."

Negotiation serves two distinct, vital life functions—information gathering and behavior influencing—and includes almost any interaction where each party wants something from the other side. Your career, your finances, your reputation, your love life, even the fate of your kids—at some point all of these hinge on your ability to negotiate.

Negotiation as you'll learn it here is nothing more than communication with results. Getting what you want out of life is all about getting what you want from—and with—other people. Conflict between two parties is inevitable in all relationships. So it's useful—crucial, even—to know how to engage in that conflict to get what you want without inflicting damage.

In this book, I draw on my more than two-decade career in the Federal Bureau of Investigation to distill the principles and practices I deployed in the field into an exciting new approach designed to help you disarm, redirect, and dismantle your counterpart in virtually any negotiation. And to do so in a relationship-affirming way.

Yes, you'll learn how we negotiated the safe release of countless hostages. But you'll also learn how to use a deep understanding of human psychology to negotiate a lower car price, a bigger raise, and a child's bedtime. This book will teach you to reclaim control of the conversations that inform your life and career.

The first step to achieving a mastery of daily negotiation is to get over your aversion to negotiating. You don't need to like it; you just need to understand that's how the world works. Negotiating does not mean browbeating or grinding someone down. It simply means playing the emotional game that human society is set up for. In this world, you get what you ask for; you just have to ask correctly. So claim your prerogative to ask for what you think is right.

What this book is really about, then, is getting you to accept negotiation and in doing so learn how to get what you want in a psychologically aware way. You'll learn to use your emotions, instincts, and insights in any encounter to connect better with others, influence them, and achieve more.

Effective negotiation is applied people smarts, a psychological edge in every domain of life: how to size someone up, how to influence their sizing up of you, and how to use that knowledge to get what you want.

But beware: this is not another pop-psych book. It's a deep and thoughtful (and most of all, practical) take on leading psychological theory that distills lessons from a twenty-four-year career in the FBI and ten years teaching and consulting in the best business schools and corporations in the world.

And it works for one simple reason: it was designed in and for the real world. It was not born in a classroom or a training hall, but built from years of experience that improved it until it reached near perfection.

Remember, a hostage negotiator plays a unique role: he *has* to win. Can he say to a bank robber, "Okay, you've taken four hostages. Let's split the difference—give me two, and we'll call it a day?"

No. A successful hostage negotiator has to get everything he asks for, without giving anything back of substance, and do so in a way that leaves the adversaries feeling as if they have a great relationship. His work is emotional intelligence on steroids. Those are the tools you'll learn here.

THE BOOK

Like a contractor building a house, this book is constructed from the ground up: first comes the big slabs of foundation, then the necessary load-bearing walls, the elegant but impermeable roof, and the lovely interior decorations.

Each chapter expands on the previous one. First you'll learn the refined techniques of this approach to *Active Listening* and then you'll move on to specific tools, turns of phrase, the ins and outs of the final act—haggling—and, finally, how to discover the rarity that can help you achieve true negotiating greatness: the Black Swan.

In Chapter 2, you'll learn how to avoid the assumptions that blind neophyte negotiators and replace them with *Active Listening* techniques like *Mirroring, Silences*, and the *Late-Night FM DJ Voice*. You'll discover how to slow things down and make your counterpart feel safe enough to reveal themselves; to discern between wants (aspirations) and needs (the bare minimum for a deal); and to laser-focus on what the other party has to say.

Chapter 3 will delve into *Tactical Empathy*. You'll learn how to recognize your counterpart's perspective and then gain trust and understanding through *Labeling*—that is, by repeating that perspective back to them. You'll also learn how to defuse negative dynamics by bringing them into the open. Finally, I'll explain how to disarm your counterpart's complaints about you by speaking them aloud in an *Accusation Audit*.

Next, in Chapter 4, I'll examine ways to make your counterpart feel understood and positively affirmed in a negotiation in order to create an atmosphere of unconditional positive regard. Here, you'll learn why you should strive for "That's right" instead of "Yes" at every stage of a negotiation, and how to identify, rearticulate, and emotionally affirm your counterpart's worldview with *Summaries* and *Paraphrasing*.

Chapter 5 teaches the flip side of *Getting to Yes*. You'll learn why it's vitally important to get to "No" because "No" starts the negotiation. You'll also discover how to step out of your ego and negotiate in your counterpart's world, the only way to achieve an agreement the other side will implement. Finally, you'll see how to engage your counterpart by acknowledging their right to choose, and you'll learn an email technique that ensures that you'll never be ignored again.

In Chapter 6, you'll discover the art of bending reality. That is, I'll explain a variety of tools for framing a negotiation in such a way that your counterpart will unconsciously accept the limits you place on the discussion. You'll learn how to navigate deadlines to create urgency; employ the idea of fairness to nudge your counterpart; and anchor their emotions so that *not* accepting your offer feels like a loss.

After this, Chapter 7 is dedicated to that incredibly powerful tool I used at Harvard: *Calibrated Questions*, the queries that begin with "How?" or "What?" By eliminating "Yes" and "No" answers they force your counterpart to apply their mental energy to solving your problems.

In Chapter 8 I demonstrate how to employ these *Calibrated Questions* to guard against failures in the implementation phase. "Yes," as I always say, is nothing without "How?" You'll also discover the importance of nonverbal communication; how to use "How" questions to gently say "No"; how to get your counterparts to bid against themselves; and how to influence the deal killers when they're not at the table.

At a certain point, every negotiation gets down to the brass tacks: that is, to old-school haggling. Chapter 9 offers a step-by-step process for effective bargaining, from how to prepare to how to dodge an aggressive counterpart and how to go on the offensive. You'll learn the Ackerman system, the most effective process the FBI has for setting and making offers.

Finally, Chapter 10 explains how to find and use those most rare of negotiation animals: the Black Swan. In every negotiation there are between three and five pieces of information that, were they to be uncovered, would change everything. The concept is an absolute gamechanger; so much so, I've named my company The Black Swan Group. In this chapter, you'll learn how to recognize the markers that show the Black Swan's hidden nest, as well as simple tools for employing Black Swans to gain leverage over your counterpart and achieve truly amazing deals.

Each chapter will start with a fast-paced story of a hostage negotiation, which will then be dissected with an eye to explaining what worked and what didn't. After I explain the theory and the tools, you'll read real-life case studies from me and others who've used these tools to prevail while negotiating a salary, purchasing a car, or working out nettlesome problems at home.

When you finish this book, I will have succeeded if you've applied these crucial techniques to improve your career and life. I'm sure you will. Just remember, to successfully negotiate it is critical to prepare. Which is why in the Appendix you'll find an invaluable tool I use with all my students and clients called the Negotiation One Sheet: a concise primer of nearly all our tactics and strategies for you to think through and customize for whatever kind of deal you're looking to close.

Most important to me is that you understand how urgent, essential, and even beautiful negotiation can be. When we embrace negotiating's transformative possibilities, we learn how to get what we want and how to move others to a better place.

Negotiation is the heart of collaboration. It is what makes conflict potentially meaningful and productive for all parties. It can change your life, as it has changed mine.

I've always thought of myself as just a regular guy. Hardworking and willing to learn, yes, but not particularly talented. And I've always felt that life holds amazing possibilities. In my much younger days, I just didn't know how to unlock those possibilities.

But with the skills I've learned, I've found myself doing extraordinary things and watching the people I've taught achieve truly life-changing results. When I use what I've learned over the last thirty years, I know I actually have the power to change the course of where my life is going, and to help others do that as well. Thirty years ago, while I felt like that could be done, I didn't know *how*.

Now I do. Here's how.

CHAPTER 2

BE A MIRROR

SEPTEMBER 30, 1993

A brisk autumn morning, around eight thirty. Two masked bank robbers trigger an alarm as they storm into the Chase Manhattan Bank at Seventh Avenue and Carroll Street in Brooklyn. There are only two female tellers and a male security guard inside. The robbers crack the unarmed sixty-year-old security guard across the skull with a .357, drag him to the men's room, and lock him inside. One of the tellers gets the same pistol-whipping treatment.

Then one of the robbers turns to the other teller, puts the barrel in her mouth, and pulls the trigger—click, goes the empty chamber.

"Next one is real," says the robber. "Now open the vault."

A bank robbery, with hostages. Happens all the time in the movies, but it had been almost twenty years since there'd been one of these standoffs in New York, the city with more hostage negotiation jobs than any other jurisdiction in the country.

And this happened to be my very first feet-to-the-fire, in-your-face hostage job.

I had been training for about a year and a half in hostage negotiations, but I hadn't had a chance to use my new skills. For me, 1993 had already been a very busy and incredible ride. Working on the FBI's Joint Terrorism Task Force, I had been the co-case agent in an investigation that thwarted a plot to set off bombs in the Holland and Lincoln Tunnels, the United Nations, and 26 Federal Plaza, the home of the FBI in New York City. We broke it up just as terrorists were mixing bombs in a safe house. The plotters were associated with an Egyptian cell that had ties to the "Blind Sheikh," who later would be found guilty of masterminding the plot that we uncovered.

You might think a bank robbery would be small potatoes after we busted up a terrorist plot, but by then I had already come to realize that negotiation would be my lifelong passion. I was eager to put my new skills to the test. And besides, there was nothing small about this situation.

When we got the call, my colleague Charlie Beaudoin and I raced to the scene, bailed out of his black Crown Victoria, and made our way to the command post. The whole cavalry showed up for this one— NYPD, FBI, SWAT—all the muscle and savvy of law enforcement up against the knee-jerk desperation of a couple of bank robbers seemingly in over their heads.

New York police, behind a wall of blue and white trucks and patrol cars, had set up across the street inside another bank. SWAT team members, peering through rifle scopes from the roofs of nearby brownstone buildings, had their weapons trained on the bank's front and rear doors.

ASSUMPTIONS BLIND, HYPOTHESES GUIDE

Good negotiators, going in, know they have to be ready for possible surprises; great negotiators aim to use their skills to reveal the surprises they are certain exist.

Experience will have taught them that they are best served by holding multiple hypotheses—about the situation, about the counterpart's wants, about a whole array of variables—in their mind at the same time. Present and alert in the moment, they use all the new information that comes their way to test and winnow true hypotheses from false ones.

In negotiation, each new psychological insight or additional piece of information revealed heralds a step forward and allows one to discard one hypothesis in favor of another. You should engage the process with a mindset of discovery. Your goal at the outset is to extract and observe as much information as possible. Which, by the way, is one of the reasons that really smart people often have trouble being negotiators—they're so smart they think they don't have anything to discover.

Too often people find it easier just to stick with what they believe. Using what they've heard or their own biases, they often make assumptions about others even before meeting them. They even ignore their own perceptions to make them conform to foregone conclusions. These assumptions muck up our perceptual windows onto the world, showing us an unchanging—often flawed—version of the situation.

Great negotiators are able to question the assumptions that the rest of the involved players accept on faith or in arrogance, and thus remain more emotionally open to all possibilities, and more intellectually agile to a fluid situation.

Unfortunately, back in 1993, I was far from great.

Everyone thought the crisis would be over quickly. The bank robbers had little choice but to surrender—or so we thought. We actually started the day with intelligence that the bank robbers wanted to surrender. Little did we know that was a ruse their ringleader planted to buy time. And throughout the day, he constantly referred to the influence the other four bank robbers exerted on him. I hadn't yet learned to be aware of a counterpart's overuse of personal pronouns—*we/they* or *me/I*. The less important he makes himself, the more important he probably is (and vice versa). We would later find out there was only one other bank robber, and he had been tricked into the robbery. Actually, three robbers, if you counted the getaway driver, who got away before we even entered the scene.

The "lead" hostage-taker was running his own "counterintelligence operation," feeding us all kinds of misinformation. He wanted us to think he had a bunch of co-conspirators with him—from a number of different countries. He also wanted us to think that his partners were much more volatile and dangerous than he was.

Looking back, of course, his game plan was clear—he wanted to confuse us as much as he could until he could figure a way out. He would constantly tell us that he wasn't in charge and that every decision was the responsibility of the other guys. He would indicate that he was scared—or, at least, a little tentative—when we asked him to pass along certain information. And yet he always spoke with a voice of complete calm and absolute confidence. It was a reminder to my colleagues and me that until you know what you're dealing with, you don't know what you're dealing with.

Though the call had come in about 8:30 a.m., by the time we arrived across the street from the bank and made contact it was probably about 10:30 a.m. The word when we came on the scene was that this was going to be cookie-cutter, by the book, short and sweet. Our commanders thought we'd be in and out of there in ten minutes, because the bad guys supposedly wanted to give themselves up. This would later become a problem, when negotiations stalled and Command became embarrassed, because they'd made the mistake of sharing this early optimism with the press, based on all the early misinformation.

We arrived on the scene to take a surrender, but the situation went sideways almost immediately.

Everything we *assumed* we knew was wrong.

CALM THE SCHIZOPHRENIC

Our Negotiation Operation Center (NOC) was set up in an office in a bank immediately across a narrow street from the Chase branch. We were way too close to the hostage site, so right away we were at a disadvantage. We were less than thirty yards from the crisis point, where ideally you want to have a little more of a buffer than that. You want to put some distance between you and whatever worst-case scenario might be waiting at the other end of the deal.

When my partner and I arrived, I was immediately assigned to coach the police department negotiator on the phone. His name was Joe, and he was doing fine—but in these types of situations, nobody worked alone. We always worked in teams. The thinking behind this policy was that all these extra sets of ears would pick up extra information. In some standoffs, we had as many as five people on the line, analyzing the information as it came in, offering behind-the-scenes input and guidance to our man on the phone—and that's how we were set up here. We had Joe taking the lead on the phone, and another three or four of us were listening in, passing notes back and forth, trying to make sense of a confusing situation. One of us was trying to gauge the mood of the bad guy taking the lead on the other end, and another was listening in for clues or "tells" that might give us a better read on what we were facing, and so on.

Students of mine balk at this notion, asking, "Seriously, do you really need a whole team to . . . hear someone out?" The fact that the FBI has come to that conclusion, I tell them, should be a wake-up call. It's really not that easy to listen well.

We are easily distracted. We engage in selective listening, hearing only what we want to hear, our minds acting on a cognitive bias for consistency rather than truth. And that's just the start.

Most people approach a negotiation so preoccupied by the arguments that support their position that they are unable to listen attentively. In one of the most cited research papers in psychology,[1] George A. Miller persuasively put forth the idea that we can process only about seven pieces of information in our conscious mind at any given moment. In other words, we are easily overwhelmed.

For those people who view negotiation as a battle of arguments, it's the voices in their own head that are overwhelming them. When they're not talking, they're thinking about their arguments, and when they are talking, they're making their arguments. Often those on both sides of the table are doing the same thing, so you have what I call a state of schizophrenia: everyone just listening to the voice in their head (and not well, because they're doing seven or eight other things at the same time). It may look like there are only two people in a conversation, but really it's more like four people all talking at once.

There's one powerful way to quiet the voice in your head and the voice in their head at the same time: treat two schizophrenics with just one pill. Instead of prioritizing your argument—in fact, instead of doing any thinking at all in the early goings about what you're going to say—make your sole and all-encompassing focus the other person and what they have to say. In that mode of true active listening—aided by the tactics you'll learn in the following chapters—you'll disarm your counterpart. You'll make them feel safe. The voice in their head will begin to quiet down.

The goal is to identify what your counterparts actually need (monetarily, emotionally, or otherwise) and get them feeling safe enough to talk and talk and talk some more about what they want. The latter will help you discover the former. Wants are easy to talk about, representing the aspiration of getting our way, and sustaining any illusion of control we have as we begin to negotiate; needs imply survival, the very minimum required to make us act, and so make us vulnerable. But neither wants nor needs are where we start; it begins with listening, making it about the other people, validating their emotions, and creating enough trust and safety for a real conversation to begin.

We were far from that goal with the lead hostage-taker on the call. He kept putting up these weird smoke screens. He wouldn't give up his name, he tried to disguise his voice, he was always telling Joe he was being put on speaker so everyone around him in the bank could hear, and then he would abruptly announce that he was putting Joe on "hold" and hang up the phone. He was constantly asking about a van, saying he and his partners wanted us to arrange one for them so they could drive themselves and the hostages to the local precinct to surrender. That was where the surrender nonsense had come from— but, of course, this wasn't a surrender plan so much as it was an escape plan. In the back of his mind, this guy thought he could somehow leave the bank without being taken into custody, and now that his getaway driver had fled the scene he needed access to a vehicle.

After it was all over, a couple of other details came clear. We weren't the only ones who had been lied to. Apparently, this lead bank robber hadn't told his partners they were going to rob a bank that morning. It turned out he was a cash courier who serviced the bank, and his partners were under the impression that they were going to burglarize the ATM. They didn't sign up for taking hostages, so we learned that this guy's co-conspirators were also hostages, in a way. They were caught up in a bad situation they didn't see coming—and, in the end, it was this "disconnect" among the hostage-takers that helped us to drive a wedge between them and put an end to the stalemate.

SLOW. IT. DOWN.

The leader wanted to make us think he and his partners were taking good care of his hostages, but in reality the security guard was out of the picture and the second bank teller had run to the bank base- ment to hide. Whenever Joe said he wanted to talk to the hostages, the hostage-taker would stall, and make it seem like there was this frenzy of activity going on inside the bank, going to ridiculous lengths to tell us how much time and energy he and his cohorts were spending on taking good care of the hostages. Very often, the leader would use this as a reason to put Joe on hold, or to end a call. He'd say, "The girls need to go to the bathroom." Or, "The girls want to call their families." Or, "The girls want to get something to eat."

Joe was doing a good job keeping this guy talking, but he was slightly limited by the negotiating approach that police departments were using at the time. The approach was half MSU—Making Shit Up—and half a sort of sales approach—basically trying to persuade, coerce, or manipulate in any way possible. The problem was, we were in too much of a hurry, driving too hard toward a quick solution; trying to be a problem solver, not a *people mover*.

Going too fast is one of the mistakes all negotiators are prone to making. If we're too much in a hurry, people can feel as if they're not being heard and we risk undermining the rapport and trust we've built. There's plenty of research that now validates the passage of time as one of the most important tools for a negotiator. When you slow the process down, you also calm it down. After all, if someone is talking, they're not shooting.

We caught a break when the robbers started to make noise about food. Joe was going back and forth with them for a while on what they were going to have and how we were going to get it to them. It became a negotiation in and of itself. We got it all set up, prepared to send the food in on a kind of robot device, because that's what this guy was comfortable with, but then he did an about-face, said to forget about it. Said they'd found some food inside, so it was just one brick wall after another, one smoke screen after another. It would feel to us like we were making a little progress, then this guy would take an abrupt turn, or hang up on us, or change his mind.

Meanwhile, our investigators used the time to run the registration of every one of the dozens of vehicles found nearby on the street, and managed to speak to the owners of every one of them except one—a car belonging to someone named Chris Watts. This became our one and only lead, at the time, and as our endless back-and-forth continued on the phone we sent a group of investigators to the address on Chris Watts's registration, where they found someone who knew Chris Watts and agreed to come down to the scene of the standoff to possibly identify him.

We still didn't have a visual on the inside, so our eyewitness had to be more of an "earwitness"—and he was able to identify Chris Watts by his voice.

We now knew more about our adversary than he *thought* we knew, which put us at a momentary advantage. We were putting together all the puzzle pieces, but it didn't get us any closer to our endgame, which was to determine for sure who was inside the building, to ensure the health and well-being of the hostages, and to get them all out safely— the good guys *and* the bad guys.

THE VOICE

After five hours, we were stuck, so the lieutenant in charge asked me to take over. Joe was out; I was in. Basically, it was the only strategic play at our disposal that didn't involve an escalation in force.

The man we now knew as Chris Watts had been in the habit of ending his calls abruptly, so my job was to find a way to keep him talking. I switched into my *Late-Night, FM DJ Voice*: deep, soft, slow, and reassuring. I had been instructed to confront Watts as soon as possible about his identity. I also came onto the phone with no warning, replacing Joe, against standard protocol. It was a shrewd move by the NYPD lieutenant to shake things up, but it easily could have backfired. This soothing voice was the key to easing the confrontation.

Chris Watts heard my voice on the line and cut me off immediately—said, "Hey, what happened to Joe?"

I said, "Joe's gone. This is Chris. You're talking to me now."

I didn't put it like a question. I made a downward-inflecting statement, in a downward-inflecting tone of voice. The best way to describe the late-night FM DJ's voice is as the voice of calm and reason.

When deliberating on a negotiating strategy or approach, people tend to focus all their energies on what to say or do, but it's how we *are* (our general demeanor and delivery) that is both the easiest thing to enact and the most immediately effective mode of influence. Our brains don't just process and understand the actions and words of others but their feelings and intentions too, the social meaning of their behavior and their emotions. On a mostly unconscious level, we can understand the minds of others not through any kind of thinking but through quite literally grasping what the other is feeling.

Think of it as a kind of involuntary neurological telepathy—each of us in every given moment signaling to the world around us whether we are ready to play or fight, laugh or cry.

When we radiate warmth and acceptance, conversations just seem to flow. When we enter a room with a level of comfort and enthusiasm, we attract people toward us. Smile at someone on the street, and as a reflex they'll smile back. Understanding that reflex and putting it into practice is critical to the success of just about every negotiating skill there is to learn.

That's why your most powerful tool in any verbal communication is your voice. You can use your voice to intentionally reach into someone's brain and flip an emotional switch. Distrusting to trusting. Nervous to calm. In an instant, the switch will flip just like that with the right delivery.

There are essentially three voice tones available to negotiators: the late-night FM DJ voice, the positive/playful voice, and the direct or assertive voice. Forget the assertive voice for now; except in very rare circumstances, using it is like slapping yourself in the face while you're trying to make progress. You're signaling dominance onto your counterpart, who will either aggressively, or passive-aggressively, push back against attempts to be controlled.

Most of the time, you should be using the positive/playful voice. It's the voice of an easygoing, good-natured person. Your attitude is light and encouraging. The key here is to relax and smile while you're talking. A smile, even while talking on the phone, has an impact tonally that the other person will pick up on.

The effect these voices have are cross-cultural and never lost in translation. On a vacation to Turkey with his girlfriend, one of our instructors at The Black Swan Group was befuddled—not to mention a little embarrassed—that his partner was repeatedly getting better deals in their backstreet haggling sessions at the spice markets in Istanbul. For the merchants in such markets throughout the Middle East, bargaining is an art form. Their emotional intelligence is finely honed, and they'll use hospitality and friendliness in a powerful way to draw you in and create reciprocity that ends in an exchange of money. But it works both ways, as our instructor discovered while observing his girlfriend in action: she approached each encounter as a fun game, so that no matter how aggressively she pushed, her smile and playful demeanor primed her merchant friends to settle on a successful outcome.

When people are in a positive frame of mind, they think more quickly, and are more likely to collaborate and problem-solve (instead of fight and resist). It applies to the smile-er as much as to the smile-ee: a smile on your face, and in your voice, will increase your own mental agility.

Playful wasn't the move with Chris Watts. The way the late-night FM DJ voice works is that, when you inflect your voice in a downward way, you put it out there that you've got it covered. Talking slowly and clearly you convey one idea: *I'm in control.* When you inflect in an upward way, you invite a response. Why? Because you've brought in a measure of uncertainty. You've made a statement sound like a question. You've left the door open for the other guy to take the lead, so I was careful here to be quiet, self-assured.

It's the same voice I might use in a contract negotiation, when an item isn't up for discussion. If I see a work-for-hire clause, for example, I might say, "We don't do work-for-hire." Just like that, plain, simple, and friendly. I don't offer up an alternative, because it would beg further discussion, so I just make a straightforward declaration.

That's how I played it here. I said, "Joe's gone. You're talking to me now."

Done deal.

You can be very direct and to the point as long as you create safety by a tone of voice that says I'm okay, you're okay, let's figure things out.

The tide was turning. Chris Watts was rattled, but he had a few moves left in him. One of the bad guys went down to the basement and collected one of the female bank tellers. She'd disappeared into the bowels of the bank at some point, but Chris Watts and his accomplice hadn't chased after her because they knew she wasn't going anywhere. Now one of the bank robbers dragged her back upstairs and put her on the phone.

She said, "I'm okay." That's all.

I said, "Who is this?"

She said, "I'm okay."

I wanted to keep her talking, so I asked her name—but then, just like that, she was gone.

This was a brilliant move on Chris Watts's part. It was a threat, teasing us with the woman's voice, but subtly and indirectly. It was a way for the bad guy to let us know he was calling the shots on his end of the phone without directly escalating the situation. He'd given us a "proof of life," confirming that he did indeed have hostages with him who were in decent enough shape to talk on the phone, but stopped short of allowing us to gather any useful information.

He'd managed to take back a measure of control.

MIRRORING

Chris Watts came back on the phone trying to act like nothing had happened. He was a little rattled, that's for sure, but now he was talking.

"We've identified every car on the street and talked to all the owners except one," I said to Watts. "We've got a van out here, a blue and gray van. We've been able to get a handle on the owners of all of the vehicles except this one in particular. Do you know anything about it?"

"The other vehicle's not out there because you guys chased my driver away . . ." he blurted.

"We chased your driver away?" I mirrored.

"Well, when he seen the police he cut."

"We don't know anything about this guy; is he the one who was driving the van?" I asked.

The mirroring continued between me and Watts, and he made a series of damaging admissions. He started vomiting information, as we now refer to it in my consulting business. He talked about an accomplice we had no knowledge of at the time. That exchange helped us nail the driver of the getaway car.

Mirroring, also called isopraxism, is essentially imitation. It's another neurobehavior humans (and other animals) display in which we copy each other to comfort each other. It can be done with speech patterns, body language, vocabulary, tempo, and tone of voice. It's generally an unconscious behavior—we are rarely aware of it when it's happening— but it's a sign that people are bonding, in sync, and establishing the kind of rapport that leads to trust.

It's a phenomenon (and now technique) that follows a very basic but profound biological principle: We fear what's different and are drawn to what's similar. As the saying goes, birds of a feather flock together. Mirroring, then, when practiced consciously, is the art of insinuating similarity. "Trust me," a mirror signals to another's unconscious, "You and I—we're alike."

Once you're attuned to the dynamic, you'll see it everywhere: couples walking on the street with their steps in perfect synchrony; friends in conversation at a park, both nodding their heads and crossing the legs at about the same time. These people are, in a word, connected.

While mirroring is most often associated with forms of nonverbal communication, especially body language, as negotiators a "mirror" focuses on the words and nothing else. Not the body language. Not the accent. Not the tone or delivery. Just the words.

It's almost laughably simple: for the FBI, a "mirror" is when you repeat the last three words (or the critical one to three words) of what someone has just said. Of the entirety of the FBI's hostage negotiation skill set, mirroring is the closest one gets to a Jedi mind trick. Simple, and yet uncannily effective.

By repeating back what people say, you trigger this mirroring instinct and your counterpart will inevitably elaborate on what was just said and sustain the process of connecting. Psychologist Richard Wiseman created a study using waiters to identify what was the more effective method of creating a connection with strangers: mirroring or positive reinforcement.

One group of waiters, using positive reinforcement, lavished praise and encouragement on patrons using words such as "great," "no problem," and "sure" in response to each order. The other group of waiters mirrored their customers simply by repeating their orders back to them. The results were stunning: the average tip of the waiters who mirrored was 70 percent more than of those who used positive reinforcement.

• • •

I decided it was time to hit him with his name—to let him know we were on to him. I said, "There's a vehicle out here, and it's registered to a Chris Watts."

He said, "Okay." Not letting anything on.

I said, "Is he there? Is this you? Are you Chris Watts?"

It was a stupid question, on my part. A mistake. For a mirror to be effective, you've got to let it sit there and do its work. It needs a bit of silence. I stepped all over my mirror. As soon as I said it, I wanted to take it back.

"Are you Chris Watts?"

What the hell could this guy say to that? Of course, he replied, "No."

I'd made a bone-headed move and given Chris Watts a way to dodge this confrontation, but he was nevertheless rattled. Up until this moment, he'd thought he was anonymous. Whatever fantasy he had running through his head, there was a way out for him, a do-over button. Now he knew different. I composed myself, slowed it down a little, and this time shut my mouth after the mirror—I said, "No? You said 'okay.'"

Now I had him, I thought. His voice went way up. He ended up blurting a few things out, vomiting more information, and became so flustered he stopped talking to me. Suddenly his accomplice, who we later learned was Bobby Goodwin, came onto the phone.

We hadn't heard from this second hostage-taker, until now. We'd known all along that Chris Watts wasn't acting alone, but we hadn't gotten a good read on how many people he had working with him on this, and now here was his unwitting accomplice, thinking our original police department negotiator was still handling our end. We knew this because he kept calling me "Joe," which told us he'd been in the loop early on, and somewhat less involved as the stalemate dragged on.

At the very least, the disconnect told me these guys weren't exactly on the same page—but I didn't jump to correct him.

Another thing: it sounded like this second guy was speaking through a towel, or a sweatshirt—like he was biting on some kind of fabric, even. Going to all these lengths to mask his voice, which meant he was clearly scared. He was nervous, jumpy as hell, anxious over how this standoff was going down.

I tried to set him at ease—still with the downward-inflecting DJ voice. I said, "Nobody's going anywhere." I said, "Nobody's gonna get hurt."

After about a minute and a half, the jumpiness seemed to disappear. The muffled voice, too. His voice came through much more clearly as he said, "I trust you, Joe."

The more I kept this second guy on the phone, the more it became clear he was someplace he did not want to be. Bobby wanted out—and, of course, he wanted out without getting hurt. He was already in deep, but he didn't want it to get any deeper. He didn't start out that day planning to rob a bank, but it took hearing my calm voice on the other end of the phone for him to start to see a way out. The seventh-largest standing army in the world was at the ready outside the bank doors—that's the size and scope of the NYPD, in full force, and their guns were fixed on him and his partner. Obviously, Bobby was desperate to step out those doors unharmed.

I didn't know where Bobby was, inside the bank. To this day, I don't know if he managed to step away from his partner, or if he was talking to me in plain sight of Chris Watts. I only know that I had his full attention, and that he was looking for a way to end the standoff—or, at least, to end his role in it.

I learned later that in between phone calls Chris Watts was busy squirreling cash inside the bank walls. He was also burning piles of cash, in full view of the two female hostages. On the face of it, this was bizarre behavior, but to a guy like Chris Watts there was a certain logic to it. Apparently, he'd gotten it in his head that he could burn, say, $50,000, and if $300,000 was reported missing bank officials wouldn't think to go looking for the other $250,000. It was an interesting deception—not exactly clever, but interesting. It showed a weird attention to detail. In his own mind at least, if Chris Watts managed to escape this box he'd made for himself, he could lie low for a while and come back at some future date for the money he'd stashed away—money that would no longer be on the bank's ledgers.

What I liked about this second guy, Bobby, was that he didn't try to play any games with me on the phone. He was a straight shooter, so I was able to respond as a straight shooter in kind. The same way I'd get back whatever I put out, he was getting back whatever he was putting out, so I was with him on this. Experience told me all I had to do was keep him talking and he'd come around. We'd find a way to get him out of that bank—with or without Chris Watts.

Someone on my team handed me a note: "Ask him if he wants to come out."

I said, "Do you want to come out first?"

I paused, remaining silent.

"I don't know how I'd do it," Bobby said finally.

"What's stopping you from doing it right now?" I asked.

"How do I do that?" he asked again.

"Tell you what. Meet me out front right now."

This was a breakthrough moment for us—but we still had to get Bobby out of there, and find a way to let him know that I'd be waiting for him on the other side of the door. I'd given him my word that I would be the one to take his surrender, and that he wouldn't get hurt, and now we had to make that happen—and very often it's this implementation phase that can be the most difficult.

Our team scrambled to put a plan in place to bring this about. I started putting on bulletproof gear. We surveyed the scene, figuring I could position myself behind one of the big trucks we'd parked out in front of the bank, to give me a measure of cover, just in case.

Then we ran into one of those maddening situations where one hand didn't know what the other was doing. It turned out the bank door had been barricaded from the outside early on in the standoff—a precaution to ensure that none of the bank robbers could flee the scene. We all knew this, of course, on some level, but when the time came for Bobby to give himself up and walk out the door, it's like our brains went into sleep mode. No one on the SWAT team thought to remind anyone on the negotiating team of this one significant detail, so for a couple long beats Bobby couldn't get out, and I got a sick feeling in my stomach that whatever progress we'd just made with this guy would be for nothing.

So there we were, scrambling to recover. Soon, two SWAT guys moved forward toward the entrance, with ballistic shields, guns drawn, to take the locks and the barricade off the door—and at this point they still didn't know what they were facing on the other side. It was a super-tense moment. There could have been a dozen guns on these two SWAT guys, but there was nothing for them to do but make their slow approach. Those guys were rock solid. They unlocked the door, backed away, and finally we were good to go.

Bobby came out—his hands in the air. I'd walked him through a specific set of instructions on what to do when he came out the door, what to expect. A couple of SWAT guys patted him down. Bobby turned and looked and said, "Where's Chris? Take me to Chris."

Finally, they brought him around to me, and we were able to debrief him inside our makeshift command post. This was the first we learned that there was only one other hostage-taker inside—and this naturally set the commander off. I didn't learn this until later, but I could see why he would have been angry and embarrassed at this latest turn. All along, he'd been telling the media there were a bunch of bad guys inside—an international assemblage of bad guys, remember? But now that it turned out it was essentially a two-man operation, and one of the bad guys had wanted no part of it, the commander looked like he didn't have a handle on the situation.

But like I said, we didn't know about the commander's reaction just yet. All we knew was that we'd just gotten all this new intel, which told us we were closer to achieving our desired outcome than we had just thought. This was a positive development, something to celebrate. With what we now knew, it was going to be a whole lot easier to negotiate our way through the rest of it, and yet this commander was angry. He didn't like that he'd been played, so he turned to one of the guys from NYPD's Technical Assistance Response Unit (TARU) and commanded them to get a camera inside the bank, a mic . . . *something.*

Now that I was huddled with Bobby, the commander swapped me out in favor of another primary negotiator on the phone. The new negotiator played it the same way I had, a couple of hours earlier—said, "This is Dominick. You're talking to me now."

Dominick Misino was a great hostage negotiator—in my view, one of the world's great closers, which was the term often used for the guy brought in to bang out the last details and secure the deal. He didn't get rattled and he was good at what he did.

Matter-of-fact. Street smart.

Dominick plowed ahead. And then, an amazing thing happened—a nearly disastrous amazing thing. As Chris Watts was talking to Dominick, he heard an electric tool of some kind burrowing its way through the wall behind him. It was one of our TARU guys, trying to get a bug planted inside—in precisely the wrong spot, at precisely the wrong time. Chris Watts was already rattled enough as it was, his partner giving himself up like that and leaving him to play out the siege on his own. And now, to hear our guys drilling through the wall, it just about set him off.

He responded like a pit bull backed into a corner. He called Dominick a liar. Dominick was unflappable. He kept his cool as Chris Watts raged on the other end of the phone, and eventually Dominick's cool, calm demeanor brought the guy from a boil to a simmer.

In retrospect, it was a fool move to try to get a bug inside the bank at this late stage—born out of frustration and panic. We'd gotten one of the hostage-takers out of the bank, but now we'd given back a measure of control. Startling the one remaining hostage-taker, who may or may not have been a loose cannon, was absolutely not a good idea.

As Dominick went to work smoothing over the situation, Chris Watts switched things up on us. He said, "What if I let a hostage go?"

This came as if from nowhere. Dominick hadn't even thought to ask, but Chris Watts just offered up one of the tellers like it was no big deal—and to him, at this late stage in the standoff, I guess it wasn't. From his view, such a conciliatory move might buy him enough time to figure out a way to escape.

Dominick remained calm, but seized on the opportunity. He said he wanted to talk to the hostage first, to make sure everything went okay, so Chris Watts tapped one of the women and put her on the phone. The woman had been paying attention, knew there'd been some sort of snafu when Bobby wanted to give himself up, so even though she was still completely terrified she had the presence of mind to ask about the door. I remember thinking this showed a lot of brass—to be terrified, held against your will, roughed up a bit, and to still have your wits about you.

She said, "Are you sure you have a key to the front door?"

Dominick said, "The front door's open."

And it was.

Ultimately, what happened was one of the women came out, unharmed, and an hour or so later the other woman followed, also unharmed.

We were working on getting the bank guard out, but we couldn't be sure from the accounts of these bank tellers what kind of shape this guy might be in. We didn't even know if he was still alive. They hadn't seen him since first thing that morning. He could have had a heart attack and died—there was just no way to know.

But Chris Watts had one last trick up his sleeve. He pulled a fast one on us and out of the blue, offered to come out. Maybe he thought he could catch us off guard one last time. What was strange about his sudden appearance was that he seemed to be looking about, surveying the scene, like he still thought he'd somehow elude capture. Right up until the moment the cops put the handcuffs on him, his gaze was darting back and forth, scanning for some kind of opportunity. The bright lights were on this guy, he was basically surrounded, but somewhere in the back of his scheming, racing mind he still thought he had a chance.

It was a long, long day, but it went down in the books as a success. Nobody was hurt. The bad guys were in custody. And I emerged from the experience humbled by how much more there was to learn, but at the same time, awakened to and inspired by the elemental power of emotion, dialogue, and the FBI's evolving toolbox of applied psychological tactics to influence and persuade just about anyone in any situation.

In the decades since my initiation into the world of high-stakes negotiations, I've been struck again and again by how valuable these seemingly simple approaches can be. The ability to get inside the head—and eventually under the skin—of your counterpart depends on these techniques and a willingness to change your approach, based on new evidence, along the way. As I've worked with executives and students to develop these skills, I always try to reinforce the message that being right isn't the key to a successful negotiation—having the right mindset is.

HOW TO CONFRONT—AND GET YOUR WAY—
WITHOUT CONFRONTATION

I only half-jokingly refer to mirroring as magic or a Jedi mind trick because it gives you the ability to disagree without being disagreeable.

To consider just how useful that can be, think of the average workplace: invariably there is still someone in a position of authority who arrived at that position through aggressive assertiveness, sometimes outright intimidation, with "old school" top-down, command-and-control assumptions that the boss is always right. And let's not delude ourselves: whatever the enlightened rules of the "new school," in every environment (work or otherwise) you will always have to deal with forceful type A people who prefer consent to collaboration.

If you take a pit bull approach with another pit bull, you generally end up with a messy scene and lots of bruised feelings and resentment. Luckily, there's another way without all the mess.

It's just four simple steps:

1. Use the late-night FM DJ voice.

2. Start with "I'm sorry . . ."

3. Mirror.

4. Silence. At least four seconds, to let the mirror work its magic on your counterpart.

5. Repeat.

One of my students experienced the effectiveness of this simple process at her workplace, where her impulsive boss was known for his "drive-bys": an infuriating practice by which the boss would suddenly swing by one's office or cubicle unannounced with an "urgent," poorly thought out assignment that created a lot of unnecessary work. Past attempts at any kind of debate created immediate pushback. "There's a better way" was always interpreted by this boss as "the lazy way."

Such a drive-by occurred toward the end of a long consulting engagement, one that had generated literally thousands of documents. The boss, still skeptical of anything "digital," wanted the security of paper copies.

Popping his head into her office, the boss said, "Let's make two copies of all the paperwork."

"I'm sorry, two copies?" she mirrored in response, remembering not only the DJ voice, but to deliver the mirror in an inquisitive tone. The intention behind most mirrors should be "Please, help me understand." Every time you mirror someone, they will reword what they've said. They will never say it exactly the same way they said it the first time. Ask someone, "What do you mean by that?" and you're likely to incite irritation or defensiveness. A mirror, however, will get you the clarity you want while signaling respect and concern for what the other person is saying.

"Yes," her boss responded, "one for us and one for the customer."

"I'm sorry, so you are saying that the client is asking for a copy and we need a copy for internal use?"

"Actually, I'll check with the client—they haven't asked for anything. But I definitely want a copy. That's just how I do business."

"Absolutely," she responded. "Thanks for checking with the customer. Where would you like to store the in-house copy? There's no more space in the file room here."

"It's fine. You can store it anywhere," he said, slightly perturbed now.

"Anywhere?" she mirrored again, with calm concern. When another person's tone of voice or body language is inconsistent with his words, a good mirror can be particularly useful.

In this case, it caused her boss to take a nice, long pause—something he did not often do. My student sat silent. "As a matter of fact, you can put them in my office," he said, with more composure than he'd had the whole conversation. "I'll get the new assistant to print it for me after the project is done. For now, just create two digital backups."

A day later her boss emailed and wrote simply, "The two digital backups will be fine."

Not long after, I received an ecstatic email from this student: "I was shocked! I love mirrors! A week of work avoided!"

Mirroring will make you feel awkward as heck when you first try it. That's the only hard part about it; the technique takes a little practice. Once you get the hang of it, though, it'll become a conversational Swiss Army knife valuable in just about every professional and social setting.

KEY LESSONS

The language of negotiation is primarily a language of conversation and rapport: a way of quickly establishing relationships and getting people to talk and think together. Which is why when you think of the greatest negotiators of all time, I've got a surprise for you—think Oprah Winfrey.

Her daily television show was a case study of a master practitioner at work: on a stage face-to-face with someone she has never met, in front of a crowded studio of hundreds, with millions more watching from home, and a task to persuade that person in front of her, sometimes against his or her own best interests, to talk and talk and keep talking, ultimately sharing with the world deep, dark secrets that they had held hostage in their own minds for a lifetime.

Look closely at such an interaction after reading this chapter and suddenly you'll see a refined set of powerful skills: a conscious smile to ease the tension, use of subtle verbal and nonverbal language to signal empathy (and thus security), a certain downward inflection in the voice, embrace of specific kinds of questions and avoidance of others—a whole array of previously hidden skills that will prove invaluable to you, once you've learned to use them.

Here are some of the key lessons from this chapter to remember:

- A good negotiator prepares, going in, to be ready for possible surprises; a great negotiator aims to use her skills to reveal the surprises she is certain to find.

- Don't commit to assumptions; instead, view them as hypotheses and use the negotiation to test them rigorously.

- People who view negotiation as a battle of arguments become overwhelmed by the voices in their head. Negotiation is not an act of battle; it's a process of discovery. The goal is to uncover as much information as possible.

- To quiet the voices in your head, make your sole and all-encompassing focus the other person and what they have to say.

- Slow. It. Down. Going too fast is one of the mistakes all negotiators are prone to making. If we're too much in a hurry, people can feel as if they're not being heard. You risk undermining the rapport and trust you've built.

- Put a smile on your face. When people are in a positive frame of mind, they think more quickly, and are more likely to collaborate and problem-solve (instead of fight and resist). Positivity creates mental agility in both you and your counterpart.

There are three voice tones available to negotiators:

1. The late-night FM DJ voice: Use selectively to make a point. Inflect your voice downward, keeping it calm and slow. When done properly, you create an aura of authority and trustworthiness without triggering defensiveness.

2. The positive/playful voice: Should be your default voice. It's the voice of an easygoing, good-natured person. Your attitude is light and encouraging. The key here is to relax and smile while you're talking.

3. The direct or assertive voice: Used rarely. Will cause problems and create pushback.

- Mirrors work magic. Repeat the last three words (or the critical one to three words) of what someone has just said. We fear what's different and are drawn to what's similar. Mirroring is the art of insinuating similarity, which facilitates bonding. Use mirrors to encourage the other side to empathize and bond with you, keep people talking, buy your side time to regroup, and encourage your counterparts to reveal their strategy.

CHAPTER 3

DON'T FEEL THEIR PAIN, LABEL IT

It was 1998 and I was standing in a narrow hallway outside an apartment on the twenty-seventh floor of a high-rise in Harlem. I was the head of the New York City FBI Crisis Negotiation Team, and that day I was the primary negotiator.

The investigative squad had reported that at least three heavily armed fugitives were holed up inside. Several days earlier the fugitives had used automatic weapons in a shoot-out with a rival gang, so the New York City FBI SWAT team was arrayed behind me, and our snipers were on nearby rooftops with rifles trained on the apartment windows.

In tense situations like this, the traditional negotiating advice is to keep a poker face. Don't get emotional. Until recently, most academics and researchers completely ignored the role of emotion in negotiation. Emotions were just an obstacle to a good outcome, they said. "Separate the people from the problem" was the common refrain.

But think about that: How can you separate people from the problem when their emotions *are* the problem? Especially when they are scared people with guns. Emotions are one of the main things that derail communication. Once people get upset at one another, rational thinking goes out the window.

That's why, instead of denying or ignoring emotions, good negotiators identify and influence them. They are able to precisely label emotions, those of others and especially their own. And once they label the emotions they talk about them without getting wound up. For them, emotion is a tool.

Emotions aren't the obstacles, they are the means.

The relationship between an emotionally intelligent negotiator and their counterpart is essentially therapeutic. It duplicates that of a psychotherapist with a patient. The psychotherapist pokes and prods to understand his patient's problems, and then turns the responses back onto the patient to get him to go deeper and change his behavior. That's exactly what good negotiators do.

Getting to this level of emotional intelligence demands opening up your senses, talking less, and listening more. You can learn almost everything you need—and a lot more than other people would like you to know—simply by watching and listening, keeping your eyes peeled and your ears open, and your mouth shut.

Think about the therapist's couch as you read the following sections. You'll see how a soothing voice, close listening, and a calm repetition of the words of your "patient" can get you a lot further than a cold, rational argument.

It may sound touchy-feely, but if you can perceive the emotions of others, you have a chance to turn them to your advantage. The more you know about someone, the more power you have.

TACTICAL EMPATHY

We had one big problem that day in Harlem: no telephone number to call into the apartment. So for six straight hours, relieved periodically by two FBI agents who were learning crisis negotiation, I spoke through the apartment door.

I used my late-night FM DJ voice.

I didn't give orders in my DJ voice, or ask what the fugitives wanted. Instead, I imagined myself in their place.

"It looks like you don't want to come out," I said repeatedly. "It seems like you worry that if you open the door, we'll come in with guns blazing. It looks like you don't want to go back to jail."

For six hours, we got no response. The FBI coaches loved my DJ voice. But was it working?

And then, when we were almost completely convinced that no one was inside, a sniper on an adjacent building radioed that he saw one of the curtains in the apartment move.

The front door of the apartment slowly opened. A woman emerged with her hands in front of her.

I continued talking. All three fugitives came out. None of them said a word until we had them in handcuffs.

Then I asked them the question that was most nagging me: Why did they come out after six hours of radio silence? Why did they finally give in?

All three gave me the same answer.

"We didn't want to get caught or get shot, but you calmed us down," they said. "We finally believed you wouldn't go away, so we just came out."

There is nothing more frustrating or disruptive to any negotiation than to get the feeling you are talking to someone who isn't listening. Playing dumb is a valid negotiating technique, and "I don't understand" is a legitimate response. But ignoring the other party's position only builds up frustration and makes them less likely to do what you want.

The opposite of that is tactical empathy.

In my negotiating course, I tell my students that empathy is "the ability to recognize the perspective of a counterpart, and the vocalization of that recognition." That's an academic way of saying that empathy is paying attention to another human being, asking what they are feeling, and making a commitment to understanding their world.

Notice I didn't say anything about agreeing with the other person's values and beliefs or giving out hugs. That's sympathy. What I'm talking about is trying to understand a situation from another person's perspective.

One step beyond that is tactical empathy.

Tactical empathy is understanding the feelings and mindset of another in the moment and also hearing what is *behind* those feelings so you increase your influence in all the moments that follow. It's bringing our attention to both the emotional obstacles and the potential pathways to getting an agreement done.

It's emotional intelligence on steroids.

As a cop in Kansas City, I was curious about how a select handful of veteran cops managed to talk angry, violent people out of fights or to get them to put down their knives and guns.

When I asked how they did that, I rarely got more than a shrug. They couldn't articulate what they did. But now I know the answer is tactical empathy. They were able to think from another person's point of view while they were talking with that person and quickly assess what was driving them.

Most of us enter verbal combat unlikely to persuade anyone of anything because we only know and care about our own goals and perspective. But the best officers are tuned in to the other party—their audience. They know that if they empathize, they can mold their audience by how they approach and talk to them.

That's why, if a corrections officer approaches an inmate expecting him to resist, he often will. But if he approaches exuding calm, the inmate will be much more likely to be peaceful. It seems like wizardry, but it's not. It's just that when the officer has his audience clearly in mind, he can become who he needs to be to handle the situation.

Empathy is a classic "soft" communication skill, but it has a physical basis. When we closely observe a person's face, gestures, and tone of voice, our brain begins to align with theirs in a process called neural resonance, and that lets us know more fully what they think and feel.

In an fMRI brain-scan experiment,[1] researchers at Princeton University found that neural resonance disappears when people communicate poorly. The researchers could predict how well people were communicating by observing how much their brains were aligned. And they discovered that people who paid the most attention—good listeners—could actually anticipate what the speaker was about to say before he said it.

If you want to increase your neural resonance skills, take a moment right now and practice. Turn your attention to someone who's talking near you, or watch a person being interviewed on TV. As they talk, imagine that you are that person. Visualize yourself in the position they describe and put in as much detail as you can, as if you were actually there.

But be warned, a lot of classic deal makers will think your approach is softheaded and weak.

Just ask former secretary of state Hillary Clinton.

A few years ago during a speech at Georgetown University, Clinton advocated, "showing respect, even for one's enemies. Trying to understand and, insofar as psychologically possible, empathize with their perspective and point of view."

You can predict what happened next. A gaggle of pundits and politicians pounced on her. They called her statement inane and naïve, and even a sign she had embraced the Muslim Brotherhood. Some said that she had blown her chances at a presidential run.

The problem with all of that hot air is that she was right.

Politics aside, empathy is not about being nice or agreeing with the other side. It's about understanding them. Empathy helps us learn the position the enemy is in, why their actions make sense (to them), and what might move them.

As negotiators we use empathy because it works. Empathy is why the three fugitives came out after six hours of my late-night DJ voice. It's what helped me succeed at what Sun Tzu called "the supreme art of war": to subdue the enemy without fighting.

LABELING

Let's go back to the Harlem doorway for a minute.

We didn't have a lot to go on, but if you've got three fugitives trapped in an apartment on the twenty-seventh floor of a building in Harlem, they don't have to say a word for you to know that they're worried about two things: getting killed, and going to jail.

So for six straight hours in that sweltering apartment building hallway, the two FBI negotiating students and I took turns speaking. We rotated in order to avoid verbal stumbles and other errors caused by tiredness. And we stayed relentlessly on message, all three of us saying the same thing.

Now, pay close attention to exactly what we said: "It looks like you don't want to come out. It seems like you worry that if you open the door, we'll come in with guns blazing. It looks like you don't want to go back to jail."

We employed our tactical empathy by recognizing and then verbalizing the predictable emotions of the situation. We didn't just put ourselves in the fugitives' shoes. We spotted their feelings, turned them into words, and then very calmly and respectfully repeated their emotions back to them.

In a negotiation, that's called labeling.

Labeling is a way of validating someone's emotion by acknowledging it. Give someone's emotion a name and you show you identify with how that person feels. It gets you close to someone without asking about external factors you know nothing about ("How's your family?"). Think of labeling as a shortcut to intimacy, a time-saving emotional hack.

Labeling has a special advantage when your counterpart is tense. Exposing negative thoughts to daylight—"It looks like you don't want to go back to jail"—makes them seem less frightening.

In one brain imaging study,[2] psychology professor Matthew Lieberman of the University of California, Los Angeles, found that when people are shown photos of faces expressing strong emotion, the brain shows greater activity in the amygdala, the part that generates fear. But when they are asked to label the emotion, the activity moves to the areas that govern rational thinking. In other words, labeling an emotion—applying rational words to a fear—disrupts its raw intensity.

Labeling is a simple, versatile skill that lets you reinforce a good aspect of the negotiation, or diffuse a negative one. But it has very specific rules about form and delivery. That makes it less like chatting than like a formal art such as Chinese calligraphy.

For most people, it's one of the most awkward negotiating tools to use. Before they try it the first time, my students almost always tell me they expect their counterpart to jump up and shout, "Don't you dare tell me how I feel!"

Let me let you in on a secret: people never even notice.

The first step to labeling is detecting the other person's emotional state. Outside that door in Harlem we couldn't even see the fugitives, but most of the time you'll have a wealth of information from the other person's words, tone, and body language. We call that trinity "words, music, and dance."

The trick to spotting feelings is to pay close attention to changes people undergo when they respond to external events. Most often, those events are your words.

If you say, "How is the family?" and the corners of the other party's mouth turn down even when they say it's great, you might detect that all is not well; if their voice goes flat when a colleague is mentioned, there could be a problem between the two; and if your landlord unconsciously fidgets his feet when you mention the neighbors, it's pretty clear that he doesn't think much of them (we'll dig deeper into how to spot and use these cues in Chapter 9).

Picking up on these tiny pieces of information is how psychics work. They size up their client's body language and ask him a few innocent questions. When they "tell" his future a few minutes later, they're really just saying what he wants to hear based on small details they've spotted. More than a few psychics would make good negotiators for that very reason.

Once you've spotted an emotion you want to highlight, the next step is to label it aloud. Labels can be phrased as statements or questions. The only difference is whether you end the sentence with a downward or upward inflection. But no matter how they end, labels almost always begin with roughly the same words:

It seems like . . .

It sounds like . . .

It looks like . . .

Notice we said "It sounds like . . ." and not "I'm hearing that . . ." That's because the word "I" gets people's guard up. When you say "I," it says you're more interested in yourself than the other person, and it makes you take personal responsibility for the words that follow—and the offense they might cause.

But when you phrase a label as a neutral statement of understanding, it encourages your counterpart to be responsive. They'll usually give a longer answer than just "yes" or "no." And if they disagree with the label, that's okay. You can always step back and say, "I didn't say that was what it was. I just said it seems like that."

The last rule of labeling is silence. Once you've thrown out a label, be quiet and listen. We all have a tendency to expand on what we've said, to finish, "It seems like you like the way that shirt looks," with a specific question like "Where did you get it?" But a label's power is that it invites the other person to reveal himself.

If you'll trust me for a second, take a break now and try it out: Strike up a conversation and put a label on one of the other person's emotions—it doesn't matter if you're talking to the mailman or your ten-year-old daughter—and then go silent. Let the label do its work.

NEUTRALIZE THE NEGATIVE, REINFORCE THE POSITIVE

Labeling is a tactic, not a strategy, in the same way a spoon is a great tool for stirring soup but it's not a recipe. *How* you use labeling will go a long way in determining your success. Deployed well, it's how we as negotiators identify and then slowly alter the inner voices of our counterpart's consciousness to something more collaborative and trusting.

First, let's talk a little human psychology. In basic terms, people's emotions have two levels: the "presenting" behavior is the part above the surface you can see and hear; beneath, the "underlying" feeling is what motivates the behavior.

Imagine a grandfather who's grumbly at a family holiday dinner: the presenting behavior is that he's cranky, but the underlying emotion is a sad sense of loneliness from his family never seeing him.

What good negotiators do when labeling is address those underlying emotions. Labeling negatives diffuses them (or *defuses* them, in extreme cases); labeling positives reinforces them.

We'll come back to the cranky grandfather in a moment. First, though, I want to talk a little bit about anger.

As an emotion, anger is rarely productive—in you or the person you're negotiating with. It releases stress hormones and neurochemicals that disrupt your ability to properly evaluate and respond to situations. And it blinds you to the fact that you're angry in the first place, which gives you a false sense of confidence.

That's not to say that negative feelings should be ignored. That can be just as damaging. Instead, they should be teased out. Labeling is a helpful tactic in de-escalating angry confrontations, because it makes the person acknowledge their feelings rather than continuing to act out.

Early on in my hostage negotiation career, I learned how important it was to go directly at negative dynamics in a fearless but deferential manner.

It was to fix a situation I'd created myself. I'd angered the top FBI official in Canada when I entered the country without first alerting him (so he could notify the Department of State), a procedure known as "country clearance."

I knew I needed to call and assuage him to straighten out the situation, or I risked being expelled. Top guys like to feel on top. They don't want to be disrespected. All the more so when the office they run isn't a sexy assignment.

"Bless me, Father, for I have sinned," I said when he answered the phone.

There was a long pause at the other end of the line.

"Who is this?" he said.

"Bless me, Father, for I have sinned," I repeated. "It's Chris Voss."

Again there was a long silence.

"Does your boss know you're here?"

I said he did, and crossed my fingers. At this point, the FBI official would have been completely within his rights to tell me to leave Canada immediately. But by mentioning the negative dynamic, I knew I'd diffused it as much as I could. I had a chance.

"All right, you've got country clearance," he finally said. "I'll take care of the paperwork."

Try this the next time you have to apologize for a bone-headed mistake. Go right at it. The fastest and most efficient means of establishing a quick working relationship is to acknowledge the negative and diffuse it. Whenever I was dealing with the family of a hostage, I started out by saying I knew they were scared. And when I make a mistake—something that happens a lot—I always acknowledge the other person's anger. I've found the phrase "Look, I'm an asshole" to be an amazingly effective way to make problems go away.

That approach has never failed me.

Let's go back to the cranky grandfather.

He's grumpy because he never sees the family and he feels left out. So he's speaking up in his own dysfunctional way to get attention.

How do you fix that?

Instead of addressing his grumpy behavior, you acknowledge his sadness in a nonjudgmental way. You head him off before he can really get started.

"We don't see each other all that often," you could say. "It seems like you feel like we don't pay any attention to you and you only see us once a year, so why should you make time for us?"

Notice how that acknowledges the situation and labels his sadness? Here you can pause briefly, letting him recognize and appreciate your attempts to understand what he's feeling, and then turn the situation around by offering a positive solution.

"For us this is a real treat. We want to hear what you have to talk about. We want to value this time with you because we feel left out of your life."

Research shows that the best way to deal with negativity is to observe it, without reaction and without judgment. Then consciously label each negative feeling and replace it with positive, compassionate, and solution-based thoughts.

One of my Georgetown University students, a guy named TJ, who worked as an assistant controller at the Washington Redskins, put that lesson to work while he was taking my negotiations class.

The economy was in the toilet at the time, and Redskins season ticket holders were leaving in droves to avoid the cost. Worse, the team had been *terrible* the year before, and off-field player problems were alienating the fans.

The team's CFO was getting more worried—and cranky—by the day, and two weeks before the season was to start he walked by TJ's desk and slammed down a folder full of paper.

"Better yesterday than today," he said and walked away.

Inside was a list of forty season ticket holders who hadn't paid their bills, a USB drive with a spreadsheet about each one's situation, and a script to use when calling them.

TJ saw right away that the script was a disaster. It began by saying that his colleagues had been trying to call for months, and the account had been escalated to him. "I wanted to inform you," it read, "that in order to receive your tickets for the upcoming season opener against the New York Giants, you will need to pay your outstanding balance in full prior to September 10."

It was the stupidly aggressive, impersonal, tone-deaf style of communication that is the default for most business. It was all "me, me, me" from TJ, with no acknowledgment of the ticket holder's situation. No empathy. No connection. Just give me the money.

Maybe I don't need to say it, but the script didn't work. TJ left messages; no one called back.

A few weeks into the class, TJ rewrote the script. These weren't massive changes, and he didn't offer the fans any discounts. What he did was add subtle tweaks to make the call about the fans, their situation, and their love of the team.

Now the team was "YOUR Washington Redskins" and the purpose of the call was to ensure that the team's most valuable fans—the delinquent customers—would be there at the season opener. "The home-field advantage created by you each and every Sunday at FedEx Field does not go unnoticed," TJ wrote. He then told them, "In these difficult times, we understand our fans have been hit hard and we are here to work with you," and asked the ticket holders to call back to talk through their "unique situation."

Though superficially simple, the changes TJ made in the script had a deep emotional resonance with the delinquent ticket holders. It mentioned their debt to the team but also acknowledged the team's debt to them, and by labeling the tough economic times, and the stress they were causing, it diffused the biggest negative dynamic—their delinquency—and turned the issue into something solvable.

The simple changes masked a complex understanding of empathy on TJ's side. With the new script, TJ was able to set up payment plans with all the ticket holders before the Giants game. And the CFO's next visit? Well, it was far less terse.

CLEAR THE ROAD BEFORE ADVERTISING THE DESTINATION

Remember the amygdala, the part of the brain that generates fear in reaction to threats? Well, the faster we can interrupt the amygdala's reaction to real or imaginary threats, the faster we can clear the road of obstacles, and the quicker we can generate feelings of safety, well-being, and trust.

We do that by labeling the fears. These labels are so powerful because they bathe the fears in sunlight, bleaching them of their power and showing our counterpart that we understand.

Think back to that Harlem landing: I didn't say, "It seems like you want us to let you go." We could all agree on that. But that wouldn't have diffused the real fear in the apartment, or shown that I empathized with the grim complexity of their situation. That's why I went right at the amygdala and said, "It seems like you don't want to go back to jail."

Once they've been labeled and brought into the open, the negative reactions in your counterpart's amygdala will begin to soften. I promise it will shock you how suddenly his language turns from worry to optimism. Empathy is a powerful mood enhancer.

The road is not always cleared so easily, so don't be demoralized if this process seems to go slowly. The Harlem high-rise negotiation took six hours. Many of us wear fears upon fears, like layers against the cold, so getting to safety takes time.

That was the experience of another one of my students, a fundraiser for the Girl Scouts, who backed into naming her counterpart's fears almost accidentally.

We're not talking about someone who sold Girl Scout cookies: my student was an experienced fund-raiser who regularly got donors to pony up $1,000 to $25,000 a check. Over the years, she'd developed a very successful system to get her "clients," usually wealthy women, to open their checkbook.

She'd invite a potential donor to her office, serve a few Girl Scouts cookies, walk her through an album of heartwarming snapshots and handwritten letters from projects that matched the woman's profile, and then collect a check when the donor's eyes lit up. It was almost easy.

One day, though, she met the immovable donor. Once the woman sat down in her office, my student began to throw out the projects her research had said would fit. But the woman shook her head at one project after another.

My student found herself growing perplexed at the difficult donor who had no interest in donating. But she held her emotion in check and reached back to a lesson from my recent class on labeling. "I'm sensing some hesitation with these projects," she said in what she hoped was a level voice.

As if she'd been uncorked, the woman exclaimed: "I want my gift to directly support programming for Girl Scouts and not anything else."

This helped focus the conversation, but as my student put forth project after project that seemed to fulfill the donor's criteria, all she got was still rejection.

Sensing the potential donor's growing frustration, and wanting to end on a positive note so that they might be able to meet again, my student used another label. "It seems that you are really passionate about this gift and want to find the right project reflecting the opportunities and life-changing experiences the Girl Scouts gave you."

And with that, this "difficult" woman signed a check without even picking a specific project. "You understand me," she said as she got up to leave. "I trust you'll find the right project."

Fear of her money being misappropriated was the presenting dynamic that the first label uncovered. But the second label uncovered the underlying dynamic—her very presence in the office was driven by very specific memories of being a little Girl Scout and how it changed her life.

The obstacle here wasn't finding the right match for the woman. It wasn't that she was this highly finicky, hard-to-please donor. The real obstacle was that this woman needed to feel that she was understood, that the person handling her money knew why she was in that office and understood the memories that were driving her actions.

That's why labels are so powerful and so potentially transformative to the state of any conversation. By digging beneath what seems like a mountain of quibbles, details, and logistics, labels help to uncover and identify the primary emotion driving almost all of your counterpart's behavior, the emotion that, once acknowledged, seems to miraculously solve everything else.

DO AN ACCUSATION AUDIT

On the first day of negotiating class each semester, I march the group through an introductory exercise called "sixty seconds or she dies." I play a hostage-taker and a student has to convince me to release my hostage within a minute. It's an icebreaker that shows me the level of my students, and it reveals to them how much they need to learn. (Here's a little secret: the hostage never gets out.)

Sometimes students jump right in, but finding takers is usually hard because it means coming to the front of the class and competing with the guy who holds all the cards. If I just ask for a volunteer, my students sit on their hands and look away. You've been there. You can almost feel your back muscles tense as you think, Oh please, don't call on me.

So I don't ask. Instead, I say, "In case you're worried about volunteering to role-play with me in front of the class, I want to tell you in advance . . . it's going to be horrible."

After the laughter dies down, I then say, "And those of you who do volunteer will probably get more out of this than anyone else."

I always end up with more volunteers than I need.

Now, look at what I did: I prefaced the conversation by labeling my audience's fears; how much worse can something be than "horrible"? I defuse them and wait, letting it sink in and thereby making the unreasonable seem less forbidding.

All of us have intuitively done something close to this thousands of times. You'll start a criticism of a friend by saying, "I don't want this to sound harsh . . ." hoping that whatever comes next will be softened. Or you'll say, "I don't want to seem like an asshole . . ." hoping your counterpart will tell you a few sentences later that you're not that bad. The small but critical mistake this commits is denying the negative. That actually gives it credence.

In court, defense lawyers do this properly by mentioning everything their client is accused of, and all the weaknesses of their case, in the opening statement. They call this technique "taking the sting out."

What I want to do here is turn this into a process that, applied systematically, you can use to disarm your counterpart while negotiating everything from your son's bedtime to large business contracts.

The first step of doing so is listing every terrible thing your counterpart *could* say about you, in what I call an accusation audit.

This idea of an accusation audit is really, really hard for people to get their minds around. The first time I tell my students about it, they say, "Oh my God. We can't do that." It seems both artificial and self-loathing. It seems like it would make things worse. But then I remind them that it's exactly what I did the first day of class when I labeled their fears of the hostage game in advance. And they all admit that none of them knew.

As an example, I'm going to use the experience of one of my students, Anna, because I couldn't be more proud at how she turned what she learned in my class into $1 million.

At the time, Anna was representing a major government contractor. Her firm had won a competition for a sizable government deal by partnering with a smaller company, let's call it ABC Corp., whose CEO had a close relationship with the government client representative.

Problems started right after they won the contract, though. Because ABC's relationship had been instrumental in winning the deal, ABC felt that it was owed a piece of the pie whether it fulfilled its part of the contract or not.

And so, while the contract paid them for the work of nine people, they continually cut back support. As Anna's company had to perform ABC's work, the relationship between ABC and Anna's company fragmented into vituperative emails and bitter complaining. Facing an already low profit margin, Anna's company was forced into tough negotiations to get ABC to take a cut to 5.5 people. The negotiations left a bitter aftertaste on both sides. The vituperative emails stopped, but then again *all* emails stopped. And no communication is always a bad sign.

A few months after those painful talks, the client demanded a major rethink on the project and Anna's firm was faced with losing serious money if it didn't get ABC to agree to further cuts. Because ABC wasn't living up to its side of the bargain, Anna's firm would have had strong contractual grounds to cut out ABC altogether. But that would have damaged Anna's firm's reputation with a very important customer, and could have led to litigation from ABC.

Faced with this scenario, Anna set up a meeting with ABC where she and her partners planned to inform ABC that its pay was being cut to three people. It was a touchy situation, as ABC was already unhappy about the first cut. Even though she was normally an aggressive and confident negotiator, worries about the negotiations ruined Anna's sleep for weeks. She needed to extract concessions while improving the relationship at the same time. No easy task, right?

To prepare, the first thing Anna did was sit down with her negotiating partner, Mark, and list every negative charge that ABC could level at them. The relationship had gone sour long before, so the list was huge. But the biggest possible accusations were easy to spot:

"You are the typical prime contractor trying to force out the small guy."

"You promised us we would have all this work and you reneged on your promise."

"You could have told us about this issue weeks ago to help us prepare."

Anna and Mark then took turns role-playing the two sides, with one playing ABC and the other disarming these accusations with anticipatory labels. "You're going to think we are a big, bad prime contractor when we are done," Anna practiced saying slowly and naturally. "It seems you feel this work was promised to you from the beginning," Mark said. They trained in front of an observer, honing their pacing; deciding at what point they would label each fear; and planning when to include meaningful pauses. It was theater.

When the day of the meeting arrived, Anna opened by acknowledging ABC's biggest gripes. "We understand that we brought you on board with the shared goal of having you lead this work," she said. "You may feel like we have treated you unfairly, and that we changed the deal significantly since then. We acknowledge that you believe you were promised this work."

This received an emphatic nod from the ABC representatives, so Anna continued by outlining the situation in a way that encouraged the ABC reps to see the firms as teammates, peppering her statements with open-ended questions that showed she was listening: "What else is there you feel is important to add to this?"

By labeling the fears and asking for input, Anna was able to elicit an important fact about ABC's fears, namely that ABC was expecting this to be a high-profit contract because it thought Anna's firm was doing quite well from the deal.

This provided an entry point for Mark, who explained that the client's new demands had turned his firm's profits into losses, meaning that he and Anna needed to cut ABC's pay further, to three people. Angela, one of ABC's representatives, gasped.

"It sounds like you think we are the big, bad prime contractor trying to push out the small business," Anna said, heading off the accusation before it could be made.

"No, no, we don't think that," Angela said, conditioned by the acknowledgment to look for common ground.

With the negatives labeled and the worst accusations laid bare, Anna and Mark were able to turn the conversation to the contract. Watch what they do closely, as it's brilliant: they acknowledge ABC's situation while simultaneously shifting the onus of offering a solution to the smaller company.

"It sounds like you have a great handle on how the government contract *should* work," Anna said, labeling Angela's expertise.

"Yes—but I know that's not how it always goes," Angela answered, proud to have her experience acknowledged.

Anna then asked Angela how she would amend the contract so that everyone made some money, which pushed Angela to admit that she saw no way to do so without cutting ABC's worker count.

Several weeks later, the contract was tweaked to cut ABC's payout, which brought Anna's company $1 million that put the contract into the black. But it was Angela's reaction at the end of the meeting that most surprised Anna. After Anna had acknowledged that she had given Angela some bad news and that she understood how angry she must feel, Angela said:

"This is not a good situation but we appreciate the fact that you are acknowledging what happened, and we don't feel like you are mistreating us. And you are not the 'Big Bad Prime.'"

Anna's reaction to how this turned out? "Holy crap, this stuff actually works!"

She's right. As you just saw, the beauty of going right after negativity is that it brings us to a safe zone of empathy. Every one of us has an inherent, human need to be understood, to connect with the person across the table. That explains why, after Anna labeled Angela's fears, Angela's first instinct was to add nuance and detail to those fears. And that detail gave Anna the power to accomplish what she wanted from the negotiation.

GET A SEAT—AND AN UPGRADE—ON A SOLD-OUT FLIGHT

Up to this point, we've been building each skill as if they were musical instruments: first, try the saxophone mirror; now here's the bass label; and finally, why don't you blow a note on the French horn of tactical silence. But in a real negotiation the band all plays together. So you've got to learn how to conduct.

Keeping all the instruments playing is really awkward for most people. It seems to go by in such a rush. So what I'm going to do here is play a song at slow speed so you can hear each instrument note by note. I promise you'll quickly see how the skills you have been building play off one another, rising, riffing, falling, and pausing in perfect harmony.

Here is the situation (the song, if you will): My student Ryan B. was flying from Baltimore to Austin to sign a large computer-consulting contract. For six months, the client representative had gone back and forth on whether he wanted the services, but a major system collapse put the representative in a tight spot with his CEO. To shift the blame, he called Ryan with his CEO on the line and very aggressively demanded to know why it was taking Ryan so long to come ink the contract. If Ryan was not there by Friday morning, he said, the deal was off.

Ryan bought a ticket for the next morning, Thursday, but a freak lightning storm whipped up in Baltimore, closing the airport for five hours. It became painfully clear that Ryan wasn't going to make his original connection to Austin from Dallas. Worse, when he called American Airlines just before departing, he found that his connection had been automatically rebooked to 3 p.m. the next day, putting the contract in jeopardy.

When Ryan finally got to Dallas at 8 p.m., he ran to the gate where the day's final American Airlines flight to Austin was less than thirty minutes from takeoff. His goal was to get on that flight or, at worst, get an earlier flight the next day.

In front of him at the gate, a very aggressive couple was yelling at the gate agent, who was barely looking at them as she tapped on the computer in front of her; she was clearly making every effort not to scream back. After she'd said, "There's nothing I can do," five times, the angry couple finally gave up and left.

To start, watch how Ryan turns that heated exchange to his advantage. Following on the heels of an argument is a great position for a negotiator, because your counterpart is desperate for an empathetic connection. Smile, and you're already an improvement.

"Hi, Wendy, I'm Ryan. It seems like they were pretty upset."

This labels the negative and establishes a rapport based on empathy. This in turn encourages Wendy to elaborate on her situation, words Ryan then mirrors to invite her to go further.

"Yeah. They missed their connection. We've had a fair amount of delays because of the weather."

"The weather?"

After Wendy explains how the delays in the Northeast had rippled through the system, Ryan again labels the negative and then mirrors her answer to encourage her to delve further.

"It seems like it's been a hectic day."

"There've been a lot of 'irate consumers,' you know? I mean, I get it, even though I don't like to be yelled at. A lot of people are trying to get to Austin for the big game."

"The big game?"

"UT is playing Ole Miss football and every flight into Austin has been booked solid."

"Booked solid?"

Now let's pause. Up to this point, Ryan has been using labels and mirrors to build a relationship with Wendy. To her it must seem like idle chatter, though, because he hasn't asked for anything. Unlike the angry couple, Ryan is acknowledging her situation. His words ping-pong between "What's that?" and "I hear you," both of which invite her to elaborate.

Now that the empathy has been built, she lets slip a piece of information he can use.

"Yeah, all through the weekend. Though who knows how many people will make the flights. The weather's probably going to reroute a lot of people through a lot of different places."

Here's where Ryan finally swoops in with an ask. But notice how he acts: not assertive or coldly logical, but with empathy and labeling that acknowledges her situation and tacitly puts them in the same boat.

"Well, it seems like you've been handling the rough day pretty well," he says. "I was also affected by the weather delays and missed my connecting flight. It seems like this flight is likely booked solid, but with what you said, maybe someone affected by the weather might miss this connection. Is there any possibility a seat will be open?"

Listen to that riff: Label, tactical empathy, label. And only then a request.

At this point, Wendy says nothing and begins typing on her computer. Ryan, who's eager not to talk himself out of a possible deal, engages in some silence. After thirty seconds, Wendy prints a boarding pass and hands it to Ryan, explaining that there were a few seats that were supposed to be filled by people who would now arrive much later than the flight's departure. To make Ryan's success even better, she puts him in Economy Plus seating.

All that in under two minutes!

The next time you find yourself following an angry customer at a corner store or airplane line, take a moment and practice labels and mirrors on the service person. I promise they won't scream, "Don't try to control me!" and burst into flames—and you might walk away with a little more than you expected.

KEY LESSONS

As you try to insert the tools of tactical empathy into your daily life, I encourage you to think of them as extensions of natural human interactions and not artificial conversational tics.

In any interaction, it pleases us to feel that the other side is listening and acknowledging our situation. Whether you are negotiating a business deal or simply chatting to the person at the supermarket butcher counter, creating an empathetic relationship and encouraging your counterpart to expand on their situation is the basis of healthy human interaction.

These tools, then, are nothing less than emotional best practices that help you cure the pervasive ineptitude that marks our most critical conversations in life. They will help you connect and create more meaningful and warm relationships. That they might help you extract what you want is a bonus; human connection is the first goal.

With that in mind, I encourage you to take the risk of sprinkling these in every conversation you have. I promise you that they will feel awkward and artificial at first, but keep at it. Learning to walk felt awfully strange, too.

As you internalize these techniques, turning the artifice of tactical empathy into a habit and then into an integral part of your personality, keep in mind these lessons from the chapter you've just read:

- Imagine yourself in your counterpart's situation. The beauty of empathy is that it doesn't demand that you agree with the other person's ideas (you may well find them crazy). But by acknowledging the other person's situation, you immediately convey that you are listening. And once they know that you are listening, they may tell you something that you can use.

- The reasons why a counterpart will *not* make an agreement with you are often more powerful than why they *will* make a deal, so focus first on clearing the barriers to agreement. Denying barriers or negative influences gives them credence; get them into the open.

- Pause. After you label a barrier or mirror a statement, let it sink in. Don't worry, the other party will fill the silence.

- Label your counterpart's fears to diffuse their power. We all want to talk about the happy stuff, but remember, the faster you interrupt action in your counterpart's amygdala, the part of the brain that generates fear, the faster you can generate feelings of safety, well-being, and trust.

- List the worst things that the other party could say about you and say them before the other person can. Performing an accusation audit in advance prepares you to head off negative dynamics before they take root. And because these accusations often sound exaggerated when said aloud, speaking them will encourage the other person to claim that quite the opposite is true.

- Remember you're dealing with a person who wants to be appreciated and understood. So use labels to reinforce and encourage positive perceptions and dynamics.

CHAPTER 4

BEWARE "YES"—MASTER "NO"

Let me paint a scenario we've all experienced: You're at home, just before dinner, and the phone rings. It is, no surprise, a telemarketer. He wants to sell you magazine subscriptions, water filters, frozen Argentine beef—to be honest, it doesn't matter, as the script is always the same. After butchering your name, and engaging in some disingenuous pleasantries, he launches into his pitch.

The hard sell that comes next is a scripted flowchart designed to cut off your escape routes as it funnels you down a path with no exit but "Yes." "Do you enjoy a nice glass of water from time to time." "Well, yes, but . . ." "Me, too. And like me I bet you like crisp, clean water with no chemical aftertaste, like Mother Nature made it." "Well, yes, but . . ."

Who is this guy with a fake smile in his voice, you wonder, who thinks he can trick you into buying something you don't want? You feel your muscles tighten, your voice go defensive, and your heart rate accelerate.

You feel like his prey, and you are!

The last thing you want to do is say "Yes," even when it's the only way to answer, "Do you drink water?" Compromise and concession, even to the truth, feels like defeat. And "No," well, "No" feels like salvation, like an oasis. You're tempted to use "No" when it's blatantly untrue, just to hear its sweet sound. "*No*, I do *not* need water, carbon filtered or otherwise. *I'm a camel!*"

Now let's think about this selling technique. It's designed to get to "Yes" at all costs, as if "No" were death. And for many of us it is. We have all these negative connotations with "No." We talk about the rejection of "No," about the fear of hearing it. "No" is the ultimate negative word.

But at the end of the day, "Yes" is often a meaningless answer that hides deeper objections (and "Maybe" is even worse). Pushing hard for "Yes" doesn't get a negotiator any closer to a win; it just angers the other side.

So if "Yes" can be so damn uncomfortable, and "No" such a relief, why have we fetishized one and demonized the other?

We have it backward. For good negotiators, "No" is pure gold. That negative provides a great opportunity for you and the other party to clarify what you really want by eliminating what you don't want. "No" is a safe choice that maintains the status quo; it provides a temporary oasis of control.

At some point in their development, all negotiators have to come to grips with "No." When you come to realize the real psychological dynamic behind it, you'll love the word. It's not just that you lose your fear of it, but that you come to learn what it does for you and how you can build deals out of it.

"Yes" and "Maybe" are often worthless. But "No" always alters the conversation.

"NO" STARTS THE NEGOTIATION

My fascination with "No" in all its beautiful nuance began with a conversation I had a few months before my negotiation career began.

I started my career with the Bureau as a member of the FBI SWAT team in the Pittsburgh Division but after nearly two years I was transferred to New York, where the FBI attached me to the Joint Terrorism Task Force (JTTF). It was an amazing post: We spent our days and nights tracking suspected terrorists, investigating their cells, and assessing whether or how they might strike. We were untying knots of human anger in the midst of America's biggest city, making life-and-death decisions on who was dangerous and who was just blowing hot air. The work fascinated me.

Ever since my first days with the Bureau, I had been obsessed with crisis response. The immediacy of the task enthralled me. The stakes were high. Lives hung in the balance.

The emotional terrain was complex, changing, and often conflicting. To successfully gain a hostage's safe release, a negotiator had to penetrate the hostage-taker's motives, state of mind, intelligence, and emotional strengths and weaknesses. The negotiator played the role of bully, conciliator, enforcer, savior, confessor, instigator, and peacemaker—and that's just a few of the parts.

I thought I was cut out for every one of them.

A few weeks after I got to Manhattan, I showed up at the desk of Amy Bonderow, who ran the FBI's Crisis Negotiation Team in New York. I didn't know beans about negotiating, so I went for the direct approach.

"I want be a hostage negotiator," I said.

"Everyone does—got any training?" she asked.

"No," I said.

"Any credentials?"

"Nope." I answered.

"Any experience?" she asked.

"No," I answered.

"Do you have a degree in psychology, sociology, *anything* at all related to negotiation?"

"No."

"Looks like you answered your own question," she said. "No. Now go away."

"Go away?" I protested. "Really?"

"Yep. As in, 'Leave me alone.' Everybody wants to be a hostage negotiator, and you have no résumé, experience, or skills. So what would you say in my position? You got it: 'No.'"

I paused in front of her, thinking, This is not how my negotiating career ends. I had stared down terrorists; I wasn't going to just leave.

"Come on," I said. "There has to be *something* I can do."

Amy shook her head and gave one of those ironic laughs that mean the person doesn't think you've got a snowball's chance in hell.

"I'll tell you what. Yes, there is something you can do: Volunteer at a suicide hotline. Then come talk to me. No guarantees, got it?" she said. "Now, seriously, *go away*."

My conversation with Amy kicked off my awareness of the complex and hidden subtleties of conversation, the power of certain words, the seemingly unintelligible emotional truths that so often underlie intelligible exchanges.

A trap into which many fall is to take what other people say literally. I started to see that while people played the game of conversation, it was in the game beneath the game, where few played, that all the leverage lived.

In our chat, I saw how the word "No"—so apparently clear and direct—really wasn't so simple. Over the years, I've thought back repeatedly to that conversation, replaying how Amy so quickly turned me down, again and again. But her "No's" were just the gateway to "Yes." They gave her—and me—time to pivot, adjust, and reexamine, and actually created the environment for the one "Yes" that mattered.

While assigned to the JTTF, I worked with an NYPD lieutenant named Martin. He had a hard shell, and whenever asked for anything he responded with a terse negative. After I'd gotten to know him a bit, I asked him why. "Chris," he said, proudly, "a lieutenant's job is to say, 'No.'"

At first, I thought that sort of automated response signaled a failure of imagination. But then I realized I did the same thing with my teenage son, and that after I'd said "No" to him, I often found that I was open to hearing what he had to say.

That's because having protected myself, I could relax and more easily consider the possibilities.

"No" is the *start* of the negotiation, not the *end* of it. We've been conditioned to fear the word "No." But it is a statement of perception far more often than of fact. It seldom means, "I have considered all the facts and made a rational choice." Instead, "No" is often a decision, frequently temporary, to maintain the status quo. Change is scary, and "No" provides a little protection from that scariness.

Jim Camp, in his excellent book, *Start with NO*,[1] counsels the reader to give their adversary (his word for counterpart) permission to say "No" from the outset of a negotiation. He calls it "the right to veto." He observes that people will fight to the death to preserve their right to say "No," so give them that right and the negotiating environment becomes more constructive and collaborative almost immediately.

When I read Camp's book, I realized this was something we'd known as hostage negotiators for years. We'd learned that the quickest way to get a hostage-taker out was to take the time to talk them out, as opposed to "demanding" their surrender. Demanding their surrender, "telling" them to come out, always ended up creating a much longer standoff and occasionally, actually contributed to death.

It comes down to the deep and universal human need for autonomy. People need to feel in control. When you preserve a person's autonomy by clearly giving them permission to say "No" to your ideas, the emotions calm, the effectiveness of the decisions go up, and the other party can really look at your proposal. They're allowed to hold it in their hands, to turn it around. And it gives you time to elaborate or pivot in order to convince your counterpart that the change you're proposing is more advantageous than the status quo.

Great negotiators seek "No" because they know that's often when the real negotiation begins.

Politely saying "No" to your opponent (we'll go into this in more depth in Chapter 9), calmly hearing "No," and just letting the other side know that they are welcome to say "No" has a positive impact on any negotiation. In fact, your invitation for the other side to say "No" has an amazing power to bring down barriers and allow for beneficial communication.

This means you have to train yourself to hear "No" as something other than rejection, and respond accordingly. When someone tells you "No," you need to rethink the word in one of its alternative—and much more real—meanings:

- I am not yet ready to agree;

- You are making me feel uncomfortable;

- I do not understand;

- I don't think I can afford it;

- I want something else;

- I need more information; or

- I want to talk it over with someone else.

Then, after pausing, ask solution-based questions or simply label their effect:

"What about this doesn't work for you?"

"What would you need to make it work?"

"It seems like there's something here that bothers you."

People have a need to say, "No." So don't just hope to hear it at some point; get them to say it early.

PERSUADE IN THEIR WORLD

I'd like to present you with a guy named Joe Businessman as he readies himself for a negotiation. You've met him before. He's the prepared type, with all his *Getting to Yes* strategies written out and memorized. And he's *more* than ready to unleash them on the guy across the table. Joe pauses to look at his expensive suit in the mirror, fantasizing about the impressive things he'll say and the fancy charts and graphs that'll back up those things and leave his counterpart—his *opponent*—vanquished and in defeat. He is Russell Crowe in *Gladiator*. He is The Man.

Now allow me to let you in on a secret: None of that preparation will mean a damn thing. His negotiation style is all me, me, me, ego, ego, ego. And when the people on the other side of the table pick up those signals, they're going to decide that it's best to politely, even furtively, ignore this Superman . . . by saying "Yes"!

"Huh?" you say.

Sure, the word they'll say right off is "Yes," but that word is only a tool to get this blowhard to go away. They'll weasel out later, claiming changing conditions, budget issues, the weather. For now, they just want to be released because Joe isn't convincing them of anything; he's only convincing himself.

I'll let you in on a secret. There are actually three kinds of "Yes": Counterfeit, Confirmation, and Commitment.

A counterfeit "yes" is one in which your counterpart plans on saying "no" but either feels "yes" is an easier escape route or just wants to disingenuously keep the conversation going to obtain more information or some other kind of edge. A confirmation "yes" is generally innocent, a reflexive response to a black-or-white question; it's sometimes used to lay a trap but mostly it's just simple affirmation with no promise of action. And a commitment "yes" is the real deal; it's a true agreement that leads to action, a "yes" at the table that ends with a signature on the contract. The commitment "yes" is what you want, but the three types sound almost the same so you have to learn how to recognize which one is being used.

Human beings the world over are so used to being pursued for the commitment "yes" as a condition to find out more that they have become masters at giving the counterfeit "yes." That's what the people facing Joe Businessman are doing, dangling the counterfeit "yes" so they can hear more.

Whether you call it "buy-in" or "engagement" or something else, good negotiators know that their job isn't to put on a great performance but to gently guide their counterpart to discover their goal as his own.

Let me tell you, I learned that the hard way.

Two months after talking with Amy, I started answering phones for HelpLine, the crisis hotline founded by Norman Vincent Peale.

The basic rule was that you couldn't be with anybody on the phone for more than twenty minutes. If you did your job, it wasn't going to take you longer than that to get them to a better place. We had a thick book of organizations we referred them to for help. It was a paramedic approach: patch them up and send them on their way.

But people in crisis only accounted for about 40 percent of the calls we got. The majority of the calls came from frequent callers. These are highly dysfunctional people, energy vampires whom no one else would listen to anymore.

We kept a list of frequent callers and when you got one, the first thing you had to do was check to see if the person had called that day, because they were only allowed one call a day. They knew it, too. A lot of times, they'd say, "Yeah, I'm Eddie. I haven't called yet today. Go ahead and check the list. You got to talk to me."

Since I was there primarily to learn a skill, I loved the frequent callers. They were a problem, and I loved trying to figure them out. I felt I had some talent at it. I felt like a superstar.

When it came time for my performance review, they assigned me a shift supervisor named Jim Snyder. Jim was a hotline veteran and a sweetheart; the only problem was he always wanted to joke around. Jim understood that volunteer burnout was the biggest problem at a hotline, so he dedicated his time to making work fun. I became good friends with Jim.

For my review, Jim waited until I got a call and went into the monitoring room where the supervisors could listen to our calls. The call was from one of my frequent clients, a cabbie with a fear of going outside and plenty of time to tell me about it. This energy vampire (his name was Daryl) launched into his shtick about how he was going to lose his house and with it his will to live if he couldn't work.

"Seriously, when was the last time someone tried to hurt you on the streets?" I asked.

"Well, I mean, it's been a long time," Daryl said.

"Like . . . ?"

"I can't really remember a date, Chris. Maybe a year, I guess."

"So it's safe to say that the outside world hasn't been *too* hard on you, right?"

"Yes," Daryl said. "I suppose so."

We went back and forth like this for a while, as I made him admit that most of us had little to fear in the world. I was feeling good about my new skills, about listening to Daryl and then "CareFronting" him, which was the slightly goofy name we gave to assertively—but caringly—responding to frequent callers.

It was all flowing, and our rapport was great. I even got Daryl to laugh a few times. By the time I was done with him, he couldn't give me one reason not to step outside.

"Thank you, Chris," Daryl said just before he hung up. "Thanks for doing such a great job."

Before I went to see Jim, I leaned back in my chair and basked in that compliment. How often do you get that from a man in pain, I thought. Then I sprung up and strode toward the monitoring room, so proud I was practically buffing my nails on my shirt and patting my own back.

Jim motioned me to the chair in front of him and gave me his biggest smile. I must have returned it with twice the wattage.

"Well, Chris," he said, still smiling. "That was one of the worst calls I ever heard."

I stared at him, gape-jawed.

"Jim, did you hear Daryl congratulate me?" I asked. "I talked him down, man. I killed it."

Jim smiled—I hated that smile right then—and nodded.

"That's one of the signs, because they should be congratulating themselves when they get off the line," he said. "They don't need to be congratulating you. That tells me you did too much. If they think you did it—if you were the guy who killed it—how is he going to help himself? I don't want to be harsh, but you were horrible."

As I listened to what Jim said, I felt that acid stomach rush you get when you are forced to accept that the guy dumping on you is completely right. Daryl's response had been a kind of "yes," but it had been anything but a true commitment "yes." He'd made no promise to action. His "yes" had been designed to make me feel good enough to leave him alone. Daryl may not have known it, but his "yes" was as counterfeit as they came.

You see, that whole call had been about me and my ego and not the caller. But the only way to get these callers to take action was to have them own the conversation, to believe that they were coming to these conclusions, to these necessary next steps, and that the voice at the other end was simply a medium for those realizations.

Using all your skills to create rapport, agreement, and connection with a counterpart is useful, but ultimately that connection is useless unless the other person feels that they are equally as responsible, if not *solely* responsible, for creating the connection and the new ideas they have.

I nodded slowly, the fight drained out of me.

"One of the worst calls?" I said to Jim. "That's right."

I worked hard at reorienting myself from that point on. I asked so many questions and read so much about it that soon they had me teaching two classes for new volunteers at HelpLine: the opening class, on active listening; and the one on CareFrontation.

Got it, you say. It's not about me. We need to persuade from their perspective, not ours. But how?

By starting with their most basic wants.

In every negotiation, in every agreement, the result comes from someone else's decision. And sadly, if we believe that we can control or manage others' decisions with compromise and logic, we're leaving millions on the table. But while we can't control others' decisions, we can influence them by inhabiting their world and seeing and hearing exactly what they want.

Though the intensity may differ from person to person, you can be sure that everyone you meet is driven by two primal urges: the need to feel safe and secure, and the need to feel in control. If you satisfy those drives, you're in the door.

As we saw with my chat with Daryl, you're not going to logically *convince* them that they're safe, secure, or in control. Primal needs are urgent and illogical, so arguing them into a corner is just going to push your counterpart to flee with a counterfeit "Yes."

And being "nice" in the form of feigned sympathy is often equally as unsuccessful. We live in an age that celebrates niceness under various names. We are exhorted to be nice and to respect people's feelings at all times and in every situation.

But nice alone in the context of negotiation can backfire. Nice, employed as a ruse, is disingenuous and manipulative. Who hasn't received the short end of the stick in dealings with a "nice" salesman who took you for a ride? If you rush in with plastic niceness, your bland smile is going to dredge up all that baggage.

Instead of getting inside with logic or feigned smiles, then, we get there by asking for "No." It's the word that gives the speaker feelings of safety and control. "No" starts conversations and creates safe havens to get to the final "Yes" of commitment. An early "Yes" is often just a cheap, counterfeit dodge.

About five months after she'd told me to "go away," I stopped by Amy Bonderow's office and told her that I'd volunteered at HelpLine.

"You did?" she asked, smiling with surprise. "I tell everybody to do that. And nobody ever does."

It turned out that Amy had started her negotiating career by volunteering at the same place. She started naming people who were now mutual friends of ours. We laughed about Jim.

In a sudden shift, Amy stopped speaking and stared at me. I shifted in my shoes as she gave me the Pause. Then she smiled.

"You get the next position."

At that time, there were five other people aiming for the same slot, people who had psychology degrees, experience, and credentials. But I was on the road to the next hostage negotiation training course at the FBI Academy in Quantico, Virginia, ahead of everybody else. My career as a negotiator had officially begun.

"NO" IS PROTECTION

Think back to the telemarketer at the beginning of this chapter. The obvious reply to his question—"Do you enjoy a nice glass of water?"—is "Yes." But all you want to do is scream, "No!" After a question like that you just know the rest of the phone call is going to be painful.

That, in a nutshell, distills the inherent contradictions in the values we give "Yes" and "No." Whenever we negotiate, there's no doubt we want to finish with a "Yes." But we mistakenly conflate the positive value of that final "Yes" with a positive value of "Yes" in general. And because we see "No" as the opposite of "Yes," we then assume that "No" is always a bad thing.

Nothing could be further from the truth. Saying "No" gives the speaker the feeling of safety, security, and control. You use a question that prompts a "No" answer, and your counterpart feels that by turning you down he has proved that he's in the driver's seat. Good negotiators welcome—even invite—a solid "No" to start, as a sign that the other party is engaged and thinking.

Gun for a "Yes" straight off the bat, though, and your counterpart gets defensive, wary, and skittish. That's why I tell my students that, if you're trying to sell something, don't start with "Do you have a few minutes to talk?" Instead ask, "Is now a bad time to talk?" Either you get "Yes, it is a bad time" followed by a good time or a request to go away, or you get "No, it's not" and total focus.

As an exercise, the next time you get a telemarketing call, write down the questions the seller asks. I promise you'll find that your level of discomfort correlates directly to how quickly he pushes you for "Yes."

My colleague Marti Evelsizer was the one who first opened my eyes to why "No" was better than "Yes."

Marti was the FBI's Crisis Negotiation Coordinator in Pittsburgh at the time. She was a dynamo and a negotiating genius, which earned her huge respect both within the Bureau and with the local police. But human beings are innately jealous, and her immediate supervisor was no exception to that rule. Her success diminished him, and that made her a threat.

His jealousy got the better of him when the Pittsburgh Police Department's Hostage Negotiation Team asked her to sit on the selection board for their new candidates. Picking her, and doing so over her boss, was an unprecedented move.

So her boss decided to remove her from her position. For ignoring her regular duties, he said. But really it was for being a threat.

When Marti sat down with her supervisor for her official dismissal, her options were few. He had every right to do as he pleased.

Marti told me that she considered a variety of scenarios. She thought about going right at his jealousy and hashing it out, or explaining how the job would reflect well on the Bureau: "Would you like our office to be honored for its expertise?"

But by the time she sat down with him, she had picked one of the most strongly worded "No"-oriented setup questions I have ever heard.

"Do you want the FBI to be embarrassed?" she said.

"No," he answered.

"What do you want me to do?" she responded.

He leaned back in his chair, one of those 1950s faux-leather numbers that squeak meaningfully when the sitter shifts. He stared at her over his glasses and then nodded ever so slightly. He was in control.

"Look, you can keep the position," he said. "Just go back out there and don't let it interfere with your other duties."

And a minute later Marti walked out with her job intact.

When I heard Marti do that, I was like, "Bang!" By pushing for a "No," Marti nudged her supervisor into a zone where he was making the decisions. And then she furthered his feelings of safety and power with a question inviting him to define her next move.

The important thing here is that Marti not only accepted the "No"; she searched it out and embraced it.

At a recent sales conference, I asked the participants for the one word they all dread. The entire group yelled, "No!" To them—and to almost everyone—"No" means one thing: end of discussion.

But that's not what it means.

"No" is not failure. Used strategically it's an answer that opens the path forward. Getting to the point where you're no longer horrified by the word "No" is a liberating moment that every negotiator needs to reach. Because if your biggest fear is "No," you can't negotiate. You're the hostage of "Yes." You're handcuffed. You're done.

So let's undress "No." It's a reaffirmation of autonomy. It is not a use or abuse of power; it is not an act of rejection; it is not a manifestation of stubbornness; it is not the end of the negotiation.

In fact, "No" often opens the discussion up. The sooner you say "No," the sooner you're willing to see options and opportunities that you were blind to previously. Saying "No" often spurs people to action because they feel they've protected themselves and now see an opportunity slipping away.

Since I've demystified "No" for myself, I've found the ideas, perceptions, and baggage that people have with that two-letter word to be fascinating. To me, it's like watching a movie or a music video from the 1980s for the umpteenth time. You can identify with the experience—while simultaneously being conscious of the fact that the world, and you, have moved on.

Today, I coach my students to learn to see "No" for what it is. Rather than harming them or those they negotiate with, "No" protects and benefits all parties in an exchange. "No" creates safety, security, and the feeling of control. It's a requirement to implementable success. It's a pause, a nudge, and a chance for the speaker to articulate what they do want.

As you can see, "No" has a lot of skills.

- "No" allows the real issues to be brought forth;

- "No" protects people from making—and lets them correct— ineffective decisions;

- "No" slows things down so that people can freely embrace their decisions and the agreements they enter into;

- "No" helps people feel safe, secure, emotionally comfortable, and in control of their decisions;

- "No" moves everyone's efforts forward.

One of my grad school students, a political fund-raiser named Ben Ottenhoff, drove home this lesson with a bang. For years, he'd been using a traditional "Yes pattern" fund-raising script to raise money for Republican congressional candidates.

FUND-RAISER: Hello, can I speak with Mr. Smith?

MR. SMITH: Yes, this is he.

FUND-RAISER: I'm calling from the XYZ Committee, and I wanted to ask you a few important questions about your views on our economy today. Do you believe that gas prices are currently too high?

MR. SMITH: Yes, gas prices are much too high and hurting my family.

FUND-RAISER: Do you believe that the Democrats are part of the problem when it comes to high gas prices?

MR. SMITH: Yes, President Obama is a bad person

FUND-RAISER: Do you think we need change in November?

MR SMITH: Yes, I do.

FUND-RAISER: Can you give me your credit card number so you can be a part of that change?

In theory at least, the "Yes" answers built up a reservoir of positivity that exploded into donations when requested at the end of the script. The problem, in reality, was that the "Yes pattern" scripts had been giving poor rates of return for years. All the steps were "Yes," but the final answer was invariably "No."

Then Ben read Jim Camp's book *Start with NO* in my class and began to wonder if "No" could be a tool to boost donations. Ben knew that giving the potential donors a no-hard-feelings way to get off the call was going to be a tough sell to his grassroots fundraisers, because it goes against everything they had been trained to do. But Ben's a smart guy, so instead of totally swapping scripts he had a small group of his grassroots guys test-market a "No"-oriented script.

FUND-RAISER: Hello, can I speak with Mr. Smith?

MR. SMITH: Yes, this is he.

FUND-RAISER: I'm calling from the XYZ Committee, and I wanted to ask you a few important questions about your views on our economy today. Do you feel that if things stay the way they are, America's best days are ahead of it?

MR. SMITH: No, things will only get worse.

FUND-RAISER: Are you going to sit and watch President Obama take the White House in November without putting up a fight?

MR. SMITH: No, I'm going to do anything I can to make sure that doesn't happen.

FUND-RAISER: If you want do something today to make sure that doesn't happen, you can give to XYZ Committee, which is working hard to fight for you.

See how clearly that swaps "Yes" for "No" and offers to take a donation if Mr. Smith *wants*? It puts Mr. Smith in the driver's seat; he's in charge. And it works! In a truly remarkable turnaround, the "No"-oriented script got a *23 percent better rate of return.*

The only sad part of Ben's tale is that despite the huge improvement in results, he couldn't roll out the script to all his fund-raisers. It went against fund-raising orthodoxy, and longtime fund-raisers like the fake comfort of the "Yes." Genius is often missed the first time around, right?

One negotiating genius who's impossible to miss is Mark Cuban, the billionaire owner of the Dallas Mavericks. I always quote to my students one of his best lines on negotiation: "Every 'No' gets me closer to a 'Yes.'" But then I remind them that extracting those "No's" on the road to "Yes" isn't always easy.

There is a big difference between making your counterpart feel that they can say "No" and actually getting them to say it. Sometimes, if you're talking to somebody who is just not listening, the only way you can crack their cranium is to antagonize them into "No."

One great way to do this is to mislabel one of the other party's emotions or desires. You say something that you know is totally wrong, like "So it seems that you really are eager to leave your job" when they clearly want to stay. That forces them to listen and makes them comfortable correcting you by saying, "No, that's not it. This is it."

Another way to force "No" in a negotiation is to ask the other party what they *don't* want. "Let's talk about what you would say 'No' to," you'd say. And people are comfortable saying "No" here because it feels like self-protection. And once you've gotten them to say "No," people are much more open to moving forward toward new options and ideas.

"No"—or the lack thereof—also serves as a warning, the canary in the coal mine. If despite all your efforts, the other party won't say "No," you're dealing with people who are indecisive or confused or who have a hidden agenda. In cases like that you have to end the negotiation and walk away.

Think of it like this: No "No" means no go.

EMAIL MAGIC: HOW NEVER TO BE IGNORED AGAIN

There's nothing more irritating than being ignored. Being turned down is bad, but getting no response at all is the pits. It makes you feel invisible, as if you don't exist. And it's a waste of your time. We've all been through it: You send an email to someone you're trying to do business with and they ignore you. Then you send a polite follow-up and they stonewall you again. So what do you do?

You provoke a "No" with this one-sentence email.

Have you given up on this project?

The point is that this one-sentence email encapsulates the best of "No"-oriented questions and plays on your counterpart's natural human aversion to loss. The "No" answer the email demands offers the other party the feeling of safety and the illusion of control while encouraging them to define their position and explain it to you.

Just as important, it makes the implicit threat that you will walk away on your own terms. To stop that from happening—to cut their losses and prove their power—the other party's natural inclination is to reply immediately and disagree. *No, our priorities haven't changed. We've just gotten bogged down and . . .*

If you're a parent, you already use this technique instinctively. What do you do when your kids won't leave the house/park/mall? You say, "Fine. I'm leaving," and you begin to walk away. I'm going to guess that well over half the time they yell, "No, wait!" and run to catch up. No one likes to be abandoned.

Now, this may seem like a rude way to address someone in business, but you have to get over that. It's not rude, and though it's direct, it's cloaked with the safety of "No." Ignoring you is what's rude. I can tell you that I've used this successfully not just in North America, but with people in two different cultures (Arabic and Chinese) famous for never saying "No."

KEY LESSONS

Using this chapter's tools in daily life is difficult for many people because they go directly against one of society's biggest social dictums. That is, "Be nice."

We've instrumentalized niceness as a way of greasing the social wheels, yet it's often a ruse. We're polite and we don't disagree to get through daily existence with the least degree of friction. But by turning niceness into a lubricant, we've leeched it of meaning. A smile and a nod might signify "Get me out of here!" as much as it means "Nice to meet you."

That's death for a good negotiator, who gains their power by understanding their counterpart's situation and extracting information about their counterpart's desires and needs. Extracting that information means getting the other party to feel safe and in control. And while it may sound contradictory, the way to get there is by getting the other party to disagree, to draw their own boundaries, to define their desires as a function of what they do not want.

As you try to put the chapter's methods to use, I encourage you to think of them as the anti–"niceness ruse." Not in the sense that they are unkind, but in the sense that they are authentic. Triggering "No" peels away the plastic falsehood of "Yes" and gets you to what's really at stake. Along the way, keep in mind these powerful lessons:

- Break the habit of attempting to get people to say "yes." Being pushed for "yes" makes people defensive. Our love of hearing "yes" makes us blind to the defensiveness we ourselves feel when someone is pushing us to say it.

- "No" is not a failure. We have learned that "No" is the anti-"Yes" and therefore a word to be avoided at all costs. But it really often just means "Wait" or "I'm not comfortable with that." Learn how to hear it calmly. It is not the end of the negotiation, but the beginning.

- "Yes" is the final goal of a negotiation, but don't aim for it at the start. Asking someone for "Yes" too quickly in a conversation—"Do you like to drink water, Mr. Smith?"—gets his guard up and paints you as an untrustworthy salesman.

- Saying "No" makes the speaker feel safe, secure, and in control, so trigger it. By saying what they don't want, your counterpart defines their space and gains the confidence and comfort to listen to you. That's why "Is now a bad time to talk?" is always better than "Do you have a few minutes to talk?"

- Sometimes the only way to get your counterpart to listen and engage with you is by forcing them into a "No." That means intentionally mislabeling one of their emotions or desires or asking a ridiculous question—like, "It seems like you want this project to fail"—that can only be answered negatively.

- Negotiate in their world. Persuasion is not about how bright or smooth or forceful you are. It's about the other party convincing themselves that the solution you want is their own idea. So don't beat them with logic or brute force. Ask them questions that open paths to your goals. *It's not about you.*

- If a potential business partner is ignoring you, contact them with a clear and concise "No"-oriented question that suggests that you are ready to walk away. "Have you given up on this project?" works wonders.

CHAPTER 5

TRIGGER THE TWO WORDS THAT IMMEDIATELY TRANSFORM ANY NEGOTIATION

In August 2000, the militant Islamic group Abu Sayyaf, in the southern Philippines, broadcast that it had captured a CIA agent. The truth was not as newsworthy, or as valuable to the rebels.

Abu Sayyaf had kidnapped Jeffrey Schilling, a twenty-four-year-old American who had traveled near their base in Jolo Island. A California native, Schilling became a hostage with a $10 million price tag on his head.

At the time I was a Supervisory Special Agent (SSA) attached to the FBI's elite Crisis Negotiation Unit (CNU). The CNU is the equivalent of the special forces of negotiations. It's attached to the FBI's Hostage Rescue Team (HRT). Both are national counterterrorist response assets. They are the best of the best.

The CNU is based at the FBI Academy in Quantico, Virginia. The FBI Academy has come to be known by the one word, "Quantico." Rightly or wrongly, Quantico has developed the reputation as one of the centers, if not the center of knowledge, for law enforcement. When a negotiation is going badly and the negotiators involved are directed to call and find out what "Quantico" has to say, the CNU is who they call.

CNU developed what is a powerful staple in the high-stakes world of crisis negotiation, the Behavioral Change Stairway Model (BCSM). The model proposes five stages—active listening, empathy, rapport, influence, and behavioral change—that take any negotiator from listening to influencing behavior.

The origins of the model can be traced back to the great American psychologist Carl Rogers, who proposed that real change can only come when a therapist accepts the client as he or she is—an approach known as unconditional positive regard. The vast majority of us, however, as Rogers explained, come to expect that love, praise, and approval are dependent on saying and doing the things people (initially, our parents) consider correct. That is, because for most of us the positive regard we experience is conditional, we develop a habit of hiding who we really are and what we really think, instead calibrating our words to gain approval but disclosing little.

Which is why so few social interactions lead to actual behavior change. Consider the typical patient with severe coronary heart disease recovering from open-heart surgery. The doctor tells the patient: "This surgery isn't a cure. The only way to truly prolong your life is to make the following behavior changes . . ." The grateful patient responds: "Yes, yes, yes, of course, Doctor! This is my second chance. I will change!"

And do they? Study after study has shown that, no, nothing changes; two years after their operation, more than 90 percent of patients haven't changed their lifestyle at all.

Though the stakes of an everyday negotiation with your child, boss, or client are usually not as high as that of a hostage (or health crisis) negotiation, the psychological environment necessary for not just temporary in-the-moment compliance, but real gut-level change, is the same.

If you successfully take someone up the Behavioral Change Stairway, each stage attempting to engender more trust and more connection, there will be a breakthrough moment when unconditional positive regard is established and you can begin exerting influence.

After years of refining the BCSM and its tactics, I can teach anyone how to get to that moment. But as cardiologists know all too well, and legions of B-school grads weaned on the most famous negotiating book in the world, *Getting to Yes*, have ultimately discovered, you more than likely haven't gotten there yet if what you're hearing is the word "yes."

As you'll soon learn, the sweetest two words in any negotiation are actually "That's right."

CREATE A SUBTLE EPIPHANY

I was a natural for the Schilling case. I had spent some time in the Philippines and had an extensive background in terrorism from my New York City days assigned to the Joint Terrorism Task Force (JTTF).

A few days after Schilling became a hostage, my partner Chuck Regini and I flew to Manila to run the negotiations. Along with Jim Nixon, the FBI's highest official in Manila, we conferred with top Philippine military brass. They agreed to let us guide the negotiations. Then we got down to business. One of us would take charge of the negotiation strategy for the FBI and consequently for the U.S. government. That became my role. With the support of my colleagues, my job was to come up with the strategy, get it approved, and implement it.

As a result of the Schilling case, I would become the FBI's lead international kidnapping negotiator.

Our principal adversary was Abu Sabaya, the rebel leader who personally negotiated for Schilling's ransom. Sabaya was a veteran of the rebel movement with a violent past. He was straight out of the movies, a terrorist-sociopath-killer. He had a history of rape, murder, and be-headings. He liked to record his bloody deeds on video and send them to the Philippine media.

Sabaya always wore sunglasses, a bandana, a black T-shirt, and camo pants. He thought it made him a more dashing figure. If you look for any photos of Abu Sayyaf terrorists from this period, you always see one in sunglasses. That's Sabaya.

Sabaya loved, loved, loved the media. He had the Philippine reporters on speed dial. They'd call him and ask him questions in Tagalog, his native tongue. He would answer in English because he wanted the world to hear his voice on CNN. "They should make a movie about me," he would tell reporters.

In my eyes, Sabaya was a cold-blooded businessman with an ego as big as Texas. A real shark. Sabaya knew he was in the commodities game. In Jeffrey Schilling, he had an item of value. How much could he get for it? He would find out, and I intended it to be a surprise he wouldn't like. As an FBI agent, I wanted to free the hostage and bring the criminal to justice.

One crucial aspect of any negotiation is to figure out how your adversary arrived at his position. Sabaya threw out the $10 million ransom based on a business calculation.

First, the United States was offering $5 million for information leading to the arrest of any of the remaining fugitives from the 1993 World Trade Center bombing. Sabaya reasoned that if the United States would pay $5 million to get its hands on someone it didn't like, it would pay much more for a citizen.

Second, a rival faction of the Abu Sayyaf had just reportedly been paid $20 million for six Western European captives. Libyan strong-man Muammar Gaddafi had made the payment as "development aid." This absurdity had been compounded by a significant portion of the ransom being paid in counterfeit bills. It was an opportunity for Gaddafi to both embarrass Western governments and get money over-the-table to groups with whom he sympathized. I'm sure he laughed about that episode until the day he died.

Regardless, a price had been set. Sabaya did the math and figured Schilling was worth $10 million. Problem was, Jeff Schilling came from a working-class family. His mother could come up with $10,000, perhaps. The United States wasn't about to pay one dollar. But we would allow a payment to be made if it could be run as a "sting" operation.

If we could draw Sabaya into an offer-counteroffer bargaining situation, we had a bargaining system that worked every time. We could beat him down to where we wanted him, get the hostage out, and set up the "sting."

For months Sabaya refused to budge. He argued that Muslims in the Philippines had suffered five hundred years of oppression, since Spanish missionaries had brought Catholicism to the Philippines in the sixteenth century. He recited instances where atrocities had been committed against his Islamic forebears. He explained why the Abu Sayyaf wanted to establish an Islamic state in the southern Philippines. Fishing rights had been violated. You name it, he thought it up and used it.

Sabaya wanted $10 million in war damages—not ransom, but war damages. He held firm in his demand and kept us out of the offer-counteroffer system we wanted to use against him.

And he occasionally dropped in threats that he was torturing Jeff Schilling.

Sabaya negotiated directly with Benjie, a Filipino military officer. They talked in Tagalog. We reviewed transcripts translated to English and used them to advise Benjie. I rotated in and out of Manila and oversaw the talks and strategy. I instructed Benjie to ask what Schilling had to do with five hundred years of bad blood between Muslims and Filipinos. He told Sabaya that $10 million was not possible.

No matter what approach we took to "reason" with Sabaya over why Schilling had nothing to do with the "war damages," it fell on deaf ears.

Our first "that's right" breakthrough actually came when I was negotiating with Benjie. He was a true Filipino patriot and hero. He was the leader of the Philippine National Police's Special Action Force and had been in his share of firefights. On many occasions, Benjie and his men had been sent on rescue missions to save hostages, and they had a sterling record. His men were feared, for good reason. They rarely took handcuffs.

Benjie wanted to take a hard line with Sabaya and speak to him in direct, no-nonsense terms. We wanted to engage Sabaya in dialogue to discover what made the adversary tick. We actually wanted to establish rapport with an adversary. To Benjie that was distasteful.

Benjie told us he needed a break. We had been working him nearly twenty-four hours a day, seven days a week for several weeks. He wanted to spend some time with his family in the mountains north of Manila. We agreed, but only on the condition that we could accompany him and spend several hours both on Saturday and Sunday working on negotiation strategy.

That Saturday night we sat in the library of the American ambassador's summer residence working on the strategy. As I was explaining to Benjie the value of establishing a rapport-based, working relationship, even with an adversary as dangerous as Sabaya, I could see a snarl coming over his face. I realized I needed to negotiate with Benjie.

"You hate Sabaya, don't you?" I said, leading with a label.

Benjie unloaded on me. "I tell you I *do*!" he said. "He has murdered and raped. He has come up on our radio when we were lobbing mortars on his position and said 'these mortars are music to my ears.' I heard his voice come on our radio one day and celebrate that he was standing over the body of one of my men."

This outburst was Benjie's equivalent of "that's right." As he acknowledged his rage, I watched him get control of his anger and calm down. Though he had been very good up to that point, from that moment forward Benjie became a superstar. He blossomed into a truly talented negotiator.

This "negotiation" between Benjie and me was no different than any other negotiation between colleagues who disagree on a strategy. Before you convince them to see what you're trying to accomplish, you have to say the things to them that will get them to say, "That's right."

The "that's right" breakthrough usually doesn't come at the beginning of a negotiation. It's invisible to the counterpart when it occurs, and they embrace what you've said. To them, it's a subtle epiphany.

TRIGGER A "THAT'S RIGHT!" WITH A SUMMARY

After four months of negotiations, Sabaya still refused to budge. I decided it was time to hit the reset switch.

Benjie had gotten so good at extending the conversations that you could tell that there were times that Sabaya must have paced back and forth for an hour before calling Benjie, trying to figure out how to get what he wanted. He would call in and say, "Tell me yes or no! Just yes or no!"

We had to get Sabaya off this war damages nonsense. No matter what type of questioning, logic, or reasoning we tried with him, he wouldn't release it. Threats against Schilling came and went. We talked him down each time.

I decided that in order to break through this phase we needed to reposition Sabaya with his own words in a way that would dissolve barriers. We needed to get him to say, "That's right." At the time, I didn't know for sure what kind of breakthrough it was going to give us. I just knew we needed to trust the process.

I wrote a two-page document that instructed Benjie to change course. We were going to use nearly every tactic in the active listening arsenal:

1. Effective Pauses: Silence is powerful. We told Benjie to use it for emphasis, to encourage Sabaya to keep talking until eventually, like clearing out a swamp, the emotions were drained from the dialogue.

2. Minimal Encouragers: Besides silence, we instructed using simple phrases, such as "Yes," "OK," "Uh-huh," or "I see," to effectively convey that Benjie was now paying full attention to Sabaya and all he had to say.

3. Mirroring: Rather than argue with Sabaya and try to separate Schilling from the "war damages," Benjie would listen and repeat back what Sabaya said.

4. Labeling: Benjie should give Sabaya's feelings a name and identify with how he felt. "It all seems so tragically unfair, I can now see why you sound so angry."

5. Paraphrase: Benjie should repeat what Sabaya is saying back to him in Benjie's own words. This, we told him, would powerfully show him you really do understand and aren't merely parroting his concerns.

6. Summarize: A good summary is the combination of re-articulating the meaning of what is said plus the acknowledgment of the emotions underlying that meaning (paraphrasing + labeling = summary). We told Benjie he needed to listen and repeat the "world according to Abu Sabaya." He needed to fully and completely summarize all the nonsense that Sabaya had come up with about war damages and fishing rights and five hundred years of oppression. And once he did that fully and completely, the only possible response for Sabaya, and anyone faced with a good summary, would be "that's right."

Two days later Sabaya phoned Benjie. Sabaya spoke. Benjie listened. When he spoke, he followed my script: he commiserated with the rebel group's predicament. Mirroring, encouraging, labeling, each tactic worked seamlessly and cumulatively to soften Sabaya up and begin shifting his perspective. Finally, Benjie repeated in his own words Sabaya's version of history and the emotions that came with that version.

Sabaya was silent for nearly a minute. Finally he spoke.

"That's right," he said.

We ended the call.

The "war damages" demand just disappeared.

From that point forward Sabaya never mentioned money again. He never asked for another dime for the release of Jeffrey Schilling. He ultimately became so weary of this case and holding the young Californian that he let down his guard. Schilling escaped from their camp, and Philippine commandoes swooped in and rescued him. He returned safely to his family in California.

Two weeks after Jeff Schilling escaped, Sabaya called Benjie:

"Have you been promoted yet?" he asked. "If not, you should have been."

"Why?" Benjie asked.

"I was going to hurt Jeffrey," Sabaya said. "I don't know what you did to keep me from doing that, but whatever it was, it worked."

In June 2002 Sabaya was killed in a shoot-out with Philippine military units.

In the heat of negotiations for a man's life, I didn't appreciate the value of those two words: "That's right." But when I studied the transcripts and reconstructed the trajectory of the negotiations, I realized that Sabaya had changed course when he uttered those words. Benjie had used some fundamental techniques that we had developed over many years. He had reflected Sabaya's vision. He had stepped back from confrontation. He had allowed Sabaya to speak freely and exhaust his version of events.

"That's right" signaled that negotiations could proceed from deadlock. It broke down a barrier that was impeding progress. It created a realization point with our adversary where he actually agreed on a point without the feeling of having given in.

It was a stealth victory.

When your adversaries say, "That's right," they feel they have assessed what you've said and pronounced it as correct of their own free will. They embrace it.

"That's right" allowed us to draw out the talks and divert Sabaya from hurting Schilling. And it gave Philippine commandos time to mount their rescue operation.

In hostage negotiations, we never tried to get to "yes" as an endpoint. We knew that "yes" is nothing without "how." And when we applied hostage negotiating tactics to business, we saw how "that's right" often leads to the best outcomes.

"THAT'S RIGHT" IS GREAT, BUT IF "YOU'RE RIGHT," NOTHING CHANGES

Driving toward "that's right" is a winning strategy in all negotiations. But hearing "you're right" is a disaster.

Take my son, Brandon, and his development as a football player. He had been playing on the offensive and defensive lines all through high school. At six foot two and 250 pounds, he was formidable. He loved to knock every player wearing an opposing jersey to the ground.

Having played quarterback, I didn't fully appreciate the blue-collar nature of being a lineman. Linemen are like mountain goats. They put their heads down and hit things. It makes them happy.

At St. Thomas More prep school in Connecticut, Brandon's coach moved him to linebacker, and his role suddenly changed from hitting everything he saw to avoiding players who were trying to block him. He was supposed to play off blocks—dodge them, if you will—and get to the ball. But Brandon continued to confront opposing blockers head-on, which kept him from getting to the ballcarrier. His coach pleaded with him to avoid blockers, but Brandon couldn't change. He loved to hit. Flattening opposing players was a source of pride.

Both his coach and I kept trying to explain it to him. And every time we got the worst possible answer—"*You're* right." He agreed, in theory, but he didn't own the conclusion. Then he would go right back to the behavior we were trying to get him to stop. He would smash blockers and take himself out of the play.

Why is "you're right" the worst answer?

Consider this: Whenever someone is bothering you, and they just won't let up, and they won't listen to anything you have to say, what do you tell them to get them to shut up and go away? "You're right."

It works every time. Tell people "you're right" and they get a happy smile on their face and leave you alone for at least twenty-four hours. But you haven't agreed to their position. You have used "you're right" to get them to quit bothering you.

I was in the same situation with Brandon. He didn't hear me and embrace my request. What could I say to get through to this kid? How could I reach Brandon and help him change course?

I thought back to Benjie and Sabaya. I took Brandon aside before a crucial game. I had searched my mind for a way to hear the two critical words, "That's right."

"You seem to think it's unmanly to dodge a block," I told him. "You think it's cowardly to get out of someone's way that's trying to hit you."

Brandon stared at me and paused.

"That's right," he said.

With those words Brandon embraced the reality of what was holding him back. Once he understood why he was trying to knock down every blocker, he changed course. He started avoiding the blocks and became an exceptionally fine linebacker.

With Brandon on the field tackling and playing star linebacker, St. Thomas More School won every game.

USING "THAT'S RIGHT" TO MAKE THE SALE

Getting to "that's right" helped one of my students in her job as a sales representative for a large pharmaceutical company.

She was trying to sell a new product to a doctor who used similar medication. He was the largest user of this kind of medication in her territory. The sale was critical to her success.

In her first appointments, the doctor dismissed her product. He said it was no better than the ones he was already using. He was unfriendly. He didn't even want to hear her viewpoint. When she presented the positive attributes of her product, he interrupted her and knocked them down.

Making the sales pitch, she soaked up as much as possible about the doctor. She learned that he was passionate about treating his patients. Each patient was special in his eyes. Improving their sense of calm and peace was the most important outcome for him. How could she put her understanding of his needs, desires, and passions to work for her?

At her next visit, the doctor asked what medications she wanted to discuss. Rather than tout the benefits of her product, she talked about him and his practice.

"Doctor," she said, "the last time I was in we spoke about your patients with this condition. I remember thinking that you seemed very passionate about treating them, and how you worked hard to tailor the specific treatment to each and every patient."

He looked her in the eyes as if he were seeing her for the first time.

"That's right," he said. "I really feel like I'm treating an epidemic that other doctors are not picking up on—which means that a lot of patients are not getting treated adequately."

She told him he seemed to have a deep understanding of how to treat these patients, especially because some of them didn't respond to the usual medications. They talked about specific challenges he had confronted in treating his patients. He gave her examples.

When he was finished, she summarized what he had said, especially the intricacies and problems in treatment.

"You seem to tailor specific treatments and medications for each patient," she said.

"That's right," he responded.

This was the breakthrough she had hoped to reach. The doctor had been skeptical and cold. But when she recognized his passion for his patients—using a summary—the walls came down. He dropped his guard, and she was able to gain his trust. Rather than pitch her product, she let him describe his treatment and procedures. With this, she learned how her medication would fit into his practice. She then paraphrased what he said about the challenges of his practice and reflected them back to him.

Once the doctor signaled his trust and rapport, she could tout the attributes of her product and describe precisely how it would help him reach the outcomes he desired for his patients. He listened intently.

"It might be perfect for treating a patient who has not benefited from the medication I have been prescribing," he told her. "Let me give yours a try."

She made the sale.

USING "THAT'S RIGHT" FOR CAREER SUCCESS

One of my Korean students got to "that's right" in negotiating with his ex-boss for a new job.

Returning to Seoul after getting his MBA, he wanted to work in his company's consumer electronics division, rather than the semiconductor section, where he had been stationed. He was a human resources specialist. Under the company's rules, he believed he had to remain in his previous department, unless he could *also* get approval from his ex-boss. He had gotten two job offers from the consumer products division. He phoned his ex-boss from the United States.

"You should reject this offer and find your spot here with the semiconductor division," the ex-boss said.

My student hung up depressed. If he wanted to advance in the company, he had to obey his former superior. He rejected the two offers and prepared to return to the semiconductor side.

Then he contacted a friend who was a senior manager in the human resources department to check on the company's regulations. He found there was no rule that he had to stay within his division, but he did need his ex-boss's blessing to switch.

He phoned his ex-boss again. This time he asked questions to draw him out.

"Is there any reason you want me to go to the semiconductor headquarters?" he asked.

"It's the best position for you," the ex-boss said.

"The best position?" he asked. "It sounds like there's no regulation that I have to remain with the semiconductor division," he said. "Hmm," the ex-boss said. "I don't think there is any."

"Then will you please tell me what made you decide that I remain in the semiconductor headquarters?" he asked.

The ex-boss said he needed someone to help him network at

headquarters between the semiconductor and consumer products divisions.

"So it sounds like you could approve my new position no matter which division, as long as I was in headquarters and could help you communicate better with the top managers."

"That's right," he said. "I must admit I need your help in headquarters."

My student realized he had made a breakthrough. Not only had his ex-boss uttered those sweet words—"that's right"—but he had revealed his true motive: he needed an ally in headquarters.

"Is there any other help you need?" he asked.

"Let me tell you everything," the ex-boss responded.

It turns out his former superior would be up for a promotion to vice president in two years. He desperately wanted to move up into this job. He needed someone in headquarters to lobby the company CEO.

"I would help you in any way," my student said. "But I could help with the networking and also talk you up to the CEO even if I were at headquarters with the consumer products division, right?"

"That's right," he said. "If you get an offer from the consumer products unit, I will approve it."

Bingo! By asking questions that got him to "that's right," my student had achieved his goal. He also got his boss to reveal two "Black Swans," the unspoken, underlying breakthrough dynamics of a negotiation (explored in more detail in Chapter 10):

- His boss needed someone to help him network and communicate in headquarters.

- His boss would be up for a promotion and needed someone to talk him up to the CEO.

My student was able to win the job he desired on the consumer electronics division. And he's been talking up his former boss.

"I was stunned," he wrote me in an email. "In this culture it is not really possible to know what a superior is thinking."

I have many opportunities to travel the country and speak to business leaders, either in formal speaking engagements or private counseling sessions. I entertain them with war stories, then I describe some basic negotiating skills. I always impart a few techniques. Getting to "that's right" is a staple.

After a speech in Los Angeles, one of the attendees, Emily, sent me an email:

> *Hi Chris, I feel compelled to tell you that I just tried the "That's right" technique in a price negotiation with a potential new client. And, I got what I wanted. I'm so excited!*
>
> *Before I probably would have just gone with the "in-the-middle" suggested price (halfway between my initial offer and her initial counter). Instead, I believe I correctly assessed her motivations, presented her with the right statement to get to a "that's right" (in her mind) . . . and then she proposed the solution I wanted and asked if I would agree to it! So, I did of course.*
>
> *Thank you!*
> *Emily*

And I thought to myself: That's right.

KEY LESSONS

"Sleeping in the same bed and dreaming different dreams" is an old Chinese expression that describes the intimacy of partnership (whether in marriage or in business) without the communication necessary to sustain it.

Such is the recipe for bad marriages and bad negotiations.

With each party having its own set of objectives, its own goals and motivations, the truth is that the conversational niceties—the socially lubricating "yeses" and "you're rights" that get thrown out fast and furious early in any interaction—are not in any way a substitute for real understanding between you and your partner.

The power of getting to that understanding, and not to some simple "yes," is revelatory in the art of negotiation. The moment you've convinced someone that you truly understand her dreams and feelings (the whole world that she inhabits), mental and behavioral change becomes possible, and the foundation for a breakthrough has been laid.

Use these lessons to lay that foundation:

- Creating unconditional positive regard opens the door to changing thoughts and behaviors. Humans have an innate urge toward socially constructive behavior. The more a person feels understood, and positively affirmed in that understanding, the more likely that urge for constructive behavior will take hold.

- "That's right" is better than "yes." Strive for it. Reaching "that's right" in a negotiation creates breakthroughs.

- Use a summary to trigger a "that's right." The building blocks of a good summary are a label combined with paraphrasing. Identify, rearticulate, and emotionally affirm "the world according to . . ."

CHAPTER 6

BEND THEIR REALITY

One Monday morning in Haiti's capital, Port-au-Prince, a call came in to the FBI office from the nephew of a prominent Haitian political figure. He spoke so fast he had to repeat his story three times before I understood. But finally I got the basics: kidnappers had snatched his aunt from her car, and their ransom demand was $150,000.

"Give us the money," the kidnappers told him, "or your aunt is going to die."

In the lawless, chaotic wake of the 2004 rebellion that toppled President Jean-Bertrand Aristide, Haiti surpassed Colombia as the kidnap capital of the Americas. In fact, with between eight and ten people abducted every day in the Caribbean nation of eight million, Haiti earned the dubious honor of having the highest kidnapping rate in the world.

During this onslaught of abductions and death threats, I was the FBI's lead international kidnapping negotiator. And I had never seen anything like it. Reports of abductions—increasingly bold, daylight attacks right in Port-au-Prince—seemed to roll into the office hourly: fourteen students abducted on their school bus; American missionary Phillip Snyder shot in an ambush and seized along with a Haitian boy he was taking to Michigan for eye surgery; prominent Haitian politicians and businessmen bundled from their homes in broad daylight. No one was spared.

Most of the abductions went down the same way: ski-mask-clad kidnappers surrounded a house or a car, forced entry with a gun, and snatched a vulnerable victim—usually a woman, child, or elderly person.

Early on, there was the possibility that the kidnappings were driven by politically aligned gangs seeking to destabilize Haiti's new government. This proved to be wrong. Haitian criminals are famous for employing brutal means for political ends, but when it came to kidnappings, it was almost always all business.

Later on, I'll get to how we pieced together the clues to discover who the perpetrators were and what they really wanted—invaluable information when it came to negotiating with and destabilizing these gangs. But first I want to discuss the crystallizing feature of high-stakes, life-and-death negotiating: that is, how little of it is on the surface.

When that Monday ransom call came in to the politician's nephew, the guy was so petrified he could only think of doing one thing: paying the thugs. His reaction makes sense: when you get a call from brutal criminals who say they'll kill your aunt unless you pay them immediately, it seems impossible to find leverage in the situation. So you pay the ransom and they release your relative, right?

Wrong. There's always leverage. Negotiation is never a linear formula: add X to Y to get Z. We all have irrational blind spots, hidden needs, and undeveloped notions.

Once you understand that subterranean world of unspoken needs and thoughts, you'll discover a universe of variables that can be leveraged to change your counterpart's needs and expectations. From using some people's fear of deadlines and the mysterious power of odd numbers, to our misunderstood relationship to fairness, there are always ways to bend our counterpart's reality so it conforms to what we ultimately want to give them, not to what they initially think they deserve.

DON'T COMPROMISE

Let's go back to the $150,000 ransom demand. We're always taught to look for the win-win solution, to accommodate, to be reasonable. So what's the win-win here? What's the compromise? The traditional negotiating logic that's drilled into us from an early age, the kind that exalts compromises, says, "Let's just split the difference and offer them $75,000. Then everyone's happy."

No. Just, simply, no. The win-win mindset pushed by so many negotiation experts is usually ineffective and often disastrous. At best, it satisfies neither side. And if you employ it with a counterpart who has a win-lose approach, you're setting yourself up to be swindled.

Of course, as we've noted previously, you need to keep the cooperative, rapport-building, empathetic approach, the kind that creates a dynamic in which deals can be made. But you have to get rid of that naïveté. Because compromise—"splitting the difference"—can lead to terrible outcomes. Compromise is often a "bad deal" and a key theme we'll hit in this chapter is that "no deal is better than a bad deal."

Even in a kidnapping?

Yes. A bad deal in a kidnapping is where someone pays and no one comes out.

To make my point on compromise, let me paint you an example: A woman wants her husband to wear black shoes with his suit. But her husband doesn't want to; he prefers brown shoes. So what do they do? They compromise, they meet halfway. And, you guessed it, he wears one black and one brown shoe. Is this the best outcome? No! In fact, that's the *worst* possible outcome. Either of the two other outcomes—black or brown—would be better than the compromise.

Next time you want to compromise, remind yourself of those mis-matched shoes.

So why are we so infatuated with the notion of compromise if it often leads to poor results?

The real problem with compromise is that it has come to be known as this great concept, in relationships and politics and everything else. Compromise, we are told quite simply, is a sacred moral good.

Think back to the ransom demand: Fair is no ransom, and what the nephew wants is to pay nothing. So why is he going to offer $75,000, much less $150,000, for the ransom? There is no validity in the $150,000 request. With any compromise, the nephew ends up with a bizarrely bad result.

I'm here to call bullshit on compromise right now. We don't com-promise because it's right; we compromise because it is easy and be-cause it saves face. We compromise in order to say that at least we got half the pie. Distilled to its essence, we compromise to be safe. Most people in a negotiation are driven by fear or by the desire to avoid pain. Too few are driven by their actual goals.

So don't settle and—here's a simple rule—*never split the difference*. Creative solutions are almost always preceded by some degree of risk, annoyance, confusion, and conflict. Accommodation and compro-mise produce none of that. You've got to embrace the hard stuff. That's where the great deals are. And that's what great negotiators do.

DEADLINES: MAKE TIME YOUR ALLY

Time is one of the most crucial variables in any negotiation. The simple passing of time and its sharper cousin, the deadline, are the screw that pressures every deal to a conclusion.

Whether your deadline is real and absolute or merely a line in the sand, it can trick you into believing that doing a deal now is more important than getting a good deal. Deadlines regularly make people say and do impulsive things that are against their best interests, because we all have a natural tendency to rush as a deadline approaches.

What good negotiators do is force themselves to resist this urge and take advantage of it in others. It's not so easy. Ask yourself: What is it about a deadline that causes pressure and anxiety? The answer is consequences; the perception of the loss we'll incur in the future— "The deal is off!" our mind screams at us in some imaginary future scenario—should no resolution be achieved by a certain point in time.

When you allow the variable of time to trigger such thinking, you have taken yourself hostage, creating an environment of reactive behaviors and poor choices, where your counterpart can now kick back and let an imaginary deadline, and your reaction to it, do all the work for him.

Yes, I used the word "imaginary." In all the years I've been doing work in the private sector, I've made it a point to ask nearly every entrepreneur and executive I've worked with whether, over the course of their entire careers, they have ever been a witness to or a party of a negotiation in which a missed deadline had negative repercussions. Among hundreds of such clients, there's one single, solitary gentleman who gave the question serious consideration and responded affirmatively. Deadlines are often arbitrary, almost always flexible, and hardly ever trigger the consequences we think—or are told—they will.

Deadlines are the bogeymen of negotiation, almost exclusively self-inflicted figments of our imagination, unnecessarily unsettling us for no good reason. The mantra we coach our clients on is, "No deal is better than a bad deal." If that mantra can truly be internalized, and clients begin to believe they've got all the time they need to conduct the negotiation right, their patience becomes a formidable weapon.

A few weeks after the Haitian kidnapping boom began, we started to notice two patterns. First, Mondays seemed to be especially busy, as if the kidnappers had a particularly strong work ethic and wanted to get a jump on the week. And, second, the thugs grew increasingly eager to get paid as the weekend approached.

At first, this didn't make any sense. But by listening closely to the kidnappers and debriefing the hostages we rescued, we discovered something that should have been obvious: These crimes weren't politically motivated at all. Instead, these guys were garden-variety thugs who wanted to get paid by Friday so they could party through the weekend.

Once we understood the pattern and knew the kidnappers' self-imposed deadline, we had two key pieces of information that totally shifted the leverage to our side.

First, if we let the pressure build by stalling the negotiations until Thursday or Friday, we could cut the best deal. And, second, because you didn't need anything close to $150,000 to have a good weekend in Haiti, offering a lot, lot less would suffice.

How close we were getting to their self-imposed deadline would be indicated by how specific the threats were that they issued. "Give us the money or your aunt is going to die" is an early stage threat, as the time isn't specified. Increasing specificity on threats in any type of negotiations indicates getting closer to real consequences at a real specified time. To gauge the level of a particular threat, we'd pay attention to how many of the four questions—What? Who? When? And how?—were addressed. When people issue threats, they consciously or subconsciously create ambiguities and loopholes they fully intend to exploit. As the loopholes started to close as the week progressed, and did so over and over again in similar ways with different kidnappings, the pattern emerged.

With this information in hand, I came to expect the kidnappings to be orderly, four-day events. It didn't make the abductions any more pleasant for the victim, but it certainly made them more predictable—and a whole lot cheaper—for the families on the other end.

It's not just with hostage negotiations that deadlines can play into your hands. Car dealers are prone to give you the best price near the end of the month, when their transactions are assessed. And corporate salespeople work on a quarterly basis and are most vulnerable as the quarter comes to a close.

Now, knowing how negotiators use their counterpart's deadlines to gain leverage would seem to suggest that it's best to keep your own deadlines secret. And that's the advice you'll get from most old-school negotiation experts.

In his bestselling 1980 book, *You Can Negotiate Anything*,[1] negotiation expert Herb Cohen tells the story of his first big business deal, when his company sent him to Japan to negotiate with a supplier.

When he arrived, his counterparts asked him how long he was staying, and Cohen said a week. For the next seven days, his hosts proceeded to entertain him with parties, tours, and outings—everything but negotiation. In fact, Cohen's counterparts didn't start serious talks until he was about to leave, and the two sides hammered out the deal's final details in the car to the airport.

Cohen landed in the United States with the sinking feeling that he'd been played, and that he had conceded too much under deadline pressure. Would he have told them his deadline in retrospect? No, Cohen says, because it gave them a tool he didn't have: "They knew my deadline, but I didn't know theirs."

That mentality is everywhere these days. Seeing a simple rule to follow and assuming that a deadline is a strategic weakness, most negotiators follow Cohen's advice and hide their drop-dead date.

Allow me to let you in on a little secret: Cohen, and the herd of negotiation "experts" who follow his lead, are wrong. Deadlines cut both ways. Cohen may well have been nervous about what his boss would say if he left Japan without an agreement. But it's also true that Cohen's counterparts wouldn't have won if he'd left without a deal. That's the key: When the negotiation is over for one side, it's over for the other too.

In fact, Don A. Moore, a professor at the Haas School of Business at the University of California, Berkeley, says that hiding a deadline actually puts the negotiator in the worst possible position. In his research, he's found that hiding your deadlines dramatically increases the risk of an impasse. That's because having a deadline pushes you to speed up your concessions, but the other side, thinking that it has time, will just hold out for more.

Imagine if when NBA owners set a lockout deadline during contract negotiations they didn't tell the players' union. They would concede and concede as the deadline approached, inciting the union to keep negotiating past the secret deadline. In that sense, hiding a deadline means you're negotiating with yourself, and you always lose when you do so.

Moore discovered that when negotiators tell their counterparts about their deadline, they get better deals. It's true. First, by revealing your cutoff you reduce the risk of impasse. And second, when an opponent knows your deadline, he'll get to the real deal- and concession-making more quickly.

I've got one final point to make before we move on: Deadlines are almost never ironclad. What's more important is engaging in the process and having a feel for how long that will take. You may see that you have more to accomplish than time will actually allow before the clock runs out.

NO SUCH THING AS FAIR

In the third week of my negotiations class, we play my favorite type of game, that is, the kind that shows my students how much they don't understand themselves (I know—I'm cruel).

It's called the Ultimatum Game, and it goes like this: After the students split into pairs of a "proposer" and an "accepter," I give each proposer $10. The proposer then has to offer the accepter a round number of dollars. If the accepter agrees he or she receives what's been offered and the proposer gets the rest. If the accepter refuses the offer, though, they both get nothing and the $10 goes back to me.

Whether they "win" and keep the money or "lose" and have to give it back is irrelevant (except to my wallet). What's important is the offer they make. The truly shocking thing is that, almost without exception, whatever selection anyone makes, they find themselves in a minority. No matter whether they chose $6/$4, $5/$5, $7/$3, $8/$2, etc., they look around and are inevitably surprised to find no split was chosen far more than any other. In something as simple as merely splitting $10 of "found" money, there is no consensus of what constitutes a "fair" or "rational" split.

After we run this little experiment, I stand up in front of the class and make a point they don't like to hear: the reasoning each and every student used was 100 percent irrational and emotional.

"What?" they say. "I made a rational decision."

Then I lay out how they're wrong. First, how could they all be using reason if so many have made different offers? That's the point: They didn't. They assumed the other guy would reason just like them. "If you approach a negotiation thinking that the other guy thinks like you, you're wrong," I say. "That's not empathy; that's projection."

And then I push it even further: Why, I ask, did none of the proposers offer $1, which is the best rational offer for them and logically unrejectable for the accepter? And if they did and they got rejected—which happens—why did the accepter turn them down?

"Anyone who made any offer other than $1 made an emotional choice" I say. "And for you accepters who turned down $1, since when is getting $0 better than getting $1? Did the rules of finance suddenly change?"

This rocks my students' view of themselves as rational actors. But they're not. None of us are. We're all irrational, all emotional. Emotion is a necessary element to decision making that we ignore at our own peril. Realizing that hits people hard between the eyes.

In *Descartes' Error: Emotion, Reason, and the Human Brain*,[2] neuroscientist Antonio Damasio explained a groundbreaking discovery he made. Studying people who had damage in the part of the brain where emotions are generated, he found that they all had something peculiar in common: They couldn't make decisions. They could describe what they should do in logical terms, but they found it impossible to make even the simplest choice.

In other words, while we may use logic to reason ourselves toward a decision, the actual decision *making* is governed by emotion.

THE F-WORD: WHY IT'S SO POWERFUL, WHEN TO USE IT, AND HOW

The most powerful word in negotiations is "Fair." As human beings, we're mightily swayed by how much we feel we have been respected. People comply with agreements if they feel they've been treated fairly and lash out if they don't.

A decade of brain-imaging studies has shown that human neural activity, particularly in the emotion-regulating insular cortex, reflects the degree of unfairness in social interactions. Even nonhuman primates are hardwired to reject unfairness. In one famous study, two capuchin monkeys were set to perform the same task, but one was rewarded with sweet grapes while the other received cucumbers. In response to such blatant unfairness, the cucumber-fed monkey literally went bananas.

In the Ultimatum Game, years of experience has shown me that most accepters will invariably reject any offer that is less than half of the proposer's money. Once you get to a quarter of the proposer's money you can forget it and the accepters are insulted. Most people make an irrational choice to let the dollar slip through their fingers rather than to accept a derisory offer, because the negative emotional value of unfairness outweighs the positive rational value of the money.

This irrational reaction to unfairness extends all the way to serious economic deals.

Remember Robin Williams's great work as the voice of the genie in Disney's *Aladdin*? Because he wanted to leave something wonderful behind for his kids, he said, he did the voice for a cut-rate fee of $75,000, far below his usual $8 million payday. But then something happened: the movie became a huge hit, raking in $504 million.

And Williams went ballistic.

Now look at this with the Ultimatum Game in mind. Williams wasn't angry because of the money; it was the perceived unfairness that pissed him off. He didn't complain about his contract until *Aladdin* became a blockbuster, and then he and his agent went loud and long about how they got ripped off.

Lucky for Williams, Disney wanted to keep its star happy. After initially pointing out the obvious—that he'd happily signed the deal—Disney made the dramatic gesture of sending the star a Picasso painting worth a reported $1 million.

The nation of Iran was not so lucky.

In recent years, Iran has put up with sanctions that have cost it well over $100 billion in foreign investment and oil revenue in order to defend a uranium-enriching nuclear program that can only meet 2 percent of its energy needs. In other words, like the students who won't take a free $1 because the offer seems insulting, Iran has screwed itself out of its chief source of income—oil and gas revenue—in order to pursue an energy project with little expected payoff.

Why? Again, fairness.

For Iran, it's not fair that the global powers—which together have several thousand nuclear weapons—should be able to decide if it can use nuclear energy. And why, Iran wonders, is it considered a pariah for enriching uranium when India and Pakistan, which clandestinely acquired nuclear weapons, are accepted members of the international community?

In a TV interview, former Iranian nuclear negotiator Seyed Hossein Mousavian hit the nail on the head. "The nuclear issue today for Iranians is not nuclear," he said, "it's defending their integrity [as an] independent identity against the pressure of the rest."

You may not trust Iran, but its moves are pretty clear evidence that rejecting perceived unfairness, even at substantial cost, is a powerful motivation.

Once you understand what a messy, emotional, and destructive dynamic "fairness" can be, you can see why "Fair" is a tremendously powerful word that you need to use with care.

In fact, of the three ways that people drop this F-bomb, only one is positive.

The most common use is a judo-like defensive move that destabilizes the other side. This manipulation usually takes the form of something like, "We just want what's fair."

Think back to the last time someone made this implicit accusation of unfairness to you, and I bet you'll have to admit that it immediately triggered feelings of defensiveness and discomfort. These feelings are often subconscious and often lead to an irrational concession.

A friend of mine was selling her Boston home in a bust market a few years back. The offer she got was much lower than she wanted—it meant a big loss for her—and out of frustration she dropped this F-bomb on the prospective buyer.

"We just want what's fair," she said.

Emotionally rattled by the implicit accusation, the guy raised his offer immediately.

If you're on the business end of this accusation, you need to realize that the other side might not be trying to pick your pocket; like my friend, they might just be overwhelmed by circumstance. The best response either way is to take a deep breath and restrain your desire to concede. Then say, "Okay, I apologize. Let's stop everything and go back to where I started treating you unfairly and we'll fix it."

The second use of the F-bomb is more nefarious. In this one, your counterpart will basically accuse you of being dense or dishonest by saying, "We've given you a fair offer." It's a terrible little jab meant to distract your attention and manipulate you into giving in.

Whenever someone tries this on me, I think back to the last NFL lockout.

Negotiations were getting down to the wire and the NFL Players Association (NFLPA) said that before they agreed to a final deal they wanted the owners to open their books. The owners' answer?

"We've given the players a fair offer."

Notice the horrible genius of this: instead of opening their books or declining to do so, the owners shifted the focus to the NFLPA's supposed lack of understanding of fairness.

If you find yourself in this situation, the best reaction is to simply mirror the "F" that has just been lobbed at you. "Fair?" you'd respond, pausing to let the word's power do to them as it was intended to do to you. Follow that with a label: "It seems like you're ready to provide the evidence that supports that," which alludes to opening their books or otherwise handing over information that will either contradict their claim to fairness or give you more data to work with than you had previously. Right away, you declaw the attack.

The last use of the F-word is my favorite because it's positive and constructive. It sets the stage for honest and empathetic negotiation.

Here's how I use it: Early on in a negotiation, I say, "I want you to feel like you are being treated fairly at all times. So please stop me at any time if you feel I'm being unfair, and we'll address it."

It's simple and clear and sets me up as an honest dealer. With that statement, I let people know it is okay to use that word with me if they use it honestly. As a negotiator, you should strive for a reputation of being fair. Your reputation precedes you. Let it precede you in a way that paves success.

HOW TO DISCOVER THE EMOTIONAL DRIVERS BEHIND WHAT THE OTHER PARTY VALUES

A few years ago, I stumbled upon the book *How to Become a Rainmaker*,[3] and I like to review it occasionally to refresh my sense of the emotional drivers that fuel decisions. The book does a great job to explain the sales job not as a rational argument, but as an emotional framing job.

If you can get the other party to reveal their problems, pain, and unmet objectives—if you can get at what people are *really* buying— then you can sell them a vision of their problem that leaves your proposal as the perfect solution.

Look at this from the most basic level. What does a good babysitter sell, really? It's not child care exactly, but a relaxed evening. A furnace salesperson? Cozy rooms for family time. A locksmith? A feeling of security.

Know the emotional drivers and you can frame the benefits of any deal in language that will resonate.

BEND THEIR REALITY

Take the same person, change one or two variables, and $100 can be a glorious victory or a vicious insult. Recognizing this phenomenon lets you bend reality from insult to victory.

Let me give you an example. I have this coffee mug, red and white with the Swiss flag. No chips, but used. What would you pay for it, deep down in your heart of hearts?

You're probably going to say something like $3.50.

Let's say it's your mug now. You're going to sell it to me. So tell me what it's worth.

You're probably going to say something between $5 and $7.

In both cases, it was the exact same mug. All I did was move the mug in relation to you, and I totally changed its value.

Or imagine that I offer you $20 to run a three-minute errand and get me a cup of coffee. You're going to think to yourself that $20 for three minutes is $400 an hour. You're going to be thrilled.

What if then you find out that by getting you to run that errand I made a million dollars. You'd go from being ecstatic for making $400 an hour to being angry because you got ripped off.

The value of the $20, just like the value of the coffee mug, didn't change. But your perspective of it did. Just by how I position the $20, I can make you happy or disgusted by it.

I tell you that not to expose our decision making as emotional and irrational. We've already seen that. What I am saying is that while our decisions may be largely irrational, that doesn't mean there aren't consistent patterns, principles, and rules behind how we act. And once you know those mental patterns, you start to see ways to influence them.

By far the best theory for describing the principles of our irrational decisions is something called *Prospect Theory*. Created in 1979 by the psychologists Daniel Kahneman and Amos Tversky, prospect theory describes how people choose between options that involve risk, like in a negotiation. The theory argues that people are drawn to sure things over probabilities, even when the probability is a better choice. That's called the *Certainty Effect*. And people will take greater risks to avoid losses than to achieve gains. That's called *Loss Aversion*.

That's why people who statistically have no need for insurance buy it. Or consider this: a person who's told he has a 95 percent chance of receiving $10,000 or a 100 percent chance of getting $9,499 will usually avoid risk and take the 100 percent certain safe choice, while the same person who's told he has a 95 percent chance of losing $10,000 or a 100 percent chance of losing $9,499 will make the opposite choice, risking the bigger 95 percent option to avoid the loss. The chance for loss incites more risk than the possibility of an equal gain.

Over the next few pages I'll explain a few prospect theory tactics you can use to your advantage. But first let me leave you with a crucial lesson about loss aversion: In a tough negotiation, it's not enough to show the other party that you can deliver the thing they want.

To get real leverage, you have to persuade them that they have something concrete to lose if the deal falls through.

1. ANCHOR THEIR EMOTIONS

To bend your counterpart's reality, you have to start with the basics of empathy. So start out with an accusation audit acknowledging all of their fears. By anchoring their emotions in preparation for a loss, you inflame the other side's loss aversion so that they'll jump at the chance to avoid it.

On my first consulting project after leaving the FBI, I received the honor to train the national hostage negotiation team for the United Arab Emirates. Unfortunately, the prestige of the assignment was tempered during the project by problems with the general contractor (I was a subcontractor). The problems became so bad that I was going to have to go back to the contractors I'd signed up, who normally got $2,000 a day, and tell them that for several months, I could only offer $500.

I knew exactly what they would do if I just told them straight out: they'd laugh me out of town. So I got each of them on the phone and hit them hard with an accusation audit.

"I got a lousy proposition for you," I said, and paused until each asked me to go on. "By the time we get off the phone, you're going to think I'm a lousy businessman. You're going to think I can't budget or plan. You're going to think Chris Voss is a big talker. His first big project ever out of the FBI, he screws it up completely. He doesn't know how to run an operation. And he might even have lied to me."

And then, once I'd anchored their emotions in a minefield of low expectations, I played on their loss aversion.

"Still, I wanted to bring this opportunity to you before I took it to someone else," I said.

Suddenly, their call wasn't about being cut from $2,000 to $500 but how not to lose $500 to some other guy.

Every single one of them took the deal. No counteroffers, no complaints. Now, if I hadn't anchored their emotions low, their perception of $500 would have been totally different. If I'd just called and said, "I can give you $500 per day. What do you think?" they'd have taken it as an insult and slammed down the phone.

2. LET THE OTHER GUY GO FIRST . . . MOST OF THE TIME.

Now, it's clear that the benefits of anchoring emotions are great when it comes to bending your counterpart's reality. But going first is not necessarily the best thing when it comes to negotiating price.

When the famous film director Billy Wilder went to hire the famous detective novelist Raymond Chandler to write the 1944 classic *Double Indemnity*, Chandler was new to Hollywood. But he came ready to negotiate, and in his meeting with Wilder and the movie's producer, Chandler made the first salary offer: he bluffly demanded $150 per week and warned Wilder that it might take him three weeks to finish the project.

Wilder and the producer could barely stop from laughing, because they had been planning to pay Chandler $750 per week and they knew that movie scripts took months to write. Lucky for Chandler, Wilder and the producer valued their relationship with Chandler more than a few hundred dollars, so they took pity on him and called an agent to represent Chandler in the negotiations.

Similarly, I had a student named Jerry who royally screwed up his salary negotiation by going first (let me say that this happened before he was my student).

In an interview at a New York financial firm, he demanded $110,000, in large part because it represented a 30 percent raise. It was only after he started that he realized that the firm had started everybody else in his program at $125,000.

That's why I suggest you let the other side anchor monetary negotiations.

The real issue is that neither side has perfect information going to the table. This often means you don't know enough to open with confidence. That's especially true anytime you don't know the market value of what you are buying or selling, like with Jerry or Chandler.

By letting them anchor you also might get lucky: I've experienced many negotiations when the other party's first offer was higher than the *closing* figure I had in mind. If I'd gone first they would have agreed and I would have left with either the winner's curse or buyer's remorse, those gut-wrenching feelings that you've overpaid or undersold.

That said, you've got to be careful when you let the other guy anchor. You have to prepare yourself psychically to withstand the first offer. If the other guy's a pro, a shark, he's going to go for an extreme anchor in order to bend *your* reality. Then, when they come back with a merely absurd offer it will seem reasonable, just like an expensive $400 iPhone seems reasonable after they mark it down from a crazy $600.

The tendency to be anchored by extreme numbers is a psychological quirk known as the "anchor and adjustment" effect. Researchers have discovered that we tend to make adjustments from our first reference points. For example, most people glimpsing 8 × 7 × 6 × 5 × 4 × 3 × 2 × 1 estimate that it yields a higher result than the same string in reverse order. That's because we focus on the first numbers and extrapolate.

That's not to say, "Never open." Rules like that are easy to remember, but, like most simplistic approaches, they are not always good advice. If you're dealing with a rookie counterpart, you might be tempted to be the shark and throw out an extreme anchor. Or if you really know the market and you're dealing with an equally informed pro, you might offer a number just to make the negotiation go faster.

Here's my personal advice on whether or not you want to be the shark that eats a rookie counterpart. Just remember, your reputation precedes you. I've run into CEOs whose reputation was to always badly beat their counterpart and pretty soon no one would deal with them.

3. ESTABLISH A RANGE

While going first rarely helps, there is one way to *seem* to make an offer and bend their reality in the process. That is, by alluding to a range.

What I mean is this: When confronted with naming your terms or price, counter by recalling a similar deal which establishes your "ballpark," albeit the best possible ballpark you wish to be in. Instead of saying, "I'm worth $110,000," Jerry might have said, "At top places like X Corp., people in this job get between $130,000 and $170,000."

That gets your point across without moving the other party into a defensive position. And it gets him thinking at higher levels. Research shows that people who hear extreme anchors unconsciously adjust their expectations in the direction of the opening number. Many even go directly to their price limit. If Jerry had given this range, the firm probably would have offered $130,000 because it looked so cheap next to $170,000.

In a recent study,[4] Columbia Business School psychologists found that job applicants who named a range received significantly higher overall salaries than those who offered a number, especially if their range was a "bolstering range," in which the low number in the range was what they actually wanted.

Understand, if you offer a range (and it's a good idea to do so) expect them to come in at the low end.

4. PIVOT TO NONMONETARY TERMS

People get hung up on "How much?" But don't deal with numbers in isolation. That leads to bargaining, a series of rigid positions defined by emotional views of fairness and pride. Negotiation is a more intricate and subtle dynamic than that.

One of the easiest ways to bend your counterpart's reality to your point of view is by pivoting to nonmonetary terms. After you've anchored them high, you can make your offer seem reasonable by offering things that aren't important to you but could be important to them. Or if their offer is low you could ask for things that matter more to you than them. Since this is sometimes difficult, what we often do is throw out examples to start the brainstorming process.

Not long ago I did some training for the Memphis Bar Association. Normally, for the training they were looking for, I'd charge $25,000 a day. They came in with a much lower offer that I balked at. They then offered to do a cover story about me in their association magazine. For me to be on the cover of a magazine that went out to who knows how many of the country's top lawyers was priceless advertising. (Plus my mom is really proud of it!)

They had to put something on the cover anyway, so it had zero cost to them and I gave them a steep discount on my fee. I constantly use that as an example in my negotiations now when I name a price. I want to stimulate my counterpart's brainstorming to see what valuable nonmonetary gems they might have that are cheap to them but valuable to me.

5. WHEN YOU DO TALK NUMBERS, USE ODD ONES

Every number has a psychological significance that goes beyond its value. And I'm not just talking about how you love 17 because you think it's lucky. What I mean is that, in terms of negotiation, some numbers appear more immovable than others.

The biggest thing to remember is that numbers that end in 0 inevitably feel like temporary placeholders, guesstimates that you can easily be negotiated off of. But anything you throw out that sounds less rounded—say, $37,263—feels like a figure that you came to as a result of thoughtful calculation. Such numbers feel serious and permanent to your counterpart, so use them to fortify your offers.

6. SURPRISE WITH A GIFT

You can get your counterpart into a mood of generosity by staking an extreme anchor and then, after their inevitable first rejection, offering them a wholly unrelated surprise gift.

Unexpected conciliatory gestures like this are hugely effective because they introduce a dynamic called reciprocity; the other party feels the need to answer your generosity in kind. They will suddenly come up on their offer, or they'll look to repay your kindness in the future. People feel obliged to repay debts of kindness.

Let's look at it in terms of international politics. In 1977 Egyptian president Anwar Sadat dramatically pushed negotiations on the Egypt-Israel peace treaty forward by making a surprise address to the Israeli Knesset, a generous gesture that did not involve making any actual concessions but did signify a big step toward peace.

Back in Haiti, a few hours after the kidnappers had snatched his aunt, I was on the phone with the politician's nephew.

There was no way their family could come up with $150,000, he told me, but they could pay between $50,000 and $85,000. But since learning that the ransom was just party money, I was aiming much lower: $5,000. We were not going to compromise. It was a matter of professional pride.

I advised him to start off by anchoring the conversation in the idea that he didn't have the money, but to do so without saying "No" so as not to hit their pride head-on.

"How am I supposed to do that?" he asked in the next call.

The kidnapper made another general threat against the aunt and again demanded the cash.

That's when I had the nephew subtly question the kidnapper's fairness.

"I'm sorry," the nephew responded, "but how are we supposed to pay if you're going to hurt her?"

That brought up the aunt's death, which was the thing the kidnappers most wanted to avoid. They needed to keep her unharmed if they hoped to get any money. They were commodity traders, after all.

Notice that to this point the nephew hadn't named a price. This game of attrition finally pushed the kidnappers to name a number first. Without prodding, they dropped to $50,000.

Now that the kidnappers' reality had been bent to a smaller number, my colleagues and I told the nephew to stand his ground.

"How can I come up with that kind of money?" we told him to ask.

Again, the kidnapper dropped his demand, to $25,000.

Now that we had him in our sights, we had the nephew make his first offer, an extreme low anchor of $3,000.

The line went silent and the nephew began to sweat profusely, but we told him to hold tight. This always happened at the moment the kidnapper's economic reality got totally rearranged.

When he spoke again, the kidnapper seemed shell-shocked. But he went on. His next offer was lower, $10,000. Then we had the nephew answer with a strange number that seemed to come from deep calculation of what his aunt's life was worth: $4,751.

His new price? $7,500. In response, we had the cousin "spontaneously" say he'd throw in a new portable CD stereo and repeated the $4,751. The kidnappers, who didn't really want the CD stereo felt there was no more money to be had, said yes.

Six hours later, the family paid that sum and the aunt came back home safely.

HOW TO NEGOTIATE A BETTER SALARY

One of the critical factors in business school rankings is how well their graduates are compensated. So I tell every MBA class I lecture that my first objective is to single-handedly raise the ranking of their school by teaching them how to negotiate a better salary.

I break down the process into three parts that blend this chapter's dynamics in a way that not only brings you better money, but convinces your boss to fight to get it for you.

BE PLEASANTLY PERSISTENT ON NONSALARY TERMS

Pleasant persistence is a kind of emotional anchoring that creates empathy with the boss and builds the right psychological environment for constructive discussion. And the more you talk about nonsalary terms, the more likely you are to hear the full range of their options. If they can't meet your nonsalary requests, they may even counter with more money, like they did with a French-born American former student of mine. She kept asking—with a big smile—for an extra week of vacation beyond what the company normally gave. She was "French," she said, and that's what French people did. The hiring company was completely handcuffed on the vacation issue, but because she was so darned delightful, and because she introduced a nonmonetary variable into the notion of her value, they countered by increasing her salary offer.

SALARY TERMS WITHOUT SUCCESS TERMS IS RUSSIAN ROULETTE

Once you've negotiated a salary, make sure to define success for your position—as well as metrics for your next raise. That's meaningful for you and free for your boss, much like giving me a magazine cover story was for the bar association. It gets you a planned raise and, by defining your success in relation to your boss's supervision, it leads into the next step . . .

SPARK THEIR INTEREST IN YOUR SUCCESS AND GAIN AN UNOFFICIAL MENTOR

Remember the idea of figuring what the other side is *really* buying? Well, when you are selling yourself to a manager, sell yourself as more than a body for a job; sell yourself, and your success, as a way they can validate their own intelligence and broadcast it to the rest of the company. Make sure they know you'll act as a flesh-and-blood argument for their importance. Once you've bent their reality to include you as their ambassador, they'll have a stake in your success.

Ask: "What does it take to be successful here?"

Please notice that this question is similar to questions that are suggested by many MBA career counseling centers, yet not *exactly* the same. And it's the exact wording of this question that's critical.

Students from my MBA courses who have asked this question in job interviews have actually had interviewers lean forward and say, "No one ever asked us that before." The interviewer then gave a great and detailed answer.

The key issue here is if someone gives you guidance, they will watch to see if you follow their advice. They will have a personal stake in seeing you succeed. You've just recruited your first unofficial mentor.

To show how this can be done to near perfection, I can think of no better example than my former MBA student Angel Prado.

While Angel was finishing up his MBA, he went to his boss and began to lay the groundwork for his work post-MBA (which the company was paying). During his last semester, he set a nonspecific anchor—a kind of range—by suggesting to his boss that once he graduated and the company was done investing in his MBA (around $31,000 per year), that money should go to him as salary.

His boss made no commitment, but Angel was pleasantly persistent about it, which set the idea as an anchor in his boss's mind.

Upon graduation, Angel and his boss had their big sit-down. In an assertive and calm manner, Angel broached a nonfinancial issue to move the focus away from "How much?": he asked for a new title.

Angel's boss readily agreed that a new role was a no-brainer after Angel's new degree.

At that point, Angel and his manager defined what his roles and responsibilities would be in his new role, thereby setting success metrics. Then Angel took a breath and paused so that his boss would be the first to throw out a number. At last, he did. Curiously enough, the number showed that Angel's earlier efforts at anchoring had worked: he proposed to add $31,000 to Angel's base salary, almost a 50 percent raise.

But Angel was no rookie negotiator, not after taking my class. So instead of countering and getting stuck in "How much?" he kept talking, labeling the boss's emotions and empathizing with his situation (at the time the company was going through difficult negotiations with its investors).

And then Angel courteously asked for a moment to step away and print up the agreed-upon job description. This pause created a dynamic of pre-deadline urgency in his boss, which Angel exploited when he returned with the printout. On the bottom, he'd added his desired compensation: "$134.5k—$143k."

In that one little move, Angel weaved together a bunch of the lessons from this chapter. The odd numbers gave them the weight of thoughtful calculation. The numbers were high too, which exploited his boss's natural tendency to go directly to his price limit when faced by an extreme anchor. And they were a range, which made Angel seem less aggressive and the lower end more reasonable in comparison.

From his boss's body language—raised eyebrows—it was clear that he was surprised by the compensation request. But it had the desired effect: after some comments about the description, he countered with $120,000.

Angel didn't say "No" or "Yes," but kept talking and creating empathy. Then, in the middle of a sentence, seemingly out of the blue, his boss threw out $127,000. With his boss obviously negotiating with himself, Angel kept him going. Finally his boss said he agreed with the $134,500 and would pay that salary starting in three months, contingent on the board of directors' approval.

As the icing on the cake, Angel worked in a positive use of the word "Fair" ("That's fair," he said), and then sold the raise to his boss as a marriage in which his boss would be the mentor. "I'm asking you, not the board, for the promotion, and all I need is for you to agree with it," he said.

And how did Angel's boss reply to his new ambassador?

"I'll fight to get you this salary."

So follow Angel's lead and make it rain!

KEY LESSONS

Compared to the tools discussed in previous chapters, the techniques here seem concrete and easy to use. But many people shy away from them because they seem manipulative. Something that bends your counterpart's reality must be cheating, right?

In response, let me just say that these tools are used by all the best negotiators because they simply recognize the human psyche as it is. We are emotional, irrational beasts who are emotional and irrational in predictable, pattern-filled ways. Using that knowledge is only, well, rational.

As you work these tools into your daily life, remember the following powerful lessons:

- All negotiations are defined by a network of subterranean desires and needs. Don't let yourself be fooled by the surface. Once you know that the Haitian kidnappers just want party money, you will be miles better prepared.

- Splitting the difference is wearing one black and one brown shoe, so don't compromise. Meeting halfway often leads to bad deals for both sides.

- Approaching deadlines entice people to rush the negotiating process and do impulsive things that are against their best interests.

- The F-word—"Fair"—is an emotional term people usually exploit to put the other side on the defensive and gain concessions. When your counterpart drops the F-bomb, don't get suckered into a concession. Instead, ask them to explain how you're mistreating them.

- You can bend your counterpart's reality by anchoring his starting point. Before you make an offer, emotionally anchor them by saying how bad it will be. When you get to numbers, set an extreme anchor to make your "real" offer seem reasonable, or use a range to seem less aggressive. The real value of anything depends on what vantage point you're looking at it from.

- People will take more risks to avoid a loss than to realize a gain. Make sure your counterpart sees that there is something to lose by inaction.

CHAPTER 7

CREATE THE ILLUSION OF CONTROL

A month after I'd finished working the case of Jeffrey Schilling in May 2001, I got orders from headquarters to head back to Manila. The same bad guys who'd taken Schilling, a brutal group of radical Islamists named the Abu Sayyaf, had raided the Dos Palmas private diving resort and taken twenty hostages, including three Americans: Martin and Gracia Burnham, a missionary couple from Wichita, Kansas; and Guillermo Sobero, a guy who ran a California waterproofing firm.

Dos Palmas was a negotiator's nightmare from the start. The day after the kidnappings, the recently elected Philippine president, Gloria Macapagal-Arroyo, set up the most confrontational, nonconstructive dynamic possible by publicly declaring "all-out war" on the Abu Sayyaf.

Not exactly empathetic discourse, right?

It got a lot worse.

The Philippine army and marines had a turf war in the midst of the negotiations, pissing off the kidnappers with several botched raids. Because American hostages were involved, the CIA, the FBI, and U.S. military intelligence were all called in and we too squabbled among ourselves. Then the kidnappers raped and killed several hostages, 9/11 happened, and the Abu Sayyaf was linked to Al Qaeda.

By the time the crisis concluded in an orgy of gunshots in June 2002, Dos Palmas had officially become the biggest failure in my professional life. To call it a train wreck would be generous, if you know what I mean.

But failures plant the seeds of future success, and our failure in the Philippines was no exception.

If the Dos Palmas calamity showed me anything, it was that we all were still suffering under the notion that negotiation was a wrestling match where the point is to exhaust your opponent into submission, hope for the best, and never back down.

As my disappointment with Dos Palmas forced me to reckon with our failed techniques, I took a deep look into the newest negotiating theories—some great and some completely harebrained—and I had a chance encounter with a case in Pittsburgh that completely changed how I looked at the interpersonal dynamics of negotiation conversations.

From the ashes of Dos Palmas, then, we learned a lesson that would forever change how the FBI negotiated kidnappings. We learned that negotiation was coaxing, not overcoming; co-opting, not defeating. Most important, we learned that successful negotiation involved getting your counterpart to do the work for you and suggest your solution himself. It involved giving him the illusion of control while you, in fact, were the one defining the conversation.

The tool we developed is something I call the calibrated, or open-ended, question. What it does is remove aggression from conversations by acknowledging the other side openly, without resistance. In doing so, it lets you introduce ideas and requests without sounding pushy. It allows you to nudge.

I'll explain it in depth later on, but for now let me say that it's really as simple as removing the hostility from the statement "You can't leave" and turning it into a question.

"What do you hope to achieve by going?"

DON'T TRY TO NEGOTIATE IN A FIREFIGHT

The moment I arrived in Manila on the Burnham-Sobero case I was sent down to the Mindanao region, where the Philippine military was lobbing bullets and rockets into a hospital complex where the Abu Sayyaf and the hostages were holed up.

This was no place for a negotiator, because it's impossible to have a dialogue in the middle of a firefight. Then things got worse: when I woke up the next morning, I learned that during the night the kidnappers had taken their hostages and escaped.

The "escape" was the first sign that this operation was going to be a rolling train wreck and that the Philippine military was less than a trustworthy partner.

During debriefings following the episode, it was revealed that during a cease-fire a military guy had collected a suitcase from the thugs in the hospital, and not long after that all the soldiers on the rear perimeter of the hospital had been called away for a "meeting." Coincidentally—or not—the bad guys chose that moment to slip away.

Things really blew up two weeks later, on the Philippines' Independence Day, when Abu Sabaya announced that he was going to behead "one of the whites" unless the government called off its manhunt by midday. We knew this meant one of the Americans and anticipated it would be Guillermo Sobero.

We didn't have any direct contact with the kidnappers at the time because our partners in the Philippine military had assigned us an intermediary who always "forgot" to make sure we were present for his phone calls with the kidnappers (and similarly "forgot" to tape them). All we could do was send text messages offering to schedule a time to speak.

What ended up happening was that just before the noon deadline, Sabaya and a member of the Philippine presidential cabinet had a conversation on a radio talk show, and the government conceded to

Sabaya's demand to name a Malaysian senator as a negotiator. In exchange, Sabaya agreed not to kill a hostage.

But it was too late to fix this atmosphere of confrontation, distrust, and lies. That afternoon, the hostages heard Sabaya on the phone yelling, "But that was part of the agreement! That was a part of the agreement!" Not long after, the Abu Sayyaf beheaded Guillermo Sobero and for good measure the group took fifteen more hostages.

With none of the important moving parts anywhere near under our control and the United States largely uninterested in spite of Sobero's murder, I headed back to Washington, D.C. It seemed like there was little we could do.

Then 9/11 changed everything.

Once a minor terrorist outfit, the Abu Sayyaf was suddenly linked to Al Qaeda. And then a Philippine TV reporter named Arlyn dela Cruz got into the Abu Sayyaf camp and videotaped Sabaya as he taunted the American missionaries Martin and Gracia Burnham, who were so emaciated they looked like concentration camp survivors. The video hit the U.S. news media like thunder. Suddenly, the case became a major U.S. government priority.

THERE IS ALWAYS A TEAM ON THE OTHER SIDE

The FBI sent me back in. Now I was sent in to make sure a deal got made. It was all very high profile, too. Some of my contacts reported that FBI director Robert Mueller was personally briefing President George W. Bush every morning on what we were doing. When Director Mueller showed up in the U.S. Embassy in Manila and I was introduced to him, a look of recognition came over his face. That was a very heady moment.

But all the support in the world won't work if your counterpart's team is dysfunctional. If your negotiation efforts don't reach past your counterpart and into the team behind him, then you've got a "hope"-based deal—and hope is not a strategy.

One of the things I failed to fully appreciate then was that the kidnappers had changed negotiators themselves. Sabaya had been replaced.

My boss Gary Noesner had, in a previous kidnapping, pointed out to me that a change in negotiators by the other side almost always signaled that they meant to take a harder line. What I didn't realize at the time was this meant Sabaya was going to play a role as a deal breaker if he wasn't accounted for.

Our new tack was to buy the Burnhams back. Although the United States officially doesn't pay ransoms, a donor had been found who would provide $300,000. The new Abu Sayyaf negotiator agreed to a release.

The ransom drop was a disaster. The kidnappers decided that they wouldn't release the Burnhams: or, rather, Sabaya, who was physically in charge of the hostages, refused to release them. He had cut his own side-deal—one we didn't know about—and it had fallen through. The new negotiator, now embarrassed and in a foul mood, covered himself by claiming that the payment was short $600. We were baffled—"Six hundred dollars? You won't let hostages go because of six hundred dollars?"—and we tried to argue that if the money was missing, it must have been the courier who had stolen the money. But we had no dynamic of trust and cooperation to back us up. The $300,000 was gone and we were back to rarely answered text messages.

The slow-motion wreck culminated about two months later with a botched "rescue." A team of Philippine Scout Rangers walking around in the woods came across the Abu Sayyaf camp, or so they said. Later we heard another government agency had tipped them off. That other government agency (OGA) had not told us about their location because . . . because . . . why? That's something I will never understand.

The Scout Rangers formed a skirmish line from a tree line above the camp and opened fire, indiscriminately pouring bullets into the area. Gracia and Martin were taking a nap in their hammocks when the fire started raining down. They both fell out of their hammocks and started to roll down the hill toward safety. But as a sheet of bullets from their rescuers fell on them, Gracia felt a searing burn flare through her right thigh. And then, she felt Martin go limp.

Minutes later, after the last rebels fled, the squad of Philippine soldiers tried to reassure Gracia that her husband was fine, but she shook her head. After a year in captivity, she had no time for fantasies. Gracia knew her husband was dead, and she was right: he'd been hit in the chest, three times, by "friendly" fire.

In the end, the supposed rescue mission killed two of the three hostages there that day (a Philippine nurse named Ediborah Yap also died), and the big fish—Sabaya—escaped to live a few more months. From beginning to end, the thirteen-month mission was a complete failure, a waste of lives and treasure. As I sat in the dark at home a few days later, dispirited and spent, I knew that something had to change. We couldn't let this happen again.

If the hostages' deaths were going to mean something, we would have to find a new way to negotiate, communicate, listen, and speak, both with our enemies and with our friends. Not for communication's sake, though.

No. We had to do it to *win*.

AVOID A SHOWDOWN

No two ways about it, my return to the United States was a time of reckoning. I questioned—I even doubted—some of what we were doing at the FBI. If what we knew wasn't enough, we had to get better.

The real kick in the pants came after my return, when I was reviewing information about the case, a lot of which we hadn't had in the field. Among the piles of information was one fact that totally blew my mind.

Martin Burnham had been overheard on a phone call to *someone*. I wondered what in God's name our hostage was doing talking on the phone without us knowing. And with whom was he talking? There's only one reason a hostage ever gets on a phone. It's to provide proof of life. Someone else had been trying to ransom the Burnhams out.

It turned out to be someone working for a crooked Philippine politician who'd been running a parallel negotiation for the Burnhams' release. He wanted to buy the hostages out himself in order to show up Philippine president Arroyo.

But it wasn't so much that this guy was going behind our backs that bothered me. As is pretty clear already, there were a whole lot of underhanded things going on. What really ate at me was that this schmuck, who wasn't an FBI-trained hostage negotiator, had pulled off something that I hadn't been able to.

He'd gotten to speak to Martin Burnham on the phone. For free.

That's when I realized that this crooked pol's success where we had failed was a kind of metaphor for everything that was wrong with our one-dimensional mindset.

Beyond our problems with the Philippine military, the big reason we had no effective influence with the kidnappers and hostages was that we had this very tit-for-tat mentality. Under that mentality, if we called up the bad guys we were asking for something, and if they gave it to us we had to give them something back. And so, because we were positive that the Burnhams were alive, we'd never bothered to call and ask for proof of life. We were afraid to go into debt.

If we made an "ask" and they granted it, we'd owe. Not making good on a debt risked the accusation of bad-faith negotiation and bad faith in kidnappings gets people killed.

And of course we didn't ask the kidnappers to talk directly to the hostage because we knew they'd say "no" and we were afraid of being embarrassed.

That fear was a major flaw in our negotiating mindset. There is some information that you can only get through direct, extended interactions with your counterpart.

We also needed new ways to get things without asking for them. We needed to finesse making an "ask" with something more sophisticated than closed-ended questions with their yes-no dynamic.

That's when I realized that what we had been doing wasn't communication; it was verbal flexing. We wanted them to see things our way and they wanted us to see it their way. If you let this dynamic loose in the real world, negotiation breaks down and tensions flare. That whole ethos permeated everything the FBI was doing. Everything was a showdown. And it didn't work.

Our approach to proof-of-life questions embodied all these problems.

At the time, we proved that our hostages were alive by devising questions that asked for a piece of information only the hostage could know. Computer-security style questions, like, "What's the name of Martin's first dog?" or "What's Martin's dad's middle name?"

This particular type of question had many failings, however. For one thing, it had sort of become a signature of law enforcement in the kidnapping world. When a family starts asking a question of that type, it's a near certainty that the cops are coaching them. And that makes kidnappers very nervous.

Even beyond the nerves, you had the problem that answering questions like those required little, if any, effort. The bad guys go and get the fact and give it to you right away, because it's so easy. Bang, bang, bang! It happens so fast that you didn't gain any tactical advantage, any usable information, any effort on their part toward a goal that serves you. And all negotiation, done well, should be an information-gathering process that vests your counterpart in an outcome that serves you.

Worst of all, the bad guys know that they have just given you something—a proof of life—which triggers this whole human reciprocity gene. Whether we like to recognize it or not, a universal rule of human nature, across all cultures, is that when somebody gives you something, they expect something in return. And they won't give anything else until you pay them back.

Now, we didn't want to trigger this whole reciprocity thing because we didn't want to give anything. So what happened? All of our conversations became these paralyzed confrontations between two parties who wanted to extract something from each other but didn't want to give. We didn't communicate, out of pride and fear.

That's why we failed, while numbskulls like this crooked Philippine politician just stumbled in and got what we so desperately needed. That is, communication without reciprocity. I sat back and wondered to myself, How the hell do *we* do that?

SUSPEND UNBELIEF

While I was racking my brains over how this sleazy politician managed to get Martin Burnham on the phone while we never could, FBI Pittsburgh had a kidnapping case.

My partner Chuck brought me the tapes from the case because he thought it was funny. You see, one Pittsburgh drug dealer had kidnapped the girlfriend of another Pittsburgh drug dealer, and for whatever reason the victim drug dealer came to the FBI for help. Coming to the FBI seemed kind of contrary to his best interests, being a drug dealer and all, but he did it because no matter who you are, when you need help you go to the FBI. Right?

On the tapes, our hostage negotiators are riding around with this drug dealer while he's negotiating with the other drug dealer. Normally we would have had the guy ask a bulletproof proof-of-life question, like, "What was the name of the girlfriend's teddy bear when she was little?" But in this situation, this drug dealer hadn't yet been coached on asking a "correct" question. So in the middle of the conversation with the kidnapper, he just blurts, "Hey, dog, how do I know she's all right?"

And the funniest thing happened. The kidnapper actually went silent for ten seconds. He was completely taken aback. Then he said, in a much less confrontational tone of voice, "Well, I'll put her on the phone." I was floored because this unsophisticated drug dealer just pulled off a phenomenal victory in the negotiation. To get the kidnapper to *volunteer* to put the victim on the phone is massively huge.

That's when I had my "Holy shit!" moment and realized that this is the technique I'd been waiting for. Instead of asking some closed-ended question with a single correct answer, he'd asked an open-ended, yet calibrated one that forced the other guy to pause and actually think about how to solve *the* problem. I thought to myself, This is perfect! It's a natural and normal question, not a request for a fact. It's a "how" question, and "how" engages because "how" asks for help.

Best of all, he doesn't owe the kidnapper a damn thing. The guy volunteers to put the girlfriend on the phone: he thinks it's his idea. The guy who just offered to put the girlfriend on the line thinks he's in control. And the secret to gaining the upper hand in a negotiation is giving the other side the illusion of control.

The genius of this technique is really well explained by something that the psychologist Kevin Dutton says in his book *Split-Second Persuasion*.[1] He talks about what he calls "unbelief," which is active resistance to what the other side is saying, complete rejection. That's where the two parties in a negotiation usually start.

If you don't ever get off that dynamic, you end up having showdowns, as each side tries to impose its point of view. You get two hard skulls banging against each other, like in Dos Palmas. But if you can get the other side to drop their unbelief, you can slowly work them to *your* point of view on the back of *their* energy, just like the drug dealer's question got the kidnapper to volunteer to do what the drug dealer wanted. You don't directly persuade them to see your ideas. Instead, you ride them to your ideas. As the saying goes, the best way to ride a horse is in the direction in which it is going.

Our job as persuaders is easier than we think. It's not to get others believing what we say. It's just to stop them unbelieving. Once we achieve that, the game's half-won. "Unbelief is the friction that keeps persuasion in check," Dutton says. "Without it, there'd be no limits."

Giving your counterpart the illusion of control by asking calibrated questions—by asking for help—is one of the most powerful tools for suspending unbelief. Not long ago, I read this great article in the *New York Times*[2] by a medical student who was faced with a patient who had ripped out his IV, packed his bags, and was making a move to leave because his biopsy results were days late and he was tired of waiting.

Just then a senior physician arrived. After calmly offering the patient a glass of water and asking if they could chat for a minute, he said he understood why the patient was pissed off and promised to call the lab to see why the results were delayed.

But what he did next is what really suspended the patient's unbelief: he asked a calibrated question—what he felt was so important about leaving—and then when the patient said he had errands to handle, the doctor offered to connect the patient with services that could help him get them done. And, boom, the patient volunteered to stay.

What's so powerful about the senior doctor's technique is that he took what was a showdown—"I'm going to leave" versus "You can't leave"—and asked questions that led the patient to solve his own problem . . . in the way the doctor wanted.

It was still a kind of showdown, of course, but the doctor took the confrontation and bravado out of it by giving the patient the illusion of control. As an old *Washington Post* editor named Robert Estabrook once said, "He who has learned to disagree without being disagreeable has discovered the most valuable secret of negotiation."

This same technique for suspending unbelief that you use with kidnappers and escaping patients works for anything, even negotiating prices. When you go into a store, instead of telling the salesclerk what you "need," you can describe what you're looking for and ask for suggestions.

Then, once you've picked out what you want, instead of hitting them with a hard offer, you can just say the price is a bit more than you budgeted and ask for help with one of the greatest-of-all-time calibrated questions: "How am I supposed to do that?" The critical part of this approach is that you really are asking for help and your delivery must convey that. With this negotiating scheme, instead of bullying the clerk, you're asking for their advice and giving them the illusion of control.

Asking for help in this manner, after you've already been engaged in a dialogue, is an incredibly powerful negotiating technique for transforming encounters from confrontational showdowns into joint problem-solving sessions. And calibrated questions are the best tool.

CALIBRATE YOUR QUESTIONS

A few years ago, I was consulting with a client who had a small firm that did public relations for a large corporation. The folks at the big company were not paying their bills, and as time went on, they owed my client more and more money. They kept her on the hook by promising lots of repeat business, implying that she would get a pile of revenue if she just kept working. She felt trapped.

My advice for her was simple: I told her to engage them in a conversation where she summarized the situation and then asked, "How am I supposed to do that?"

She shook her head. No way. The idea of having to ask this question just terrified her. "If they tell me I have to, then I'm trapped!" was her reaction.

She also heard the question as "You're screwing me out of money and it has to stop." That sounded like the first step to her getting fired as a consultant.

I explained to her that this implication, though real, was in her mind. Her client would hear the words and not the implication as long as she kept calm and avoided making it sound by her delivery like an accusation or threat. As long as she stayed cool, they would hear it as a problem to be solved.

She didn't quite believe me. We walked through the script several times, but she was still afraid. Then a few days later she called me, totally giddy with happiness. The client had called with another request and she had finally gotten up the courage to summarize the situation, and ask, "How am I supposed to do that?"

And you know what? The answer she got was "You're right, you can't and I apologize." Her client explained that they were going through some internal problems, but she was given a new accounting contact and told she'd be paid within forty-eight hours. And she was.

Now, think about how my client's question worked: without accusing them of anything, it pushed the big company to understand her problem and offer the solution she wanted. That in a nutshell is the whole point of open-ended questions that are calibrated for a specific effect.

Like the softening words and phrases "perhaps," "maybe," "I think," and "it seems," the calibrated open-ended question takes the aggression out of a confrontational statement or close-ended request that might otherwise anger your counterpart. What makes them work is that they are subject to interpretation by your counterpart instead of being rigidly defined. They allow you to introduce ideas and requests without sounding overbearing or pushy.

And that's the difference between "You're screwing me out of money, and it has to stop" and "How am I supposed to do that?"

The real beauty of calibrated questions is the fact that they offer no target for attack like statements do. Calibrated questions have the power to educate your counterpart on what the problem is rather than causing conflict by *telling* them what the problem is.

But calibrated questions are not just random requests for comment. They have a direction: once you figure out where you want a conversation to go, you have to design the questions that will ease the conversation in that direction while letting the other guy think it's his choice to take you there.

That's why I refer to these questions as *calibrated* questions. You have to calibrate them carefully, just like you would calibrate a gun sight or a measuring scale, to target a specific problem.

The good news is that there are rules for that.

First off, calibrated questions avoid verbs or words like "can," "is," "are," "do," or "does." These are closed-ended questions that can be answered with a simple "yes" or a "no." Instead, they start with a list of words people know as reporter's questions: "who," "what," "when," "where," "why," and "how." Those words inspire your counterpart to think and then speak expansively.

But let me cut the list even further: it's best to start with "what," "how," and *sometimes* "why." Nothing else. "Who," "when," and "where" will often just get your counterpart to share a fact without thinking. And "why" can backfire. Regardless of what language the word "why" is translated into, it's accusatory. There are very rare moments when this is to your advantage.

The only time you can use "why" successfully is when the defensiveness that is created supports the change you are trying to get them to see. "Why would you ever change from the way you've always done things and try my approach?" is an example. "Why would your company ever change from your long-standing vendor and choose our company?" is another. As always, tone of voice, respectful and deferential, is critical.

Otherwise, treat "why" like a burner on a hot stove—don't touch it.

Having just two words to start with might not seem like a lot of ammunition, but trust me, you can use "what" and "how" to calibrate nearly any question. "Does this look like something you would like?" can become "How does this look to you?" or "What about this works for you?" You can even ask, "What about this doesn't work for you?" and you'll probably trigger quite a bit of useful information from your counterpart.

Even something as harsh as "Why did you do it?" can be calibrated to "What caused you to do it?" which takes away the emotion and makes the question less accusatory.

You should use calibrated questions early and often, and there are a few that you will find that you will use in the beginning of nearly every negotiation. "What is the biggest challenge you face?" is one of those questions. It just gets the other side to teach you something about themselves, which is critical to any negotiation because all negotiation is an information-gathering process.

Here are some other great standbys that I use in almost every negotiation, depending on the situation:

- What about this is important to you?

- How can I help to make this better for us?

- How would you like me to proceed?

- What is it that brought us into this situation?

- How can we solve this problem?

- What's the objective? / What are we trying to accomplish here?

- How am I supposed to do that?

The implication of any well-designed calibrated question is that you want what the other guy wants but you need his intelligence to overcome the problem. This really appeals to very aggressive or egotistical counterparts.

You've not only implicitly asked for help—triggering goodwill and less defensiveness—but you've engineered a situation in which your formerly recalcitrant counterpart is now using his mental and emotional resources to overcome *your* challenges. It is the first step in your counterpart internalizing your way—and the obstacles in it—as his own. And that guides the other party toward designing a solution.

Your solution.

Think back to how the doctor used calibrated questions to get his patient to stay. As his story showed, the key to getting people to see things your way is not to confront them on their ideas ("You can't leave") but to acknowledge their ideas openly ("I understand why you're pissed off") and then guide them toward solving the problem ("What do you hope to accomplish by leaving?").

Like I said before, the secret to gaining the upper hand in a negotiation is giving the other side the illusion of control. That's why calibrated questions are ingenious: Calibrated questions make your counterpart feel like they're in charge, but it's really you who are framing the conversation. Your counterpart will have no idea how constrained they are by your questions.

Once I was negotiating with one of my FBI bosses about attending a Harvard executive program. He had already approved the expenditure for the travel, but on the day before I was supposed to leave he called me into his office and began to question the validity of the trip.

I knew him well enough to know that he was trying to show me that he was in charge. So after we talked for a while, I looked at him and asked, "When you originally approved this trip, what did you have in mind?"

He visibly relaxed as he sat back in his chair and brought the top of his fingers and thumbs together in the shape of a steeple. Generally this is a body language that means the person feels superior and in charge.

"Listen," he said, "just make sure you brief everyone when you get back."

That question, calibrated to acknowledge his power and nudge him toward explaining himself, gave him the illusion of control.

And it got me just what I wanted.

HOW *NOT* TO GET PAID

Let's pause for a minute here, because there's one vitally important thing you have to remember when you enter a negotiation armed with your list of calibrated questions. That is, all of this is great, but there's a rub: without self-control and emotional regulation, it doesn't work.

The very first thing I talk about when I'm training new negotiators is the critical importance of self-control. If you can't control your own emotions, how can you expect to influence the emotions of another party?

To show you what I mean, let me tell you a story.

Not long ago, a freelance marketing strategist came to me with a problem. One of her clients had hired a new CEO, a penny pincher whose strategy was to cut costs by offshoring everything he could. He was also a male chauvinist who didn't like the assertive style in which the strategist, a woman, conducted herself.

Immediately my client and the CEO started to go at each other on conference calls in that passive-aggressive way that is ever present in corporate America. After a few weeks of this, my client decided she'd had enough and invoiced the CEO for the last bit of work she'd done (about $7,000) and politely said that the arrangement wasn't working out. The CEO answered by saying the bill was too high, that he'd pay half of it and that they would talk about the rest.

After that, he stopped answering her calls.

The underlying dynamic was that this guy didn't like being questioned by anyone, especially a woman. So she and I developed a strategy that showed him she understood where she went wrong and acknowledged his power, while at the same time directing his energy toward solving her problem.

The script we came up with hit all the best practices of negotiation we've talked about so far. Here it is by steps:

1. A "No"-oriented email question to reinitiate contact: "Have you given up on settling this amicably?"

2. A statement that leaves only the answer of "That's right" to form a dynamic of agreement: "It seems that you feel my bill is not justified."

3. Calibrated questions about the problem to get him to reveal his thinking: "How does this bill violate our agreement?"

4. More "No"-oriented questions to remove unspoken barriers: "Are you saying I misled you?" "Are you saying I didn't do as you asked?" "Are you saying I reneged on our agreement?" or "Are you saying I failed you?"

5. Labeling and mirroring the essence of his answers if they are not acceptable so he has to consider them again: "It seems like you feel my work was subpar." Or ". . . my work was subpar?"

6. A calibrated question in reply to any offer other than full payment, in order to get him to offer a solution: "How am I supposed to accept that?"

7. If none of this gets an offer of full payment, a label that flatters his sense of control and power: "It seems like you are the type of person who prides himself on the way he does business—rightfully so—and has a knack for not only expanding the pie but making the ship run more efficiently."

8. A long pause and then one more "No"-oriented question: "Do you want to be known as someone who doesn't fulfill agreements?"

From my long experience in negotiation, scripts like this have a 90 percent success rate. That is, if the negotiator stays calm and rational. And that's a big *if*.

In this case, she didn't.

The first step—the magic email—worked better than she imagined, and the CEO called within ten minutes, surprising her. Almost immediately her anger flared at the sound of his patronizing voice. Her only desire became to show him how he was wrong, to impose her will, and the conversation became a showdown that went nowhere.

You probably don't need me to tell you that she didn't even get half.

With that in mind, I want to end this chapter with some advice on how to remain rational in a negotiation. Even with all the best techniques and strategy, you need to regulate your emotions if you want to have any hope of coming out on top.

The first and most basic rule of keeping your emotional cool is to bite your tongue. Not literally, of course. But you have to keep away from knee-jerk, passionate reactions. Pause. Think. Let the passion dissipate. That allows you to collect your thoughts and be more circumspect in what you say. It also lowers your chance of saying more than you want to.

The Japanese have this figured out. When negotiating with a foreigner, it's common practice for a Japanese businessman to use a translator even when he understands perfectly what the other side is saying. That's because speaking through a translator forces him to step back. It gives him time to frame his response.

Another simple rule is, when you are verbally assaulted, do not counterattack. Instead, disarm your counterpart by asking a calibrated question. The next time a waiter or salesclerk tries to engage you in a verbal skirmish, try this out. I promise you it will change the entire tenor of the conversation.

The basic issue here is that when people feel that they are not in control, they adopt what psychologists call a hostage mentality. That is, in moments of conflict they react to their lack of power by either becoming extremely defensive or lashing out.

Neurologically, in situations like this the fight-or-flight mechanism in the reptilian brain or the emotions in the limbic system overwhelm the rational part of our mind, the neocortex, leading us to overreact in an impulsive, instinctive way.

In a negotiation, like in the one between my client and the CEO, this always produces a negative outcome. So we have to train our neocortex to override the emotions from the other two brains.

That means biting your tongue and learning how to mindfully change your state to something more positive. And it means lowering the hostage mentality in your counterpart by asking a question or even offering an apology. ("You're right. That was a bit harsh.")

If you were able to take an armed kidnapper who'd been surrounded by police and hook him up to a cardiac monitor, you'd find that every calibrated question and apology would lower his heart rate just a little bit. And that's how you get to a dynamic where solutions can be found.

KEY LESSONS

Who has control in a conversation, the guy listening or the guy talking?

The listener, of course.

That's because the talker is revealing information while the listener, if he's trained well, is directing the conversation toward his own goals. He's harnessing the talker's energy for his own ends.

When you try to work the skills from this chapter into your daily life, remember that these are listener's tools. They are not about strong-arming your opponent into submission. Rather, they're about using the counterpart's power to get to your objective. They're listener's judo.

As you put listener's judo into practice, remember the following powerful lessons:

- Don't try to force your opponent to admit that you are right. Aggressive confrontation is the enemy of constructive negotiation.

- Avoid questions that can be answered with "Yes" or tiny pieces of information. These require little thought and inspire the human need for reciprocity; you will be expected to give something back.

- Ask calibrated questions that start with the words "How" or "What." By implicitly asking the other party for help, these questions will give your counterpart an illusion of control and will inspire them to speak at length, revealing important information.

- Don't ask questions that start with "Why" unless you want your counterpart to defend a goal that serves you. "Why" is always an accusation, in any language.

- Calibrate your questions to point your counterpart toward solving your problem. This will encourage them to expend their energy on devising a solution.

- Bite your tongue. When you're attacked in a negotiation, pause and avoid angry emotional reactions. Instead, ask your counterpart a calibrated question.

- There is always a team on the other side. If you are not influencing those behind the table, you are vulnerable.

CHAPTER 8

GUARANTEE EXECUTION

During a dangerous and chaotic prison siege in St. Martin Parish, Louisiana, a few years ago, a group of inmates armed with makeshift knives took the warden and some of his staff hostage. The situation was especially nervy because the prisoners were both tense and disorganized, a worrisome mix that meant anything could happen.

The negotiators sensed that, beneath the bluster, the prisoners didn't really want to hurt the staff. They knew that they felt backed into a corner and, more than anything, they wanted the situation to end.

But there was a stumbling block: the inmates were afraid that the prisoners who gave up after taking correctional officers hostage, not to mention the warden, would end up beaten, and badly.

So the negotiators delivered a pair of walkie-talkies to the inmates and designed this elaborate surrender ritual to get the hostage-takers to end the siege. The idea was elegantly simple:

The inmates would send out one of their guys with a walkie-talkie, and he'd walk past the three perimeters of combined multiagency law enforcement that were stationed outside the prison. Once he'd walked past the final perimeter, he'd get into the paddy wagon and be transferred to jail. There, he'd use the walkie-talkie to call the guys back in the prison and say, essentially, "They didn't kick my ass." And they'd know it was okay to come out just like he did, one at a time.

After some haggling, the inmates agreed with the plan and the first inmate comes out. It starts off great. He walks past the federal zone, then the SWAT zone, and then he makes it to the outer perimeter. But just as he's about to climb into the paddy wagon, some guy sees the walkie-talkie and says, "What the hell are you doing with that?" and confiscates it before sending the guy off to the jail.

The inmates back in the prison start to freak out because their buddy hasn't called. The one with the other walkie-talkie calls the negotiators and starts yelling, "Why didn't he call? They're kicking his ass. We told you!" He starts talking about cutting off a hostage's finger, just to make sure the negotiators know the inmates are for real.

Now it's the negotiators who are freaking out. They sprint to the perimeter and start screaming at everyone. It's life and death at stake. Or at least an amputated finger.

Finally, fifteen nail-biting minutes later, this SWAT guy comes striding up, all proud of himself. "Some idiot gave this dude a radio," he says, and sort of smiles as he hands the negotiators the walkie-talkie. The negotiators barely stop themselves from slugging the guy before they tear off to the jail to have the first inmate call in.

Crisis averted, but barely.

The point here is that your job as a negotiator isn't just to get to an agreement. It's getting to one that can be implemented and making sure that happens. Negotiators have to be decision architects: they have to dynamically and adaptively design the verbal and nonverbal elements of the negotiation to gain both consent *and* execution.

"Yes" is nothing without "How." While an agreement is nice, a contract is better, and a signed check is best. You don't get your profits with the agreement. They come upon implementation. Success isn't the hostage-taker saying, "Yes, we have a deal"; success comes afterward, when the freed hostage says to your face, "Thank you."

In this chapter, I'll show how to drive toward and achieve consent, both with those at the negotiating table and with the invisible forces "underneath" it; distinguish true buy-in from fake acquiescence; and guarantee execution using the Rule of Three.

"YES" IS NOTHING WITHOUT "HOW"

About a year after the Dos Palmas crisis, I was teaching at the FBI Academy in Quantico when the Bureau got an urgent call from the State Department: an American had been kidnapped in the Ecuadoran jungle by a Colombia-based rebel group. As the FBI's lead international hostage negotiator, this was my baby, so I put a team together and set up operation headquarters in Quantico.

For a few years, José and his wife, Julie, had been guiding tour groups through the jungle near the Colombian border. Born in Ecuador, José had become an American citizen and was working as a paramedic in New York City when he and Julie decided to set up an ecotourism business in his native country. José loved the Ecuadoran jungle, and he'd long dreamed of teaching visitors about the monkeys that swung through the trees and the flowers that perfumed the trails.

The business grew as ecotourists fell for the pair's obvious passion, and on August 20, 2003, José and Julie took eleven people on a whitewater rafting trip down the Mira River. After a great day on the water, everyone was smiling and soaked as they piled into Jeeps and pickups for the ride to an inn in a nearby village. José told tall tales as he drove the lead truck, Julie to his right with their eleven-month-old baby in her lap.

They were five minutes from the inn when three men jumped into the road and aimed guns at the truck. A fourth man emerged and held a revolver to Julie's head as the thugs pulled José from the car and forced him into the truck bed. The kidnappers then ordered the caravan through several small towns to a fork in the road, where they got out and walked José past Julie's seat in the cab.

"Just remember," Julie said, "no matter what happens, I love you."

"Don't worry. I'll be fine," José answered.

And then he and his captors disappeared into the jungle.

The captors wanted $5 million. We wanted to buy time.

Ever since the Dos Palmas debacle and the Pittsburgh epiphany, I had been raring to employ the lessons we'd learned about calibrated questions. So when José was kidnapped, I sent my guys down to Ecuador and told them that we had a new strategy. The kidnapping would provide an opportunity to prove this approach.

"All we're going to say is, 'Hey, how do we know José is okay? How are we supposed to pay until we know José is okay?' Again and again," I told them.

Although they were queasy about untested techniques, my guys were game. The local cops were livid, though, because they always did proof of life the old-fashioned way (which the FBI had taught them in the first place). Luckily Julie was with us 100 percent because she saw how the calibrated questions would stall for time, and she was convinced that with enough time her husband would find a way to get home.

The day after the kidnapping, the rebels marched José into the mountains along the Colombian border and settled in a cabin high in the jungle. There José built a rapport with the kidnappers to make himself harder for them to kill. He impressed them with his knowledge of the jungle and, with a black belt in karate, he filled the time by teaching them martial arts.

My negotiators coached Julie every day as we waited for contact from the rebels. We learned later that the designated negotiator from José's captors had to walk to town to negotiate by phone.

My guys told Julie to answer every one of the kidnappers' demands with a question. My strategy was to keep the kidnappers engaged but off balance.

"How do I know José is alive?" she asked the first time they talked.

To their demand for $5 million, she said, "We don't have that kind of money. How can we raise that much?"

"How can we pay you anything until we know José is okay?" Julie asked the next time they talked.

Questions, always questions.

The kidnapper who was negotiating with Julie seemed extremely perplexed by her persistent questions, and he kept asking for time to think. That slowed everything down, but he never got angry with Julie. Answering questions gave him the illusion that he had control of the negotiation.

By constantly asking questions and making minuscule offers, Julie drove the ransom down to $16,500. When they came to that number, the kidnappers demanded she get it to them immediately.

"How can I do that when I have to sell my cars and trucks?" she asked.

Always buying more time.

We were starting to grin because success was within reach; we were really close to a ransom that the family could afford.

And then I got a phone call in the middle of the night from one of my deployed guys in Ecuador, Kevin Rust. Kevin is a terrific negotiator and the same guy who'd called to tell me a year earlier that Martin Burnham had been killed. My stomach tied into a knot when I heard his voice.

"We just got a call from José," Kevin said. "He's still in guerrilla territory but he escaped and he's on a bus and he's making his way out."

It took me half a minute to respond, and when I did all I could say was "Holy shit! That's fantastic news!"

What had happened, we learned later, was that with all the delays and questions, some of the guerrillas peeled off and didn't return. Pretty soon there was only one teenager guarding José at night. He saw an opening late one evening when it began to chuck down rain. Pounding on the metal roof, the rain drowned out all other sound as the lone guard slept. Knowing the wet leaves outside would absorb the sound of his footsteps, José climbed through the window, ran down jungle paths to a dirt road, and worked his way to a small town.

Two days later he was back with Julie and their baby, just a few days before his daughter's first birthday.

Julie was right: with enough time he had found a way home.

Calibrated "How" questions are a surefire way to keep negotiations going. They put the pressure on your counterpart to come up with answers, and to contemplate your problems when making their demands.

With enough of the right "How" questions you can read and shape the negotiating environment in such a way that you'll eventually get to the answer you want to hear. You just have to have an idea of where you want the conversation to go when you're devising your questions.

The trick to "How" questions is that, correctly used, they are gentle and graceful ways to say "No" and guide your counterpart to develop a better solution—*your* solution. A gentle How/No invites collaboration and leaves your counterpart with a feeling of having been treated with respect.

Look back at what Julie did when the Colombian rebel kidnappers made their first demands.

"How can we raise that much?" she asked.

Notice that she did not use the word "No." But she still managed to elegantly deny the kidnappers' $5 million demand.

As Julie did, the first and most common "No" question you'll use is some version of "How am I supposed to do that?" (for example, "How can we raise that much?"). Your tone of voice is critical as this phrase can be delivered as either an accusation or a request for assistance. So pay attention to your voice.

This question tends to have the positive effect of making the other side take a good look at your situation. This positive dynamic is what I refer to as "forced empathy," and it's especially effective if leading up to it you've already been empathic with your counterpart. This engages the dynamic of reciprocity to lead them to do something for you. Starting with José's kidnapping, "How am I supposed to do that?" became our primary response to a kidnapper demanding a ransom. And we never had it backfire.

Once I was working with an accounting consultant named Kelly who was owed a pile of money by a corporate client. She kept consulting because she believed she was developing a useful contact, and because the promise of a future payday seemed to justify continuing in good faith.

But at a certain point Kelly was so far behind on her own bills that she was in a bind. She couldn't continue to work with only a vague idea of when she'd get paid, but she worried that if she pushed too hard she wouldn't get paid at all.

I told her to wait until the client asked for more work, because if she made a firm payment demand right away she would be vulnerable if they refused.

Luckily for Kelly, the client soon called to ask her for more work. Once he finished his request, she calmly asked a "How" question:

"I'd love to help," she said, "but how am I supposed to do that?"

By indicating her willingness to work but asking for help finding a way to do so, she left her deadbeat customer with no choice but to put her needs ahead of everything else.

And she got paid.

Besides saying "No," the other key benefit of asking "How?" is, quite literally, that it forces your counterpart to consider and explain how a deal will be implemented. A deal is nothing without good implementation. Poor implementation is the cancer that eats your profits.

By making your counterparts articulate implementation in their own words, your carefully calibrated "How" questions will convince them that the final solution is *their* idea. And that's crucial. People always make more effort to implement a solution when they think it's theirs. That is simply human nature. That's why negotiation is often called "the art of letting someone else have your way."

There are two key questions you can ask to push your counterparts to think they are defining success *their* way: "How will we know we're on track?" and "How will we address things if we find we're off track?" When they answer, you summarize their answers until you get a "That's right." Then you'll know they've bought in.

On the flip side, be wary of two telling signs that your counterpart *doesn't* believe the idea is theirs. As I've noted, when they say, "*You're* right," it's often a good indicator they are not vested in what is being discussed. And when you push for implementation and they say, "I'll try," you should get a sinking feeling in your stomach. Because this really means, "I plan to fail."

When you hear either of these, dive back in with calibrated "How" questions until they define the terms of successful implementation in their own voice. Follow up by summarizing what they have said to get a "That's right."

Let the other side feel victory. Let them think it was their idea. Subsume your ego. Remember: "Yes" is nothing without "How." So keep asking "How?" And succeed.

INFLUENCING THOSE BEHIND THE TABLE

A few weeks after José got back to the United States, I drove to his family's place in upstate New York.

I was thrilled when José escaped, but the case left me with one nagging worry: Had my new strategy failed? You see, José had gotten home safely, but not because we'd negotiated his release. I worried that our winning had less to do with our brilliant strategy than with dumb luck.

After being greeted warmly by Julie and her parents, José and I grabbed some coffee and sat down. I'd gone there to do what CNU referred to as a hostage survival debriefing. I was after insights into how to better advise people facing potential kidnappings how best to survive, not just physically, but psychologically. I was also burning to find out what had occurred behind the scenes because it seemed as if my new strategy hadn't worked.

Finally the conversation came around to our use of calibrated questions.

"You know what?" he said. "The craziest thing was that their negotiator was supposed to stay in town and negotiate the deal but because Julie kept asking him questions he didn't really know for sure how to answer, he kept coming out to the jungle. They all would get together and have a huge discussion about how to respond. They even thought about taking me into town and putting me on the phone because Julie was so persistent with asking how did she know if I was okay."

Right then I knew we had the right tool. It was exactly the opposite of the Burnham case, where our negotiator cut the deal with one of the guys and then the rest of them took the $300,000 and said, "No, we're not doing that." Causing the other side to work that hard and forcing that much internal coordination in service of our own goals was unprecedented.

Our negotiating strategy in Ecuador worked not just because the questions contributed to the environment that let José escape, but because they made sure the kidnappers—our counterparts—were all on the same page.

Yes, few hostage-takers—and few business deal makers—fly solo. But for the most part, there are almost always other players, people who can act as deal makers or deal killers. If you truly want to get to "Yes" *and* get your deal implemented, you have to discover how to affect these individuals.

When implementation happens by committee, the support of that committee is key. You always have to identify and unearth their motivations, even if you haven't yet identified each individual on that committee. That can be easy as asking a few calibrated questions, like "How does this affect the rest of your team?" or "How on board are the people not on this call?" or simply "What do your colleagues see as their main challenges in this area?"

The larger concept I'm explaining here is that in any negotiation you have to analyze the entire negotiation space.

When other people will be affected by what is negotiated and can assert their rights or power later on, it's just stupid to consider only the interests of those at the negotiation table. You have to beware of "behind the table" or "Level II" players—that is, parties that are not directly involved but who can help implement agreements they like and block ones they don't. You can't disregard them even when you're talking to a CEO. There could always be someone whispering into his ear. At the end of the day, the deal killers often are more important than the deal makers.

Think back to the prison siege: it was almost ruined because one bit player on our side was not totally on board. That's what our use of calibrated questions in Ecuador avoided, and that's why José's case was a home run.

It only takes one bit player to screw up a deal.

A few years into private practice I'd lost sight of the importance of assessing and influencing the hidden negotiation that happens "behind the table," and I paid a substantial price.

We were closing a deal with a big company in Florida that wanted negotiation training for one of its divisions. We'd been on the phone a bunch of times with the CEO and the head of HR, and they were both

100 percent gung ho on our offering. We were elated—we had what we thought was total buy-in from the top decision makers for an incredibly lucrative deal.

And then, as we were figuring out the small print, the deal fell off the table.

It turns out that the head of the division that needed the training killed the deal. Maybe this guy felt threatened, slighted, or otherwise somehow personally injured by the notion that he and his people "needed" any training at all. (A surprisingly high percentage of negotiations hinge on something outside dollars and cents, often having more to do with self-esteem, status, and other nonfinancial needs.) We'll never know now.

The point is, we didn't care until too late because we convinced ourselves that we were on the phone with the only decision makers that mattered.

We could have avoided all that had we asked a few calibrated questions, like: How does this affect everybody else? How on board is the rest of your team? How do we make sure that we deliver the right material to the right people? How do we ensure the managers of those we're training are fully on board?

If we had asked questions like that, the CEO and HR head would have checked with this guy, maybe even brought him into the conversation. And saved us all a lot of pain.

SPOTTING LIARS, DEALING WITH JERKS, AND CHARMING EVERYONE ELSE

As a negotiator, you're going to run into guys who lie to your face and try to scare you into agreement. Aggressive jerks and serial fabricators come with the territory, and dealing with them is something you have to do.

But learning how to handle aggression and identify falsehood is just part of a larger issue: that is, learning how to spot and interpret the subtleties of communication—both verbal and nonverbal—that reveal the mental states of your counterparts.

Truly effective negotiators are conscious of the verbal, paraverbal (how it's said), and nonverbal communications that pervade negotiations and group dynamics. And they know how to employ those subtleties to their benefit. Even changing a single word when you present options—like using "not lose" instead of "keep"—can unconsciously influence the conscious choices your counterpart makes.

Here I want to talk about the tools you need to ID liars, disarm jerks, and charm everybody else. Of course, the open-ended "How" question is one of them—maybe the most important one—but there are many more.

Alastair Onglingswan was living in the Philippines when, one evening in 2004, he hailed a taxi and settled in for a long ride home from Manila's Greenhills shopping center.

He dozed off.

And he woke up in chains.

Unfortunately for Alastair, the cabbie had a second business as a kidnapper. He kept a bottle of ether in his front seat, and when a target fell asleep he would drug him, imprison him, and ask for ransom.

Within hours, the kidnapper used Alastair's phone to contact his girlfriend in New York. He demanded a daily payment to "take care" of Alastair while he researched the family's wealth.

"It's okay if you don't pay," he said. "I can always sell his organs in Saudi Arabia."

Within twenty-four hours, I'd been charged with heading the negotiation from Quantico. Alastair's girlfriend was too nervous to handle the family side of the negotiation, and his mother, who lived in the Philippines, just wanted to accept any demand the kidnapper made.

But Alastair's brother Aaron, in Manila, was different: he just *got* the idea of negotiation and he accepted that Alastair might die, which would make him a better and more effective negotiator. Aaron and I set up an always-on phone line and I became Aaron's guru on the other side of the world.

Through the kidnapper's comments and demands, I saw that he was experienced and patient. As a token of his intentions, he offered to cut off one of Alastair's ears and send it to the family along with a video of him severing the ear.

The demand for the daily payment was clearly a trick to quickly drain the family of as much money as possible while at the same time gauging their wealth. We had to figure out who this guy was— Was he a lone operator or part of a group? Did he plan on killing Alastair or not?—and we had to do that before the family went broke. To get there, we were going to have to engage the kidnapper in a protracted negotiation. We were going to have to slow everything down.

From Quantico, I loaded Aaron up with calibrated questions. I instructed him to keep peppering the violent jerk with "How?" How am I supposed to . . . ? How do we know . . . ? How can we . . . ? There is great power in treating jerks with deference. It gives you the ability to be extremely assertive—to say "No"—in a hidden fashion.

"How do we know if we pay you that you won't hurt Alastair?" Aaron asked.

In the Chinese martial art of tai chi, the goal is to use your opponent's aggressiveness against him—to turn his offense into your way to defeat him. That's the approach we took with Alastair's kidnapper: we wanted to absorb his threats and wear him down. We made sure that even scheduling a call with us was complex. We delayed making email responses.

Through all these tactics, we gained the upper hand while giving the kidnapper the illusion of control. He thought he was solving

Aaron's problems while we were just reading him and wasting his time. You see, it's best not to go chin to chin with aggressiveness like that of Alastair's kidnapper; rather, default to using "what" and "how" questions to avoid making bids or adjusting your own negotiating position. Dodge and weave.

Finally, following days of back-and-forth bargaining on the daily rate, Aaron got the kidnapper down to a token amount and agreed to deposit a portion of the funds in his bank account. After that partial payment was made, Aaron came up with the perfect way to nonconfrontationally confront the cabbie with a calibrated "When/What" question.

"When we run out of money, what will happen?" Aaron asked.

The kidnapper paused.

"It will be all right," he finally responded.

Yes!

Without realizing what he had just agreed to, our killer had just promised us he wouldn't hurt Alastair. A repetitive series of "What" and "How" questions can help you overcome the aggressive tactics of a manipulative adversary.

As you can see in that last exchange, the kidnapper's protracted chats with Aaron had turned Aaron almost into a friend. Over time the kidnapper had become unguarded about spending time on the phone with his "friend." Finally, the Philippine National Police investigators tracked the phone to a house and raided it. The kidnapper and Alastair were not there, but the kidnapper's wife was. She told the police about another house they owned. The police quickly raided the other house, freed Alastair, and arrested the kidnapper.

There are plenty of other tactics, tools, and methods for using subtle verbal and nonverbal forms of communication to understand and modify the mental states of your counterpart. As I run through some of them here, I want you to take a moment to internalize each one.

These are the kind of tools that can help observant negotiators hit home runs.

THE 7-38-55 PERCENT RULE

In two famous studies on what makes us like or dislike somebody,[1] UCLA psychology professor Albert Mehrabian created the 7-38-55 rule. That is, only 7 percent of a message is based on the words while 38 percent comes from the tone of voice and 55 percent from the speaker's body language and face.

While these figures mainly relate to situations where we are forming an attitude about somebody, the rule nonetheless offers a useful ratio for negotiators. You see, body language and tone of voice—not words—are our most powerful assessment tools. That's why I'll often fly great distances to meet someone face-to-face, even when I can say much of what needs to be said over the phone.

So how do you use this rule? First, pay very close attention to tone and body language to make sure they match up with the literal meaning of the words. If they don't align, it's quite possible that the speaker is lying or at least unconvinced.

When someone's tone of voice or body language does not align with the meaning of the words they say, use labels to discover the source of the incongruence.

Here's an example:

You: "So we're agreed?"

Them: "Yes . . ."

You: "I heard you say, 'Yes,' but it seemed like there was hesitation in your voice."

Them: "Oh, it's nothing really."

You: "No, this is important, let's make sure we get this right."

Them: "Thanks, I appreciate it."

This is the way to make sure your agreement gets implemented with no surprises. And your counterpart will be grateful. Your act of recognizing the incongruence and gently dealing with it through a label will make them feel respected. Consequently, your relationship of trust will be improved.

THE RULE OF THREE

I'm positive that sometime in your life you've been involved in a negotiation where you got a "Yes" that later turned out to be a "No." Maybe the other party was lying to you, or maybe they were just engaged in wishful thinking. Either way, this is not an uncommon experience.

This happens because there are actually three kinds of "Yes": Commitment, Confirmation, and Counterfeit.

As we discussed in Chapter 5, so many pushy salesman try to trap their clients into the Commitment "Yes" that many people get very good at the Counterfeit "Yes. "

One great tool for avoiding this trap is the Rule of Three.

The Rule of Three is simply getting the other guy to agree to the same thing three times in the same conversation. It's tripling the strength of whatever dynamic you're trying to drill into at the moment. In doing so, it uncovers problems before they happen. It's really hard to repeatedly lie or fake conviction.

When I first learned this skill, my biggest fear was how to avoid sounding like a broken record or coming off as really pushy.

The answer, I learned, is to vary your tactics.

The first time they agree to something or give you a commitment, that's No. 1. For No. 2 you might label or summarize what they said so they answer, "That's right." And No. 3 could be a calibrated "How" or "What" question about implementation that asks them to explain what will constitute success, something like "What do we do if we get off track?"

Or the three times might just be the same calibrated question phrased three different ways, like "What's the biggest challenge you faced? What are we up against here? What do you see as being the most difficult thing to get around?"

Either way, going at the same issue three times uncovers falsehoods as well as the incongruences between words and body language we mentioned in the last section. So next time you're not sure your counterpart is truthful and committed, try it.

THE PINOCCHIO EFFECT

With Carlo Collodi's famous character Pinocchio, it was easy to tell when he was lying: you just had to watch the nose.

It turns out that Collodi wasn't far off reality. Most people offer obvious telltale signs when they're lying. Not a growing nose, but close enough.

In a study of the components of lying,[2] Harvard Business School professor Deepak Malhotra and his coauthors found that, on average, liars use more words than truth tellers and use far more third-person pronouns. They start talking about *him*, *her*, *it*, *one*, *they*, and *their* rather than *I*, in order to put some distance between themselves and the lie.

And they discovered that liars tend to speak in more complex sentences in an attempt to win over their suspicious counterparts. It's what W. C. Fields meant when he talked about baffling someone with bullshit. The researchers dubbed this the Pinocchio Effect because, just like Pinocchio's nose, the number of words grew along with the lie. People who are lying are, understandably, more worried about being believed, so they work harder—too hard, as it were—at being believable.

PAY ATTENTION TO THEIR USAGE OF PRONOUNS

The use of pronouns by a counterpart can also help give you a feel for their actual importance in the decision and implementation chains on the other side of the table. The more in love they are with "I," "me," and "my" the less important they are.

Conversely, the harder it is to get a first person pronoun out of a negotiator's mouth, the more important they are. Just like in the Malhotra study where the liar is distancing himself from the lie, in a negotiation, smart decision makers don't want to be cornered at the table into making a decision. They will defer to the people away from the table to keep from getting pinned down.

Our cabdriver kidnapper in the Philippines of Alastair Onglingswan used "we," "they," and "them" so rigorously early on in the kidnapping I was convinced we were engaged with their leader. I just never knew how literally true it was until the rescue. In the Chase Manhattan Bank robbery from Chapter 2, the bank robber Chris Watts consistently talked out how dangerous the "others" were and how little influence he had on them, all a lie.

THE CHRIS DISCOUNT

People always talk about remembering and using (but not *overusing*) your counterpart's name in a negotiation. And that's important. The reality though is people are often tired of being hammered with their own name. The slick salesman trying to drive them to "Yes" will hit them with it over and over.

Instead, take a different tack and use your own name. That's how I get the Chris discount.

Just as using Alastair's name with the kidnapper and getting him to use it back humanized the hostage and made it less likely he would be harmed, using your own name creates the dynamic of "forced empathy." It makes the other side see you as a person.

A few years ago I was in a bar in Kansas with a bunch of fellow FBI negotiators. The bar was packed, but I saw one empty chair. I moved toward it but just as I got ready to sit the guy next to it said, "Don't even think about it."

"Why?" I asked, and he said, "Because I'll kick your ass."

He was big, burly, and already drunk, but look, I'm a lifelong hostage negotiator—I gravitate toward tense situations that need mediation like a moth to the flame.

I held out my hand to shake his and said, "My name is Chris."

The dude froze, and in the pause my fellow FBI guys moved in, patted him on the shoulders, and offered to buy him a drink. Turned out he was a Vietnam veteran at a particularly low point. He was in a packed bar where the entire world seemed to be celebrating. The only thing he could think of was to fight. But as soon as I became "Chris," everything changed.

Now take that mindset to a financial negotiation. I was in an outlet mall a few months after the Kansas experience and I picked out some shirts in one of the stores. At the front counter the young lady asked me if I wanted to join their frequent buyer program.

I asked her if I got a discount for joining and she said, "No."

So I decided to try another angle. I said in a friendly manner, "My name is Chris. What's the Chris discount?"

She looked from the register, met my eyes, and gave a little laugh.

"I'll have to ask my manager, Kathy," she said and turned to the woman who'd been standing next to her.

Kathy, who'd heard the whole exchange, said, "The best I can do is ten percent."

Humanize yourself. Use your name to introduce yourself. Say it in a fun, friendly way. Let them enjoy the interaction, too. And get your own special price.

HOW TO GET YOUR COUNTERPARTS TO
BID AGAINST THEMSELVES

Like you saw Aaron and Julie do with their kidnappers, the best way to get your counterparts to lower their demands is to say "No" using "How" questions. These indirect ways of saying "No" won't shut down your counterpart the way a blunt, pride-piercing "No" would. In fact, these responses will sound so much like counterbids that your counterparts will often keep bidding against themselves.

We've found that you can usually express "No" four times before actually saying the word.

The first step in the "No" series is the old standby:

"How am I supposed to do that?"

You have to deliver it in a deferential way, so it becomes a request for help. Properly delivered, it invites the other side to participate in your dilemma and solve it with a better offer.

After that, some version of "Your offer is very generous, I'm sorry, that just doesn't work for me" is an elegant second way to say "No."

This well-tested response avoids making a counteroffer, and the use of "generous" nurtures your counterpart to live up to the word. The "I'm sorry" also softens the "No" and builds empathy. (You can ignore the so-called negotiating experts who say apologies are always signs of weakness.)

Then you can use something like "I'm sorry but I'm afraid I just can't do that." It's a little more direct, and the "can't do that" does great double duty. By expressing an inability to perform, it can trigger the other side's empathy toward you.

"I'm sorry, no" is a slightly more succinct version for the fourth "No." If delivered gently, it barely sounds negative at all.

If you have to go further, of course, "No" is the last and most direct way. Verbally, it should be delivered with a downward inflection and a tone of regard; it's not meant to be "NO!"

One of my students, a guy named Jesus Bueno, wrote me not long ago to tell me an amazing story about how he'd used the multi-step "No" to help his brother Joaquin out of a sticky business situation.

His brother and two friends had bought a cannabis grow shop franchise in northern Spain, where the cultivation of marijuana for personal use is legal. Joaquin and his partner, Bruno, each invested 20,000 euros in the business for a 46 percent stake (a minority partner invested another €3,500 for 8 percent).

From the beginning, Joaquin and Bruno had a rocky relationship. Joaquin is an excellent salesman, while Bruno was more of a book-keeper. The minority partner was also an excellent salesman, and he and Joaquin believed that growing sales was the correct strategy. That meant offering discounts for large orders and repeat customers, which Bruno disagreed with. Their planned spending on launching a website and expanding inventory also rubbed Bruno the wrong way.

Then Bruno's wife became a problem as she started nagging Joaquin about how he should not spend so much on expansion and instead take more profits. One day, Joaquin was reviewing inventory purchases and noticed that some items they had ordered had not been placed on the store's shelves. He began searching for them online and to his surprise he found an eBay store set up with the wife's first name that was selling exactly those missing products.

This started a huge argument between Bruno and Joaquin, and soured their relationship. In the heat of the moment, Bruno told Joaquin that he was open to selling his shares because he felt the business risks they were taking were too large. So Joaquin consulted with his brother: my student Jesus.

Because they believed that pressure from Bruno's wife was why he wanted to sell, Jesus helped Joaquin craft an empathy message around that: "It seems like you are under a lot of pressure from your wife." Joaquin was also in the middle of a divorce, so they decided to use that to relate to the wife issues, and they prepared an accusation audit—"I know you think I don't care about costs and taking profits from the company"—in order to diffuse the negative energy and get Bruno talking.

It worked like a charm. Bruno immediately agreed with the accusation audit and began explaining why he thought Joaquin was careless with spending. Bruno also noted that he didn't have someone to bail him out like Joaquin did (Joaquin got a start-up loan from his mother). Joaquin used mirrors to keep Bruno talking, and he did.

Finally, Joaquin said, "I know how the pressure from your wife can feel, I'm going through a divorce myself and it really takes a lot out of you." Bruno then went on a ten-minute rant about his wife and let slip a huge piece of information: the wife was very upset because the bank that lent them the €20,000 had reviewed their loan and had given them two options: repay the loan in full, or pay a much higher interest rate.

Bingo!

Joaquin and Jesus huddled after learning that, and decided that Joaquin could reasonably pay just above the loan price because Bruno had already taken €14,000 in salary from the business. The letter from the bank put Bruno in a bad spot, and Joaquin figured he could bid low because there wasn't really a market for Bruno to sell his shares.

They decided that €23,000 would be the magic number, with €11,000 up front with the remaining €12,000 over a year period.

Then things went sideways.

Instead of waiting for Bruno to name a price, Joaquin jumped the gun and made his full offer, telling Bruno that he thought it was "very fair." If there's one way to put off your counterpart, it's by implying that disagreeing with you is *unfair*.

What happened next proved that.

Bruno angrily hung up the phone and two days later Joaquin received an email from a guy saying he'd been hired to represent Bruno. They wanted €30,812: €20,000 for the loan, €4,000 for salary, €6,230 for equity, and €582 for interest.

Nonround figures that seemed unchangeable in their specificity. This guy was a pro.

Jesus told Joaquin that he'd truly screwed up. But they both knew that Bruno was pretty desperate to sell. So they decided to use the multi-step "No" strategy to get Bruno to bid against himself. The worst-case scenario, they decided, was that Bruno would just change his mind about selling his shares and the status quo would continue. It was a risk they'd have to take.

They crafted their first "No" message:

The price you offered is very fair, and I certainly wish that I could afford it. Bruno has worked very hard for this business, and he deserves to be compensated appropriately. I am very sorry, but wish you the best of luck.

Notice how they made no counteroffer and said "No" without using the word?

Joaquin was shocked when the following day he received an email from the advisor lowering the price to €28,346.

Joaquin and Jesus then crafted their second gentle "No":

Thank you for your offer. You were generous to reduce the price, which I greatly appreciate. I really wish that I could pay you this amount, but I am sincere in that I cannot afford this amount at this time. As you know, I am in the middle of a divorce and I just cannot come up with that type of money. Again, I wish you the best of luck.

The next day Joaquin received a one-line email from the advisor dropping the price to €25,000. Joaquin wanted to take it but Jesus told him that he had some "No" steps to go. Joaquin fought him, but in the end he relented.

There's a critical lesson there: The art of closing a deal is staying focused to the very end. There are crucial points at the finale when you must draw on your mental discipline. Don't think about what time the last flight leaves, or what it would be like to get home early and play golf. Do not let your mind wander. Remain focused.

They wrote:

Thank you again for the generous offer. You have really come down on the price and I have tried very hard to come up with that amount. Unfortunately, no one is willing to lend me the money, not even my mother. I have tried various avenues but cannot come up with the funding. In the end, I can offer you €23,567, although I can only pay €15,321.37 up front. I could pay you the remainder over a one-year period, but that is really the most I can do. I wish you the best in your decision.

Brilliant use of specific numbers, and what an empathy-building way to say "No" without using the word!

And it worked. Within one hour, the advisor responded to accept.

Look at this closely: see how the mixture of mirroring and open-ended questions dragged out the information about Bruno's financial problems, and then the "No" method exploited his desperation? It might not have been a great idea to use this method if there'd been another buyer, but with no one else it was a brilliant way to get Bruno to bid against himself.

KEY LESSONS

Superstar negotiators—real rainmakers—know that a negotiation is a playing field beneath the words, where really getting to a good deal involves detecting and manipulating subtle, nonobvious signals beneath the surface. It is only by visualizing and modifying these sub-surface issues that you can craft a great deal and make sure that it is implemented.

As you put the following tools to use, remember this chapter's most important concept. That is, "Yes" is nothing without "How." Asking "How," knowing "How," and defining "How" are all part of the effective negotiator's arsenal. He would be unarmed without them.

- Ask calibrated "How" questions, and ask them again and again. Asking "How" keeps your counterparts engaged but off balance. Answering the questions will give them the illusion of control. It will also lead them to contemplate your problems when making their demands.

- Use "How" questions to shape the negotiating environment. You do this by using "How can I do that?" as a gentle version of "No." This will subtly push your counterpart to search for other solutions—*your* solutions. And very often it will get them to bid against themselves.

- Don't just pay attention to the people you're negotiating with directly; always identify the motivations of the players "behind the table." You can do so by asking how a deal will affect everybody else and how on board they are.

- Follow the 7-38-55 Percent Rule by paying close attention to tone of voice and body language. Incongruence between the words and nonverbal signs will show when your counterpart is lying or uncomfortable with a deal.

- Is the "Yes" real or counterfeit? Test it with the Rule of Three: use calibrated questions, summaries, and labels to get your counterpart to reaffirm their agreement at least three times. It's really hard to repeatedly lie or fake conviction.

- A person's use of pronouns offers deep insights into his or her relative authority. If you're hearing a lot of "I," "me," and "my," the real power to decide probably lies elsewhere. Picking up a lot of "we," "they," and "them," it's more likely you're dealing directly with a savvy decision maker keeping his options open.

- Use your own name to make yourself a real person to the other side and even get your own personal discount. Humor and humanity are the best ways to break the ice and remove roadblocks.

CHAPTER 9

BARGAIN HARD

A few years ago I fell in love with a red Toyota 4Runner. Actually not just "red," but "Salsa Red Pearl." Kind of a smoldering red that seemed to glow at night. How sexy is that? I just had to have it; getting one became my obsession.

I searched the dealers in metropolitan Washington, D.C., and I quickly realized that I wasn't the only one obsessed with getting that truck: there weren't any in that color in the entire area, none at all, save at one dealer.

You know how they tell you not to shop for groceries when you're hungry? Well, I was hungry. Very hungry. Actually, I was in love. . . . I sat down, centered myself, and strategized. This lot was my only shot. I had to make it count

I drove to the dealer on a sunny Friday afternoon. I sat down across from the salesman, a nice enough guy named Stan, and told him how gorgeous the vehicle was.

He offered me the usual smile—he had me, he thought—and mentioned the sticker price on "that beautiful vehicle": $36,000.

I gave him an understanding nod and pursed my lips. The key to beginning a haggle is to rattle the other guy ever so gently. You do it in the nicest way possible. If I could thread that needle, I had a good chance at getting my price.

"I can pay $30,000," I said. "And I can pay it up front, all cash. I'll write a check today for the full amount. I'm sorry, I'm afraid I just can't pay any more."

His smile flickered a little bit at the edges, as if it were losing focus. But he tightened it down and shook his head.

"I'm sure you can understand we can't do that. The sticker price is $36,000, after all."

"How am I supposed to do that?" I asked deferentially.

"I'm sure," he said, then paused as if he wasn't sure what he'd meant to say. "I'm sure we can figure something out with financing the $36,000."

"It's a beautiful truck. Really amazing. I can't tell you how much I'd love to have it. It's worth more than what I'm offering. I'm sorry, this is really embarrassing. I just can't do that price."

He stared at me in silence, a little befuddled now. Then he stood and went into the back for what seemed like an eternity. He was gone so long that I remember saying to myself, "Damn! I should have come in lower! They're going to come all the way down." Any response that's not an outright rejection of your offer means you have the edge.

He returned and told me like it was Christmas that his boss had okayed a new price: $34,000.

"Wow, your offer is very generous and this is the car of my dreams," I said. "I really wish I could do that. I really do. This is so embarrassing. I simply can't."

He dropped into silence and I didn't take the bait. I let the silence linger. And then with a sigh he trudged off again.

He returned after another eternity.

"You win," he said. "My manager okayed $32,500."

He pushed a paper across the desk that even said "YOU WIN" in big letters. The words were even surrounded with smiley faces.

"I am so grateful. You've been very generous, and I can't thank you enough. The truck is no doubt worth more than my price," I said. "I'm sorry, I just can't do that."

Up he stood again. No smile now. Still befuddled. After a few seconds, he walked back to his manager and I leaned back. I could taste victory. A minute later—no eternity this time—he returned and sat.

"We can do that," he said.

Two days later, I drove off in my Salsa Red Pearl Toyota 4Runner—for $30,000.

God I love that truck. Still drive it today.

Most negotiations hit that inevitable point where the slightly loose and informal interplay between two people turns to confrontation and the proverbial "brass tacks." You know the moment: you've mirrored and labeled your way to a degree of rapport; an accusation audit has cleared any lingering mental or emotional obstacles, and you've identified and summarized the interests and positions at stake, eliciting a "That's right," and . . .

Now it's time to bargain.

Here it is: the clash for cash, an uneasy dance of offers and counters that send most people into a cold sweat. If you count yourself among that majority, regarding the inevitable moment as nothing more than a necessary evil, there's a good chance you regularly get your clock cleaned by those who have learned to embrace it.

No part of a negotiation induces more anxiety and unfocused aggression than bargaining, which is why it's the part that is more often fumbled and mishandled than any other. It's simply not a comfortable dynamic for most people. Even when we have the best-laid plans, a lot of us wimp out when we get to the moment of exchanging prices.

In this chapter, I'm going to explain the tactics that make up the bargaining process, and look at how psychological dynamics determine which tactics should be used and how they should be implemented.

Now, bargaining is not rocket science, but it's not simple intuition or mathematics, either. To bargain well, you need to shed your assumptions about the haggling process and learn to recognize the subtle psychological strategies that play vital roles at the bargaining table. Skilled bargainers see more than just opening offers, counteroffers, and closing moves. They see the psychological currents that run below the surface.

Once you've learned to identify these currents, you'll be able to "read" bargaining situations more accurately and confidently answer the tactical questions that dog even the best negotiators.

You'll be ready for the "bare-knuckle bargaining." And they'll never see it coming.

WHAT TYPE ARE YOU?

A few years ago I was on my boat with one of my employees, a great guy named Keenon; I was supposed to be giving him a pep talk and performance review.

"When I think of what we do, I describe it as 'uncovering the riptide,'" I said.

"Uncovering the riptide," Keenon said.

"Yes, the idea is that we—you and I and everyone here—have the skills to identify the psychological forces that are pulling us away from shore and use them to get somewhere more productive."

"Somewhere more productive," Keenon said.

"Exactly," I said. "To a place where we can . . ."

We had talked for about forty-five minutes when my son Brandon, who runs operations for The Black Swan Group, broke out laughing.

"I can't take it anymore! Don't you see? Really, Dad, don't you see?"

I blinked. Did I see what? I asked him.

"All Keenon is doing is mirroring you. And he's been doing it for almost an hour."

"Oh," I said, my face going red as Keenon began to laugh.

He was totally right. Keenon had been playing with me the entire time, using the psychological tool that works most effectively with assertive guys like me: the mirror.

Your personal negotiation style—and that of your counterpart—is formed through childhood, schooling, family, culture, and a million other factors; by recognizing it you can identify your negotiating strengths and weaknesses (and those of your counterpart) and adjust your mindset and strategies accordingly.

Negotiation style is a crucial variable in bargaining. If you don't know what instinct will tell you or the other side to do in various circumstances, you'll have massive trouble gaming out effective strategies and tactics. You and your counterpart have habits of mind and behavior, and once you identify them you can leverage them in a strategic manner.

Just like Keenon did.

There's an entire library unto itself of research into the archetypes and behavioral profiles of all the possible people you're bound to meet at the negotiating table. It's flat-out overwhelming, so much so that it loses its utility. Over the last few years, in an effort primarily led by my son Brandon, we've consolidated and simplified all that research, cross-referencing it with our experiences in the field and the case studies of our business school students, and found that people fall into three broad categories. Some people are Accommodators; others—like me—are basically Assertive; and the rest are data-loving Analysts.

Hollywood negotiation scenes suggest that an Assertive style is required for effective bargaining, but each of the styles can be effective. And to truly be effective you need elements from all three.

A study of American lawyer-negotiators[1] found that 65 percent of attorneys from two major U.S. cities used a cooperative style while only 24 percent were truly assertive. And when these lawyers were graded for effectiveness, more than 75 percent of the effective group came from the cooperative type; only 12 percent were Assertive. So if you're not Assertive, don't despair. Blunt assertion is actually counterproductive most of the time.

And remember, your personal negotiating style is not a straitjacket. No one is exclusively one style. Most of us have the capacity to throttle up our nondominant styles should the situation call for it. But there is one basic truth about a successful bargaining style: To be good, you have to learn to be yourself at the bargaining table. To be great you have to add to your strengths, not replace them.

Here's a quick guide to classifying the type of negotiator you're facing and the tactics that will be most fitting for you.

ANALYST

Analysts are methodical and diligent. They are not in a big rush. Instead, they believe that as long as they are working toward the best result in a thorough and systematic way, time is of little consequence. Their self-image is linked to minimizing mistakes. Their motto: As much time as it takes to get it right.

Classic analysts prefer to work on their own and rarely deviate from their goals. They rarely show emotion, and they often use what is very close to the FM DJ Voice I talked about in Chapter 3, slow and measured with a downward inflection. However, Analysts often speak in a way that is distant and cold instead of soothing. This puts people off without them knowing it and actually limits them from putting their counterpart at ease and opening them up.

Analysts pride themselves on not missing any details in their extensive preparation. They will research for two weeks to get data they might have gotten in fifteen minutes at the negotiating table, just to keep from being surprised. Analysts hate surprises.

They are reserved problem solvers, and information aggregators, and are hypersensitive to reciprocity. They will give you a piece, but if they don't get a piece in return within a certain period of time, they lose trust and will disengage. This can often seem to come out of no-where, but remember, since they like working on things alone the fact that they are talking to you at all is, from their perspective, a conces-sion. They will often view concessions by their counterpart as a new piece of information to be taken back and evaluated. Don't expect im-mediate counterproposals from them.

People like this are skeptical by nature. So asking too many ques-tions to start is a bad idea, because they're not going to want to answer until they understand all the implications. With them, it's vital to be prepared. Use clear data to drive your reason; don't ad-lib; use data comparisons to disagree and focus on the facts; warn them of issues early; and avoid surprises.

Silence to them is an opportunity to think. They're not mad at you and they're not trying to give you a chance to talk more. If you feel they don't see things the way you do, give them a chance to think first.

Apologies have little value to them since they see the negotiation and their relationship with you as a person largely as separate things. They respond fairly well in the moment to labels. They are not quick to answer calibrated questions, or closed-ended questions when the answer is "Yes." They may need a few days to respond.

If you're an analyst you should be worried about cutting yourself off from an essential source of data, your counterpart. The single big-gest thing you can do is to smile when you speak. People will be more forthcoming with information to you as a result. Smiling can also become a habit that makes it easy for you to mask any moments you've been caught off guard.

ACCOMMODATOR

The most important thing to this type of negotiator is the time spent building the relationship. Accommodators think as long as there is a free-flowing continuous exchange of information time is being well spent. As long as they're communicating, they're happy. Their goal is to be on great terms with their counterpart. They love the win-win.

Of the three types, they are most likely to build great rapport without actually accomplishing anything.

Accommodators want to remain friends with their counterpart even if they can't reach an agreement. They are very easy to talk to, extremely friendly, and have pleasant voices. They will yield a concession to appease or acquiesce and hope the other side reciprocates.

If your counterparts are sociable, peace-seeking, optimistic, distractible, and poor time managers, they're probably Accommodators.

If they're your counterpart, be sociable and friendly. Listen to them talk about their ideas and use calibrated questions focused specifically on implementation to nudge them along and find ways to translate their talk into action. Due to their tendency to be the first to activate the reciprocity cycle, they may have agreed to give you something they can't actually deliver.

Their approach to preparation can be lacking as they are much more focused on the person behind the table. They want to get to know you. They have a tremendous passion for the spirit of negotiation and what it takes not only to manage emotions but also to satisfy them.

While it is very easy to disagree with an Accommodator, because they want nothing more that to hear what you have to say, uncovering their objections can be difficult. They will have identified potential problem areas beforehand and will leave those areas unaddressed out of fear of the conflict they may cause.

If you have identified yourself as an Accommodator, stick to your ability to be very likable, but do not sacrifice your objections. Not only do the other two types need to hear your point of view; if you are dealing with another Accommodator they will welcome it. Also be conscious of excess chitchat: the other two types have no use for it, and if you're sitting across the table from someone like yourself you will be prone to interactions where nothing gets done.

ASSERTIVE

The Assertive type believes time is money; every wasted minute is a wasted dollar. Their self-image is linked to how many things they can get accomplished in a period of time. For them, getting the solution perfect isn't as important as getting it done.

Assertives are fiery people who love winning above all else, often at the expense of others. Their colleagues and counterparts never question where they stand because they are always direct and candid. They have an aggressive communication style and they don't worry about future interactions. Their view of business relationships is based on respect, nothing more and nothing less.

Most of all, the Assertive wants to be heard. And not only do they want to be heard, but they don't actually have the ability to listen to you until they know that you've heard them. They focus on their own goals rather than people. And they tell rather than ask.

When you're dealing with Assertive types, it's best to focus on what they have to say, because once they are convinced you understand them, then and only then will they listen for your point of view.

To an Assertive, every silence is an opportunity to speak more. Mirrors are a wonderful tool with this type. So are calibrated questions, labels, and summaries. The most important thing to get from an Assertive will be a "that's right" that may come in the form of a "that's it exactly" or "you hit it on the head."

When it comes to reciprocity, this type is of the "give an inch/take a mile" mentality. They will have figured they deserve whatever you have given them so they will be oblivious to expectations of owing something in return. They will actually simply be looking for the opportunity to receive more. If they have given some kind of concession, they are surely counting the seconds until they get something in return.

If you are an Assertive, be particularly conscious of your tone. You will not intend to be overly harsh but you will often come off that way. Intentionally soften your tone and work to make it more pleasant. Use calibrated questions and labels with your counterpart since that will also make you more approachable and increase the chances for collaboration.

We've seen how each of these groups views the importance of time differently (time = preparation; time = relationship; time = money). They also have completely different interpretations of silence.

I'm definitely an Assertive, and at a conference this Accommodator type told me that he blew up a deal. I thought, What did you do, scream at the other guy and leave? Because that's me blowing up a deal.

But it turned out that he went silent; for an Accommodator type, silence is anger.

For Analysts, though, silence means they want to think. And Assertive types interpret your silence as either you don't have anything to say or you want them to talk. I'm one, so I know: the only time I'm silent is when I've run out of things to say.

The funny thing is when these cross over. When an Analyst pauses to think, their Accommodator counterpart gets nervous and an Assertive one starts talking, thereby annoying the Analyst, who thinks to herself, Every time I try to think you take that as an opportunity to talk some more. Won't you ever shut up?

Before we move on I want to talk about why people often fail to identify their counterpart's style.

The greatest obstacle to accurately identifying someone else's style is what I call the "I am normal" paradox. That is, our hypothesis that the world should look to others as it looks to us. After all, who wouldn't make that assumption?

But while innocent and understandable, thinking you're normal is one of the most damaging assumptions in negotiations. With it, we unconsciously project our own style on the other side. But with three types of negotiators in the world, there's a 66 percent chance your counterpart has a different style than yours. A different "normal."

A CEO once told me he expected nine of ten negotiations to fail. This CEO was likely projecting his beliefs onto the other side. In reality, he probably only matched with someone like-minded one of ten times. If he understood that his counterpart was different from him, he would most surely have increased his success rate.

From the way they prepare to the way they engage in dialogue, the three types negotiate differently. So before you can even think about bargaining effectively, you have to understand your counterpart's "normal." You have to identify their type by opening yourself to their difference. Because when it comes to negotiating, the Golden Rule is wrong.

The Black Swan rule is don't treat others the way you want to be treated; treat them the way they need to be treated.

(I've got a complementary PDF available that will help you identify your type and that of those around you. Please visit http://info.blackswanltd.com/3-types.)

TAKING A PUNCH

Negotiation academics like to treat bargaining as a rational process devoid of emotion. They talk about the ZOPA—or Zone of Possible Agreement—which is where the seller's and buyer's zones cross. Say Tony wants to sell his car and won't take less than $5,000 and Samantha wants to buy but won't pay more than $6,000. The ZOPA runs from $5,000 to $6,000. Some deals have ZOPAs and some don't. It's all very rational.

Or so they'd have you think.

You need to disabuse yourself of that notion. In a real bargaining session, kick-ass negotiators don't use ZOPA. Experienced negotiators often lead with a ridiculous offer, an extreme anchor. And if you're not prepared to handle it, you'll lose your moorings and immediately go to your maximum. It's human nature. Like the great ear-biting pugilist Mike Tyson once said, "Everybody has a plan until they get punched in the mouth."

As a well-prepared negotiator who seeks information and gathers it relentlessly, you're actually going to want the other guy to name a price first, because you want to see his hand. You're going to welcome the extreme anchor. But extreme anchoring is powerful and you're human: your emotions may well up. If they do there are ways to weather the storm without bidding against yourself or responding with anger. Once you learn these tactics, you'll be prepared to withstand the hit and counter with panache.

First, deflect the punch in a way that opens up your counterpart. Successful negotiators often say "No" in one of the many ways we've talked about ("How am I supposed to accept that?") or deflect the anchor with questions like "What are we trying to accomplish here?" Responses like these are great ways to refocus your counterpart when you feel you're being pulled into the compromise trap.

You can also respond to a punch-in-the-face anchor by simply pivoting to terms. What I mean by this is that when you feel you're being dragged into a haggle you can detour the conversation to the non-monetary issues that make any final price work.

You can do this directly by saying, in an encouraging tone of voice, "Let's put price off to the side for a moment and talk about what would make this a good deal." Or you could go at it more obliquely by asking, "What else would you be able to offer to make that a good price for me?"

And if the other side pushes *you* to go first, wriggle from his grip. Instead of naming a price, allude to an incredibly high number that someone else might charge. Once when a hospital chain wanted me to name a price first, I said, "Well, if you go to Harvard Business School, they're going to charge you $2,500 a day per student."

No matter what happens, the point here is to sponge up information from your counterpart. Letting your counterpart anchor first will give you a tremendous feel for him. All you need to learn is how to take the first punch.

One of my Georgetown MBA students, a guy named Farouq, showed how not to fold after being punched when he went to hit up the MBA dean for funds to hold a big alumni event in Dubai. It was a desperate situation, because he needed $600 and she was his last stop.

At the meeting, Farouq told the dean about how excited the students were about the trip and how beneficial it would be for the Georgetown MBA brand in the region.

Before he could even finish, the dean jumped in.

"Sounds like a great trip you guys are planning," she said. "But money is tight and I could authorize no more than $300."

Farouq hadn't expected the dean to go so quickly. But things don't always go according to plan.

"That is a very generous offer given your budget limits, but I am not sure how that would help us achieve a great reception for the alums in the region," Farouq said, acknowledging her limits but saying no without using the word. Then he dropped an extreme anchor. "I have a very high amount in my head: $1,000 is what we need."

As expected, the extreme anchor quickly knocked the dean off her limit.

"That is severely out of my range and I am sure I can't authorize that. However, I will give you $500."

Farouq was half-tempted to fold—being $100 short wasn't make-or-break—but he remembered the curse of aiming low. He decided to push forward.

The $500 got him closer to the goal but not quite there, he said; $850 would work.

The dean replied by saying that she was already giving more than what she wanted and $500 was reasonable. At this point, if Farouq had been less prepared he would have given up, but he was ready for the punches.

"I think your offer is very reasonable and I understand your restrictions, but I need more money to put on a great show for the school," he said. "How about $775?"

The dean smiled, and Farouq knew he had her.

"You seem to have a specific number in your head that you are trying to get to," she said. "Just tell it to me."

At that point Farouq was happy to give her his number as he felt she was sincere.

"I need $737.50 to make this work and you are my last stop," he said.

She laughed.

The dean then praised him for knowing what he wanted and said she'd check her budget. Two days later, Farouq got an email saying her office would put in $750.

PUNCHING BACK: USING ASSERTION WITHOUT GETTING USED BY IT

When a negotiation is far from resolution and going nowhere fast, you need to shake things up and get your counterpart out of their rigid mindset. In times like this, strong moves can be enormously effective tools. Sometimes a situation simply calls for you to be the aggressor and punch the other side in the face.

That said, if you are basically a nice person, it will be a real stretch to hit the other guy like Mike Tyson. You can't be what you're not. As the Danish folk saying goes, "You bake with the flour you have." But anyone can learn a few tools.

Here are effective ways to assert smartly:

REAL ANGER, THREATS WITHOUT ANGER, AND STRATEGIC UMBRAGE

Marwan Sinaceur of INSEAD and Stanford University's Larissa Tiedens found that expressions of anger increase a negotiator's advantage and final take.[2] Anger shows passion and conviction that can help sway the other side to accept less. However, by heightening your counterpart's sensitivity to danger and fear, your anger reduces the resources they have for other cognitive activity, setting them up to make bad concessions that will likely lead to implementation problems, thus reducing your gains.

Also beware: researchers have also found that disingenuous expressions of unfelt anger—you know, faking it—backfire, leading to intractable demands and destroying trust. For anger to be effective, it has to be real, the key for it is to be under control because anger also reduces our cognitive ability.

And so when someone puts out a ridiculous offer, one that really pisses you off, take a deep breath, allow little anger, and channel it—at the proposal, not the person—and say, "I don't see how that would ever work."

Such well-timed offense-taking—known as "strategic umbrage"—can wake your counterpart to the problem. In studies by Columbia University academics Daniel Ames and Abbie Wazlawek, people on the receiving end of strategic umbrage were more likely to rate themselves as *over*assertive, even when the counterpart didn't think so.[3] The real lesson here is being aware of how this might be used on *you*. Please don't allow yourself to fall victim to "strategic umbrage."

Threats delivered without anger but with "poise"—that is, confidence and self-control—are great tools. Saying, "I'm sorry that just doesn't work for me," with poise, works.

"WHY" QUESTIONS

Back in Chapter 7, I talked about the problems with "Why?" Across our planet and around the universe, "Why?" makes people defensive.

As an experiment, the next time your boss wants something done ask him or her "Why?" and watch what happens. Then try it with a peer, a subordinate, and a friend. Observe their reactions and tell me if you don't find some level of defensiveness across the spectrum. Don't do this too much, though, or you'll lose your job and all your friends.

The only time I say, "Why did you do that?" in a negotiation is when I want to knock someone back. It's an iffy technique, though, and I wouldn't advocate it.

There is, however, another way to use "Why?" effectively. The idea is to employ the defensiveness the question triggers to get your counterpart to defend your position.

I know it sounds weird, but it works. The basic format goes like this: When you want to flip a dubious counterpart to your side, ask them, "Why would you do *that*?" but in a way that the "*that*" favors you. Let me explain. If you are working to lure a client away from a competitor, you might say, "Why would you ever do business with me? Why would you ever change from your existing supplier? They're great!"

In these questions, the "Why?" coaxes your counterpart into working for you.

"I" MESSAGES

Using the first-person singular pronoun is another great way to set a boundary without escalating into confrontation.

When you say, "I'm sorry, that doesn't work for me," the word "I" strategically focuses your counterpart's attention onto you long enough for you to make a point.

The traditional "I" message is to use "I" to hit the pause button and step out of a bad dynamic. When you want to counteract unproductive statements from your counterpart, you can say, "I feel ___ when you ___ because ___," and that demands a time-out from the other person.

But be careful with the big "I": You have to be mindful not to use a tone that is aggressive or creates an argument. It's got to be cool and level.

NO NEEDINESS: HAVING THE READY-TO-WALK MINDSET

We've said previously that no deal is better than a bad deal. If you feel you can't say "No" then you've taken yourself hostage.

Once you're clear on what your bottom line is, you have to be willing to walk away. Never be needy for a deal.

Before we move on, I want to emphasize how important it is to maintain a collaborative relationship even when you're setting boundaries. Your response must always be expressed in the form of strong, yet empathic, limit-setting boundaries—that is, *tough love*—not as hatred or violence. Anger and other strong emotions can on rare occasions be effective. But only as calculated acts, never a personal attack. In any bare-knuckle bargaining session, the most vital principle to keep in mind is never to look at your counterpart as an enemy.

The person across the table is never the problem. The unsolved issue is. So focus on the issue. This is one of the most basic tactics for avoiding emotional escalations. Our culture demonizes people in movies and politics, which creates the mentality that if we only got rid of the person then everything would be okay. But this dynamic is toxic to any negotiation.

Punching back is a last resort. Before you go there, I always suggest an attempt at de-escalating the situation. Suggest a time-out. When your counterparts step back and take a breath, they'll no longer feel that they are hostage to a bad situation. They'll regain a sense of agency and power. And they'll appreciate you for that.

Think of punching back and boundary-setting tactics as a flattened S-curve: you've accelerated up the slope of a negotiation and hit a plateau that requires you to temporarily stop any progress, escalate or de-escalate the issue acting as the obstacle, and eventually bring the relationship back to a state of rapport and get back on the slope. Taking a positive, constructive approach to conflict involves understanding that the bond is fundamental to any resolution. Never create an enemy.

ACKERMAN BARGAINING

I've spent a lot of time talking about the psychological judo that I've made my stock in trade: the calibrated questions, the mirrors, the tools for knocking my counterpart off his game and getting him to bid against himself.

But negotiation still comes down to determining who gets which slice of the pie, and from time to time you're going to be forced into some real bare-knuckle bargaining with a hard-ass haggler.

I faced bare-knuckle bargaining all the time in the hostage world. I haggled with a lot of guys who stuck to their game plan and were used to getting their way. "Pay or we'll kill," they'd say, and they meant it. You had to have your skills drum-tight to negotiate them down. You need tools.

Back at FBI negotiation training, I learned the haggling system that I use to this day. And I swear by it.

I call the system the Ackerman model because it came from this guy Mike Ackerman, an ex-CIA type who founded a kidnap-for-ransom consulting company based out of Miami. On many kidnappings we'd constantly be paired with "Ackerman guys"—never Mike himself—who helped design the haggle.

After I retired from the FBI, I finally met Mike on a trip to Miami. When I told him I also used the system for business negotiations, he laughed and said he'd run the system by Howard Raiffa, a legendary Harvard negotiation guy, and Howard had said it would work in any situation. So I felt pretty justified by that.

The Ackerman model is an offer-counteroffer method, at least on the surface. But it is a very effective system for beating the usual lackluster bargaining dynamic, which has the predictable result of meeting in the middle.

The systematized and easy-to-remember process has only four steps:

1. Set your target price (your goal).

2. Set your first offer at 65 percent of your target price.

3. Calculate three raises of decreasing increments (to 85, 95, and 100 percent).

4. Use lots of empathy and different ways of saying "No" to get the other side to counter before you increase your offer.

5. When calculating the final amount, use precise, nonround numbers like, say, $37,893 rather than $38,000. It gives the number credibility and weight.

6. On your final number, throw in a nonmonetary item (that they probably don't want) to show you're at your limit.

The genius of this system is that it incorporates the psychological tactics we've discussed—reciprocity, extreme anchors, loss aversion, and so on—without you needing to think about them.

If you'll bear with me for a moment, I'll go over the steps so you see what I mean.

First, the original offer of 65 percent of your target price will set an extreme anchor, a big slap in the face that might bring your counterpart right to their price limit. The shock of an extreme anchor will induce a fight-or-flight reaction in all but the most experienced negotiators, limiting their cognitive abilities and pushing them into rash action.

Now look at the progressive offer increases to 85, 95, and 100 percent of the target price. You're going to drop these in sparingly: after the counterpart has made another offer on their end, and after you've thrown out a few calibrated questions to see if you can bait them into bidding against themselves.

When you make these offers, they work on various levels. First, they play on the norm of reciprocity; they inspire your counterpart to make a concession, too. Just like people are more likely to send Christmas cards to people who first send cards to them, they are more likely to make bargaining concessions to those who have made compromises in their direction.

Second, the diminishing size of the increases—notice that they decrease by half each time—convinces your counterpart that he's squeezing you to the point of breaking. By the time they get to the last one, they'll feel that they've really gotten every last drop.

This really juices their self-esteem. Researchers have found that people getting concessions often feel better about the bargaining process than those who are given a single firm, "fair" offer. In fact, they feel better even when they end up paying more—or receiving less—than they otherwise might.

Finally, the power of nonround numbers bears reiterating.

Back in Haiti, I used to use the Ackerman system ferociously. Over eighteen months we got two or three kidnappings a week, so from experience, we knew the market prices were $15,000 to $75,000 per victim. Because I was a hard-ass, I made it my goal to get in under $5,000 in every kidnapping that I ran.

One really stands out, the first one I mentioned in this book. I went through the Ackerman process, knocking them off their game with an extreme anchor, hitting them with calibrated questions, and slowly gave progressively smaller concessions. Finally, I dropped the weird number that closed the deal. I'll never forget the head of the Miami FBI office calling my colleague the next day and saying, "Voss got this guy out for $4,751? How does $1 make a difference?"

They were howling with laughter, and they had a point. That $1 is ridiculous. But it works on our human nature. Notice that you can't buy anything for $2, but you can buy a million things for $1.99. How does a cent change anything? It doesn't. But it makes a difference every time. We just like $1.99 more than $2.00 even if we know it's a trick.

NEGOTIATING A RENT CUT AFTER RECEIVING NOTICE OF AN INCREASE

Eight months after a Georgetown MBA student of mine named Mishary signed a rental contract for $1,850/month, he got some unwelcome news: his landlord informed him that if he wanted to re-up, it would be $2,100/month for ten months, or $2,000/month for a year.

Mishary loved the place and didn't think he'd find a better one, but the price was already high and he couldn't afford more.

Taking to heart our class slogan, "You fall to your highest level of preparation," he dove into the real estate listings and found that prices for comparable apartments were $1,800–$1,950/month, but none of them were in as good a building. He then examined his own finances and figured the rent he wanted to pay was $1,830.

He requested a sit-down with his rental agent.

This was going to be tough.

At their meeting, Mishary laid out his situation. His experience in the building had been really positive, he said. And, he pointed out, he always paid on time. It would be sad for him to leave, he said, and sad for the landlord to lose a good tenant. The agent nodded.

"Totally in agreement," he said. "That's why I think it will benefit both of us to agree on renewing the lease."

Here Mishary pulled out his research: buildings around the neighborhood were offering "much" lower prices, he said. "Even though your building is better in terms of location and services, **how am I supposed to pay $200 extra?**"

The negotiation was on.

The agent went silent for a few moments and then said, "You make a good point, but this is still a good price. And as you noted, we can charge a premium."

Mishary then dropped an extreme anchor.

"I fully understand, you do have a better location and amenities. But I'm sorry, I just can't," he said. "**Would $1,730 a month for a year lease sound fair to you?**"

The agent laughed and when he finished said there was no way to accept that number, because it was way below market price.

Instead of getting pulled into a haggle, Mishary smartly pivoted to calibrated questions.

"Okay, so please help me understand: **how do you price lease renewals?**"

The agent didn't say anything shocking—merely that they used factors like area prices and supply-and-demand—but that gave Mishary the opening to argue that his leaving would open the landlord to the risk of having an unrented apartment and the cost of repainting. One month unrented would be a $2,000 loss, he said.

Then he made another offer. Now, you're probably shaking your head that he's making two offers without receiving one in return. And you're right; normally that's verboten. But you have to be able to improvise. If you feel in control of a negotiation, you can do two or three moves at a time. Don't let the rules ruin the flow.

"Let me try and move along with you: **how about $1,790 for 12 months?**"

The agent paused.

"Sir, I understand your concerns, and what you said makes sense," he said. "Your number, though, is very low. However, give me time to think this out and we can meet at another time. How does that sound?"

Remember, any response that is not an outright rejection means you have the edge.

Five days later the two met again.

"I ran the numbers, and believe me this is a good deal," the agent started. "I am able to offer you $1,950 a month for a year."

Mishary knew he'd won. The agent just needed a little push. So he praised the agent and said no without saying, "No." And notice how he brilliantly mislabels in order to get the guy to open up?

"That is generous of you, but how am I supposed to accept it when I can move a few blocks away and stay for $1,800? A hundred and fifty dollars a month means a lot to me. You know I am a student. I don't know, **it seems like you would rather run the risk of keeping the place unrented**."

"It's not that," the agent answered. "But I can't give you a number lower than the market."

Mishary made a dramatic pause, as if the agent was extracting every cent he had.

"Then I tell you what, I initially went up from $1,730 to $1,790," he said, sighing. "I will bring it up to $1,810. And I think this works well for both."

The agent shook his head.

"This is still lower than the market, sir. And I cannot do that."

Mishary then prepared to give the last of his Ackerman offers. He went silent for a while and then asked the agent for a pen and paper. Then he started doing fake calculations to seem like he was really pushing himself.

Finally, he looked up at the agent and said, "I did some numbers, and the maximum I can afford is $1,829."

The agent bobbed his head from side to side, as if getting his mind around the offer. At last, he spoke.

"Wow. $1,829," he said. "You seem very precise. You must be an accountant. [Mishary was not.] Listen, I value you wanting to renew with us and for that I think we can make this work for a twelve-month lease."

Ka-ching! Notice this brilliant combination of decreasing Ackerman offers, nonround numbers, deep research, smart labeling, and saying no without saying "No"? That's what gets you a rent *discount* when a landlord wanted to raise his monthly take.

KEY LESSONS

When push comes to shove—and it will—you're going to find yourself sitting across the table from a bare-knuckle negotiator. After you've finished all the psychologically nuanced stuff—the labeling and mirroring and calibrating—you are going to have to hash out the "brass tacks."

For most of us, that ain't fun.

Top negotiators know, however, that conflict is often the path to great deals. And the best find ways to actually have fun engaging in it. Conflict brings out truth, creativity, and resolution. So the next time you find yourself face-to-face with a bare-knuckle bargainer, remember the lessons in this chapter.

- Identify your counterpart's negotiating style. Once you know whether they are Accommodator, Assertive, or Analyst, you'll know the correct way to approach them.

- Prepare, prepare, prepare. When the pressure is on, you don't rise to the occasion; you fall to your highest level of preparation. So design an ambitious but legitimate goal and then game out the labels, calibrated questions, and responses you'll use to get there. That way, once you're at the bargaining table, you won't have to wing it.

- Get ready to take a punch. Kick-ass negotiators usually lead with an extreme anchor to knock you off your game. If you're not ready, you'll flee to your maximum without a fight. So prepare your dodging tactics to avoid getting sucked into the compromise trap.

- Set boundaries, and learn to take a punch or punch back, without anger. The guy across the table is not the problem; the situation is.

- Prepare an Ackerman plan. Before you head into the weeds of bargaining, you'll need a plan of extreme anchor, calibrated questions, and well-defined offers. Remember: 65, 85, 95, 100 percent. Decreasing raises and ending on non-round numbers will get your counterpart to believe that he's squeezing you for all you're worth when you're really getting to the number *you* want.

CHAPTER 10

FIND THE BLACK SWAN

At 11:30 a.m. on June 17, 1981, a beautiful 70-degree spring day with an insistent westerly breeze, thirty-seven-year-old William Griffin left the second-floor bedroom where he lived in his parent's Rochester, New York, home and trod down the shoe-buffed stairs that led to their meticulous living room.

At the bottom he stopped, paused, and then, without a word of warning, shot off three shotgun blasts that killed his mother and a handyman who was hanging wallpaper and critically wounded his stepfather. The sound reverberated in the enclosed space.

Griffin then left the house and shot a workman and two bystanders as he jogged two blocks to the Security Trust Company, a neighborhood bank. Seconds after he entered, people began sprinting from the bank as Griffin took nine bank employees hostage and ordered the customers to leave.

For the next three and a half hours, Griffin led police and FBI agents in a violent standoff in which he shot and wounded the first two police officers who responded to the bank's silent alarm, and shot six people who happened to be walking near the bank. Griffin shot off so many rounds—more than one hundred in all—that the police used a garbage truck to shield one officer as he was being rescued.

Waving the nine bank employees into a small office at 2:30 p.m., Griffin told the manager to call the police and deliver a message.

Outside, FBI agent Clint Van Zandt stood by while Rochester police officer Jim O'Brien picked up the phone.

"Either you come to the front entrance doors of the bank at three o'clock and have a shoot-out with him in the parking lot," the manager blurted through her tears, "or he's going to start killing hostages and throwing out bodies."

Then the line went dead.

Now, never in the history of the United States had a hostage-taker killed a hostage on deadline. The deadline was always a way to focus the mind; what the bad guys really wanted was money, respect, and a helicopter. Everyone knew that. It was a permanent and inalterable *known known*. It was the truth.

But that permanent and inalterable truth was about to change.

What came next showed the power of Black Swans, those hidden and unexpected pieces of information—those *unknown unknowns*—whose unearthing has game-changing effects on a negotiation dynamic.

Negotiation breakthroughs—when the game shifts inalterably in your favor—are created by those who can identify and utilize Black Swans.

Here's how.

FINDING LEVERAGE IN THE PREDICTABLY UNPREDICTABLE

At exactly 3 p.m., Griffin gestured toward one of his hostages, a twenty-nine-year-old teller named Margaret Moore, and told her to walk to the glass bank doors. Petrified, Moore did as she was ordered, but first cried out that she was a single parent with a young son.

Griffin didn't seem to hear her, or to care. Once the weeping Moore made it to the vestibule, Griffin shot off two blasts from his twelve-gauge shotgun. Both of the heavy rounds struck Moore in the midsection, violently blowing her through the glass door and almost cutting her body in half.

Outside, law enforcement was stunned into silence. It was obvious that Griffin didn't want money or respect or an escape route. The only way he was coming out was in a body bag.

At that moment, Griffin walked over to a full-length bank window and pressed his body against the glass. He was in full view of a sniper stationed in the church across the street. Griffin knew quite well the sniper was there; earlier in the day he'd shot at him.

Less than a second after Griffin's silhouette appeared in his scope, the sniper pulled the trigger.

Griffin crumpled to the floor, dead.

Black Swan theory tells us that things happen that were previously thought to be impossible—or never thought of at all. This is not the same as saying that sometimes things happen against one-in-a-million odds, but rather that things never imagined do come to pass.

The idea of the Black Swan was popularized by risk analyst Nassim Nicholas Taleb in his bestselling books *Fooled by Randomness* (2001)[1] and *The Black Swan* (2007),[2] but the term goes back much further. Until the seventeenth century, people could only imagine white swans because all swans ever seen had possessed white feathers. In seventeenth-century London it was common to refer to impossible things as "Black Swans."

But then the Dutch explorer Willem de Vlamingh went to western Australia in 1697—and saw a black swan. Suddenly the unthinkable and unthought was real. People had always predicted that the next swan they saw would be white, but the discovery of black swans shattered this worldview.

Black Swans are just a metaphor, of course. Think of Pearl Harbor, the rise of the Internet, 9/11, and the recent banking crisis.

None of the events above was predicted—yet on reflection, the markers were all there. It's just that people weren't paying attention.

As Taleb uses the term, the Black Swan symbolizes the uselessness of predictions based on previous experience. Black Swans are events or pieces of knowledge that sit outside our regular expectations and therefore cannot be predicted.

This is a crucial concept in negotiation. In every negotiating session, there are different kinds of information. There are those things we know, like our counterpart's name and their offer and our experiences from other negotiations. Those are *known knowns*. There are those things we are certain that exist but we don't know, like the possibility that the other side might get sick and leave us with another counterpart. Those are *known unknowns* and they are like poker wild cards; you know they're out there but you don't know who has them. But most important are those things we don't know that we don't know, pieces of information we've never imagined but that would be game changing if uncovered. Maybe our counterpart wants the deal to fail because he's leaving for a competitor.

These *unknown unknowns* are Black Swans.

With their *known knowns* and prior expectations so firmly guiding their approach, Van Zandt, and really, the entire FBI, were blind to the clues and connections that showed there was something outside of the predictable at play. They couldn't see the Black Swans in front of them.

I don't mean to single out Van Zandt here. He did all of law enforcement a service by highlighting this event and he told me and a room full of agents the story of that horrible June day during a training session at Quantico. It was an introduction to the suicide-by-cop phenomenon—when an individual deliberately creates a crisis situation to provoke a lethal response from law enforcement—but there was an even greater lesson at stake: the point of the story then, and now, was how important it is to recognize the unexpected to make sure things like Moore's death never happen again.

On that day in June 1981, O'Brien kept calling the bank, but each time the bank employee who answered quickly hung up. It was at that moment they should have realized the situation was outside the *known*. Hostage-takers *always* talked because they *always* had demands; they *always* wanted to be heard, respected, and paid.

But this guy didn't.

Then, midway through the standoff, a police officer entered the command post with the news that a double homicide with a third person critically wounded had been reported a few blocks away.

"Do we need to know this?" Van Zandt said. "Is there a connection?"

No one knew or found out in time. If they had, they might have uncovered a second Black Swan: that Griffin had already killed several people without making monetary demands.

And then, a few hours in, the hostage-taker had one of the hostages read a note to the police over the phone. Curiously, there were no demands. Instead, it was a rambling diatribe about Griffin's life and the wrongs he'd endured. The note was so long and unfocused it was never read in its entirety. Because of this, one important line— another Black Swan—wasn't registered:

". . . after the police take my life . . ."

Because these Black Swans weren't uncovered, Van Zandt and his colleagues never saw the situation for what it was: Griffin wanted to die, and he wanted the police to do it for him.

Nothing like this—a shootout on a deadline?—had ever happened to the FBI, so they tried to fit the information into what had happened in the past. Into the old templates. They wondered, What does he *actually* want? After scaring them for a bit, they expected Griffin to pick up the phone and start a dialogue. No one gets killed on deadline.

Or so they thought.

UNCOVERING UNKNOWN UNKNOWNS

The lesson of what happened at 3 p.m. on June 17, 1981, in Rochester, New York, was that when bits and pieces of a case don't add up it's usually because our frames of reference are off; they will never add up unless we break free of our expectations.

Every case is new. We must let what we know—our *known knowns*—guide us but not blind us to what we do not know; we must remain flexible and adaptable to any situation; we must always retain a beginner's mind; and we must never overvalue our experience or undervalue the informational and emotional realities served up moment by moment in whatever situation we face.

But those were not the only important lessons of that tragic event. If an overreliance on *known knowns* can shackle a negotiator to assumptions that prevent him from seeing and hearing all that a situation presents, then perhaps an enhanced receptivity to the *unknown unknowns* can free that same negotiator to see and hear the things that can produce dramatic breakthroughs.

From the moment I heard the tale of June 17, 1981, I realized that I had to completely change how I approached negotiating. I began to hypothesize that in every negotiation each side is in possession of at least three Black Swans, three pieces of information that, were they to be discovered by the other side, would change everything.

My experience since has proven this to be true.

Now, I should note here that this is not just a small tweak to negotiation technique. It is not coincidence that I embraced Black Swan as the name of my company and the symbol of our approach.

Finding and acting on Black Swans mandates a shift in your mindset. It takes negotiation from being a one-dimensional move-countermove game of checkers to a three-dimensional game that's more emotional, adaptive, intuitive . . . and truly effective.

Finding Blacks Swans is no easy task, of course. We are all to some degree blind. We do not know what is around the corner until we turn it. By definition we do not know what we don't know.

That's why I say that finding and understanding Black Swans requires a change of mindset. You have to open up your established pathways and embrace more intuitive and nuanced ways of listening.

This is vital to people of all walks of life, from negotiators to inventors and marketers. What you don't know can kill you, or your deal. But to find it out is incredibly difficult. The most basic challenge is that people don't know the questions to ask the customer, the user . . . the counterpart. Unless correctly interrogated, most people aren't able to articulate the information you want. The world didn't tell Steve Jobs that it wanted an iPad: he uncovered our need, that Black Swan, without us knowing the information was there.

The problem is that conventional questioning and research techniques are designed to confirm *known knowns* and reduce uncertainty. They don't dig into the unknown.

Negotiations will always suffer from limited predictability. Your counterpart might tell you, "It's a lovely plot of land," without mentioning that it is also a Superfund site. They'll say, "Are the neighbors noisy? Well, everyone makes a bit of noise, don't they?" when the actual fact is that a heavy metal band practices there nightly.

It is the person best able to unearth, adapt to, and exploit the unknowns that will come out on top.

To uncover these unknowns, we must interrogate our world, must put out a call, and intensely listen to the response. Ask lots of questions. Read nonverbal clues and always voice your observations with your counterpart.

This is nothing beyond what you've been learning up to now. It is merely more intense and intuitive. You have to feel for the truth behind the camouflage; you have to note the small pauses that suggest discomfort and lies. Don't look to verify what you expect. If you do, that's what you'll find. Instead, you must open yourself up to the factual reality that is in front of you.

This is why my company changed its format for preparing and engaging in a negotiation. No matter how much research our team has done prior to the interaction, we always ask ourselves, "Why are they communicating what they are communicating right now?" Remember, negotiation is more like walking on a tightrope than competing against an opponent. Focusing so much on the end objective will only distract you from the next step, and that can cause you to fall off the rope. Concentrate on the next step because the rope will lead you to the end as long as all the steps are completed.

Most people expect that Black Swans are highly proprietary or closely guarded information, when in fact the information may seem completely innocuous. Either side may be completely oblivious to its importance. Your counterpart always has pieces of information whose value they do not understand.

THE THREE TYPES OF LEVERAGE

I'm going to come back to specific techniques for uncovering Black Swans, but first I'd like to examine what makes them so useful.

The answer is leverage. Black Swans are leverage multipliers. They give you the upper hand.

Now, "leverage" is the magic word, but it's also one of those concepts that negotiation experts casually throw about but rarely delve into, so I'd like to do so here.

In theory, leverage is the ability to inflict loss and withhold gain. Where does your counterpart want to gain and what do they fear losing? Discover these pieces of information, we are told, and you'll build leverage over the other side's perceptions, actions, and decisions. In practice, where our irrational perceptions are our reality, loss and

gain are slippery notions, and it often doesn't matter what leverage actually exists against you; what really matters is the leverage they think you
have on them. That's why I say there's always leverage: as an essentially
emotional concept, it can be manufactured whether it exists or not.

If they're talking to you, you have leverage. Who has leverage in a
kidnapping? The kidnapper or the victim's family? Most people think
the kidnapper has all the leverage. Sure, the kidnapper has something
you love, but you have something they lust for. Which is more powerful? Moreover, how many buyers do the kidnappers have for the commodity they are trying to sell? What business is successful if there's
only one buyer?

Leverage has a lot of inputs, like time and necessity and competition.
If you *need* to sell your house *now*, you have less leverage than if you
don't have a deadline. If you *want* to sell it but don't *have* to, you have
more. And if various people are bidding on it at once, good on you.

I should note that leverage isn't the same thing as power. Donald
Trump has tons of power, but if he's stranded in a desert and the
owner of the only store for miles has the water he wants, the vendor
has the leverage.

One way to understand leverage is as a fluid that sloshes between
the parties. As a negotiator you should always be aware of which side,
at any given moment, feels they have the most to lose if negotiations
collapse. The party who feels they have more to lose and are the most
afraid of that loss has less leverage, and vice versa. To get leverage, you
have to persuade your counterpart that they have something real to
lose if the deal falls through.

At a taxonomic level, there are three kinds: Positive, Negative, and
Normative.

POSITIVE LEVERAGE

Positive leverage is quite simply your ability as a negotiator to
provide—or withhold—things that your counterpart wants. Whenever

the other side says, "I want . . ." as in, "I want to buy your car," you have positive leverage.

When they say that, you have power: you can make their desire come true; you can withhold it and thereby inflict pain; or you can use their desire to get a better deal with another party.

Here's an example:

Three months after you've put your business on the market, a potential buyer finally tells you, "Yes, I'd like to buy it." You're thrilled, but a few days later your joy turns to disappointment when he delivers an offer so low it's insulting. This is the only offer you have, so what do you do?

Now, hopefully you've had contact with other buyers, even casually. If you have, you can use the offer to create a sense of competition, and thereby kick off a bidding war. At least you'll force them to make a choice.

But even if you don't have other offers or the interested buyer is your first choice, you have more power than before your counterpart revealed his desire. You control what they want. That's why experienced negotiators delay making offers—they don't want to give up leverage.

Positive leverage should improve your psychology during negotiation. You've gone from a situation where you want something from the investor to a situation where you both want something from each other.

Once you have it, you can then identify other things your opponent wants. Maybe he wants to buy your firm over time. Help him do that, if he'll increase the price. Maybe his offer is all the money he has. Help him get what he wants—your business—by saying you can only sell him 75 percent for his offer.

NEGATIVE LEVERAGE

Negative leverage is what most civilians picture when they hear the word "leverage." It's a negotiator's ability to make his counterpart suffer. And it is based on threats: you have negative leverage if you can tell your counterpart, "If you don't fulfill your commitment/pay your bill/etc., I will destroy your reputation."

This sort of leverage gets people's attention because of a concept we've discussed: *loss aversion.* As effective negotiators have long known and psychologists have repeatedly proved, potential losses loom larger in the human mind than do similar gains. Getting a good deal may push us toward making a risky bet, but saving our reputation from destruction is a much stronger motivation.

So what kind of Black Swans do you look to be aware of as negative leverage? Effective negotiators look for pieces of information, often obliquely revealed, that show what is important to their counterpart: Who is their audience? What signifies status and reputation to them? What most worries them? To find this information, one method is to go outside the negotiating table and speak to a third party that knows your counterpart. The most effective method is to gather it from interactions with your counterpart.

That said, a word of warning: I do not believe in making direct threats and am extremely careful with even subtle ones. Threats can be like nuclear bombs. There will be a toxic residue that will be difficult to clean up. You have to handle the potential of negative consequences with care, or you will hurt yourself and poison or blow up the whole process.

If you shove your negative leverage down your counterpart's throat, it might be perceived as you taking away their autonomy. People will often sooner die than give up their autonomy. They'll at least act irrationally and shut off the negotiation.

A more subtle technique is to label your negative leverage and thereby make it clear without attacking. Sentences like "It seems like you strongly value the fact that you've always paid on time" or "It seems like you don't care what position you are leaving me in" can really open up the negotiation process.

NORMATIVE LEVERAGE

Every person has a set of rules and a moral framework.

Normative leverage is using the other party's norms and standards to advance your position. If you can show inconsistencies between their beliefs and their actions, you have normative leverage. No one likes to look like a hypocrite.

For example, if your counterpart lets slip that they generally pay a certain multiple of cash flow when they buy a company, you can frame your desired price in a way that reflects that valuation.

Discovering the Black Swans that give you normative valuation can be as easy as asking what your counterpart believes and listening openly. You want to see what language they speak, and speak it back to them.

KNOW THEIR RELIGION

In March 2003 I led the negotiation with a farmer who became one of the most unlikely post-9/11 terrorists you can imagine.

The drama started when Dwight Watson, a North Carolina tobacco grower, hooked up his jeep to a John Deere tractor festooned with banners and an inverted U.S. flag and towed it to Washington, D.C., to protest government policies he thought were putting tobacco farmers out of business.

When Watson got to the capital, he pulled his tractor into a pond between the Washington Monument and the Vietnam Veterans Memorial and threatened to blow it up with the "organophosphate" bombs he claimed were inside.

The capital went into lockdown as the police blocked off an eight-block area from the Lincoln Memorial to the Washington Monument. Coming just months after the Beltway sniper attacks and alongside the buildup to the Iraq War, the ease with which Watson threw the nation's capital into turmoil freaked people out.

Talking on his cell phone, Watson told the *Washington Post* that he was on a do-or-die mission to show how reduced subsidies were killing tobacco farmers. He told the *Post* that God had instructed him to stage his protest and he wasn't going to leave.

"If this is the way America will be run, the hell with it," he said. "I will not surrender. They can blow [me] out of the water. I'm ready to go to heaven."

The FBI deployed me to a converted RV on the National Mall, where I was to guide a team of FBI agents and U.S. Park Police as we tried to talk Watson out of killing himself and who knows how many others.

And then we got down to business.

Like you'd expect of a negotiation with a guy threatening to destroy a good part of the U.S. capital, it was righteously tense. Sharpshooters had their weapons trained on Watson, and they had the "green light" to shoot if he made any crazy moves.

In any negotiation, but especially in a tense one like this, it's not how well you speak but how well you listen that determines your success. Understanding the "other" is a precondition to be able to speak persuasively and develop options that resonate for them. There is the visible negotiation and then all the things that are hidden under the surface (the secret negotiation space wherein the Black Swans dwell).

Access to this hidden space very often comes through understanding the other side's worldview, their *reason for being*, their religion. Indeed, digging into your counterpart's "religion" (sometimes involving God but not always) inherently implies moving beyond the negotiating table and into the life, emotional and otherwise, of your counterpart.

Once you've understood your counterpart's worldview, you can build influence. That's why as we talked with Watson I spent my energy trying to unearth who he was rather than logically arguing him into surrender.

From this we learned that Watson had been finding it increasingly hard to make a living on his 1,200-acre tobacco farm, which had been in his family for five generations. After being hit by a drought and having his crop quota cut by half, Watson decided he couldn't afford the farm anymore and drove to Washington to make his point. He wanted attention, and knowing what he wanted gave us positive leverage.

Watson also told us he was a veteran, and veterans had rules. This is the kind of music you want to hear, as it provides normative leverage. He told us that he would be willing to surrender, but not right away. As a military police officer in the 82nd Airborne in the 1970s, he'd learned that if he was trapped behind enemy lines, he could withdraw with honor if reinforcements didn't arrive within three days. But not before.

Now, we had articulated rules we could hold him to, and the admission that he could withdraw also implied that, despite his bluster about dying, he wanted to live. One of the first things you try to decide in a hostage negotiation is whether your counterpart's vision of the future involves them living. And Watson had answered yes.

We used this information—a piece of negative leverage, as we could take away something he wanted: life—and started working it alongside the positive leverage of his desire to be heard. We emphasized to Watson that he had already made national news and if he wanted his message to survive he was going to have to live.

Watson was smart enough to understand that there was a real chance he wouldn't make it out alive, but he still had his rules of military honor. His own desires and fears helped generate some positive and negative leverage, but they were secondary to the norms by which he lived his life.

It was tempting to just wait until the third day, but I doubted we'd get that far. With each passing hour the atmosphere was growing tenser. The capital was under siege and we had reason to believe he might have explosives. If he made one wrong move, one spastic freak-out, the snipers would kill him. He'd already had several angry out-bursts, so every hour that passed endangered him. He could still get himself killed.

But we couldn't hit on that at all; we couldn't threaten to kill him and expect that to work. The reason for that is something called the "paradox of power"—namely, the harder we push the more likely we are to be met with resistance. That's why you have to use negative leverage sparingly.

Still, time was short and we had to speed things up.

But how?

What happened next was one of those glorious examples of how deeply listening to understand your counterpart's worldview can reveal a Black Swan that transforms a negotiation dynamic. Watson didn't directly tell us what we needed to know, but by close attention we uncovered a subtle truth that informed everything he said.

About thirty-six hours in, Winnie Miller, an FBI agent on our team who'd been listening intently to subtle references Watson had been making, turned to me.

"He's a devout Christian," she told me. "Tell him tomorrow is the Dawn of the Third Day. That's the day Christians believe Jesus Christ left his tomb and ascended to Heaven. If Christ came out on the Dawn of the Third Day, why not Watson?"

It was a brilliant use of deep listening. By combining that subtext of Watson's words with knowledge of his worldview she let us show Watson that we not only were *listening*, but that we had also *heard* him.

If we'd understood his subtext correctly, this would let him end the standoff honorably and to do so with the feeling that he was surrendering to an adversary that respected him and his beliefs.

By positioning your demands within the worldview your counterpart uses to make decisions, you show them respect and that gets you attention and results. Knowing your counterpart's religion is more than just gaining normative leverage per se. Rather, it's gaining a holistic understanding of your counterpart's worldview—in this case, literally a religion—and using that knowledge to inform your negotiating moves.

Using your counterpart's religion is extremely effective in large part because it has authority over them. The other guy's "religion" is what the market, the experts, God, or society—whatever matters to him—has determined to be fair and just. And people defer to that authority.

In the next conversation with Watson, we mentioned that the next morning was the Dawn of the Third Day. There was a long moment of silence on the other end of the line. Our Negotiation Operation Center was so quiet you could hear the heartbeat of the guy next to you.

Watson coughed.

"I'll come out," he said.

And he did, ending a forty-eight-hour standoff, saving himself from harm, and allowing the nation's capital to resume its normal life.

No explosives were found.

While the importance of "knowing their religion" should be clear from Watson's story, here are two tips for reading religion correctly:

- Review everything you hear. You will not hear everything the first time, so double-check. Compare notes with your team members. You will often discover new information that will help you advance the negotiation.

- Use backup listeners whose only job is to listen between the lines. They will hear things you miss.

In other words: listen, listen again, and listen some more.

We've seen how a holistic understanding of your counterpart's "religion"—a huge Black Swan—can provide normative leverage that leads to negotiating results. But there are other ways in which learning your counterpart's "religion" enables you to achieve better outcomes.

THE SIMILARITY PRINCIPLE

Research by social scientists has confirmed something effective negotiators have known for ages: namely, we trust people more when we view them as being similar or familiar.

People trust those who are in their in-group. Belonging is a primal instinct. And if you can trigger that instinct, that sense that, "Oh, we see the world the same way," then you immediately gain influence.

When our counterpart displays attitudes, beliefs, ideas—even modes of dress—that are similar to our own, we tend to like and trust them more. Similarities as shallow as club memberships or college alumni status increase rapport.

That's why in many cultures negotiators spend large amounts of time building rapport before they even think of offers. Both sides know that the information they glean could be vital to effective deal making and leverage building. It's a bit like dogs circling each other, smelling each other's behind.

I once worked a deal for our services with this CEO in Ohio where the similarity principle played a major role.

My counterpart was constantly making references that I recognized as being sort of born-again Christian material. As we talked he kept going back and forth on whether he should bring in his advisors. The whole issue of his advisors clearly pained him; at one point he even said, "Nobody understands me."

At that moment I began to rack my brain for the Christian word that captured the essence of what he was saying. And then the term came to my mind, a term people often used in church to describe the duty one had to administer our own and our world's—and therefore God's—resources with honesty, accountability, and responsibility.

"This is really stewardship for you, isn't it?" I said.

His voice immediately strengthened.

"Yes! You're the only one who understands," he said.

And he hired us at that moment. By showing that I understood his deeper reasons for being and accessing a sense of similarity, of mutual belongingness, I was able to bring him to the deal. The minute I established a kind of shared identity with this Christian, we were in. Not simply because of similarity alone, but because of the understanding implied by that moment of similarity.

THE POWER OF HOPES AND DREAMS

Once you know your counterpart's religion and can visualize what he truly wants out of life, you can employ those aspirations as a way to get him to follow you.

Every engineer, every executive, every child—all of us want to believe we are capable of the extraordinary. As children, our daydreams feature ourselves as primary players in great moments: an actor winning an Oscar, an athlete hitting the game-winning shot. As we grow older, however, our parents, teachers, and friends talk more of what we can't and shouldn't do than what is possible. We begin to lose faith.

But when someone displays a passion for what we've always wanted and conveys a purposeful plan of how to get there, we allow our perceptions of what's possible to change. We're all hungry for a map to joy, and when someone is courageous enough to draw it for us, we naturally follow.

So when you ascertain your counterpart's unattained goals, invoke your own power and follow-ability by expressing passion for their goals—and for their ability to achieve them.

Ted Leonsis is great at this. As the owner of the Washington Wizards professional basketball team and the Washington Capitals professional hockey team, he is always talking about creating the immortal moments in sports that people will tell their grandchildren about. Who doesn't want to come to an agreement with someone who is going to make them immortal?

RELIGION AS A REASON

Research studies have shown that people respond favorably to requests made in a reasonable tone of voice and followed with a "because" reason.

In a famous study from the late 1970s,[3] Harvard psychology professor Ellen Langer and her colleagues approached people waiting for copy machines and asked if they could cut the line. Sometimes they gave a reason; sometimes they didn't. What she found was crazy: without her giving a reason, 60 percent let her through, but when she did give one, more than 90 percent did. And it didn't matter if the reason made sense. ("Excuse me, I have five pages. May I cut in line because I have to make copies?" worked great.) People just responded positively to the framework.

While idiotic reasons worked with something simple like photocopying, on more complicated issues you can increase your effectiveness by offering reasons that reference your counterpart's religion. Had that Christian CEO offered me a lowball offer when he agreed to hire my firm, I might have answered, "I'd love to but I too have a duty to be a responsible steward of my resources."

IT'S NOT CRAZY, IT'S A CLUE

It's not human nature to embrace the unknown. It scares us. When we are confronted by it, we ignore it, we run away, or we label it in ways that allow us to dismiss it. In negotiations, that label most often takes the form of the statement, "They're crazy!"

That's one reason I've been highly critical of some of the implementation of America's hostage negotiation policy—which is that we don't negotiate with those we refer broadly to as "the Terrorists," including groups from the Taliban to ISIS.

The rationale for this nonengagement is summarized well by the journalist Peter Bergen, CNN's national security analyst: "Negotiations with religious fanatics who have delusions of grandeur generally do not go well."

The alternative we've chosen is to *not* understand their religion, their fanaticism, and their delusions. Instead of negotiations that don't go well, we shrug our shoulders and say, "They're crazy!"

But that's absolutely wrongheaded. We must understand these things. I'm not saying that because I'm a softheaded pacifist (the FBI doesn't hire agents like that) but because I know understanding such things is the best way to discover the other side's vulnerabilities and wants and thereby gain influence. You can't get that stuff unless you talk.

No one is immune to "They're crazy!" You can see it rear its head in every kind of negotiation, from parenting to congressional deal making to corporate bargaining.

But the moment when we're most ready to throw our hands up and declare "They're crazy!" is often the best moment for discovering Black Swans that transform a negotiation. It is when we hear or see something that doesn't make sense—something "crazy"—that a crucial fork in the road is presented: push forward, even more forcefully, into that which we initially can't process; or take the other path, the one to guaranteed failure, in which we tell ourselves that negotiating was useless anyway.

In their great book *Negotiation Genius*,[4] Harvard Business School professors Deepak Malhotra and Max H. Bazerman provide a look at the common reasons negotiators mistakenly call their counterparts crazy. I'd like to talk through them here.

MISTAKE #1: THEY ARE ILL-INFORMED

Often the other side is acting on bad information, and when people have bad information they make bad choices. There's a great computer industry term for this: GIGO—Garbage In, Garbage Out.

As an example, Malhotra talks about a student of his who was in a dispute with an ex-employee who claimed he was owed $130,000 in commissions for work he had done before being fired; he was threatening a lawsuit.

Confused, the executive turned to the company's accountants. There he discovered the problem: the accounts had been a mess when the employee was fired but had since been put into order. With the clean information, the accountants assured the executive that in fact the employee owed the company $25,000.

Eager to avoid a lawsuit, the executive called the employee, explained the situation, and made an offer: if the employee dropped the lawsuit he could keep the $25,000. To his surprise, the employee said that he was going forward with the suit anyway; he acted irrational, crazy.

Malhotra told his student that the problem was not craziness, but a lack of information and trust. So the executive had an outside accounting firm audit the numbers and send the results to the employee.

The result? The employee dropped the suit.

The clear point here is that people operating with incomplete information appear crazy to those who have different information. Your job when faced with someone like this in a negotiation is to discover what they do not know and supply that information.

MISTAKE #2: THEY ARE CONSTRAINED

In any negotiation where your counterpart is acting wobbly, there exists a distinct possibility that they have things they can't do but aren't eager to reveal. Such constraints can make the sanest counterpart seem irrational. The other side might not be able to do something because of legal advice, or because of promises already made, or even to avoid setting a precedent.

Or they may just not have the power to close the deal.

That last situation is one that a client of mine faced as he was trying to land Coca-Cola as a client for his marketing firm.

The guy had been negotiating a deal for months and it was getting on to November. He was petrified that if he didn't close it before the calendar year ended he would have to wait for Coca-Cola to set a new budget and he might lose the client.

The problem was that his contact had suddenly stopped responding. So we told him to send a version of our classic email for nonresponders, the one that *always* works: "Have you given up on finalizing this deal this year?"

Then something weird happened. The Coca-Cola contact *didn't* respond to the perfect email. What was up?

This was superficially quite irrational, but the contact had been a straight-up guy until then. We told our client this could mean only one thing: that the guy *had* given up on closing the deal by the end of the year, but he didn't want to admit it. There had to be some constraint.

With this knowledge in hand, we had our client dig deep. After a batch of phone calls and emails he tracked down someone who knew his contact. And it turned out we had been right: the contact's division had been in chaos for weeks, and in the midst of corporate infighting he had completely lost influence. Not surprisingly, he was embarrassed to admit it. That's why he was avoiding my client.

To put it simply, he had major constraints.

MISTAKE #3: THEY HAVE OTHER INTERESTS

Think back to William Griffin, the first man ever to kill a hostage on deadline.

What the FBI and police negotiators on the scene simply did not know was that his main interest was not negotiating a deal to release the hostages for money. He wanted to be killed by a cop. Had they been able to dig up that hidden interest, they might have been able to avoid some of that day's tragedy.

The presence of hidden interests isn't as rare as you might think. Your counterpart will often reject offers for reasons that have nothing to do with their merits.

A client may put off buying your product so that their calendar year closes before the invoice hits, increasing his chance for a promotion. Or an employee might quit in the middle of a career-making project, just before bonus season, because he or she has learned that colleagues are making more money. For that employee, fairness is as much an interest as money.

Whatever the specifics of the situation, these people are not acting irrationally. They are simply complying with needs and desires that you don't yet understand, what the world looks like to them based on their own set of rules. Your job is to bring these Black Swans to light.

• • •

As we've seen, when you recognize that your counterpart is not irrational, but simply ill-informed, constrained, or obeying interests that you do not yet know, your field of movement greatly expands. And that allows you to negotiate much more effectively.

Here are a few ways to unearth these powerful Black Swans:

GET FACE TIME

Black Swans are incredibly hard to uncover if you're not literally at the table.

No matter how much research you do, there's just some information that you are not going to find out unless you sit face-to-face.

Today, a lot of younger people do almost everything over email. It's just how things are done. But it's very difficult to find Black Swans with email for the simple reason that, even if you knock your counterpart off their moorings with great labels and calibrated questions, email gives them too much time to think and re-center themselves to avoid revealing too much.

In addition, email doesn't allow for tone-of-voice effects, and it doesn't let you read the nonverbal parts of your counterpart's response (remember 7-38-55).

Let's return now to the tale of my client who was trying to get Coca-Cola as a client, only to learn that his contact at the company had been pushed aside.

I realized that the only way my client was going to get a deal with Coca-Cola was by getting his contact to admit that he was useless for the situation and pass my client on to the correct executive. But there was no way this guy wanted to do that, because he still imagined that he could be important.

So I told my client to get his contact out of the Coca-Cola complex. "You got to get him to dinner. You're going to say, 'Would it be a bad idea for me to take you to your favorite steak house and we just have a few laughs, and we don't talk business?'"

The idea was that no matter the reason—whether the contact was embarrassed, or didn't like my client, or just didn't want to discuss the situation—the only way the process was going to move forward was through direct human interaction.

So my client got this guy out for dinner and as promised he didn't bring up business. But there was no way not to talk about it, and just because my client created personal, face-to-face interaction, the contact admitted he was the wrong guy. He admitted that his division was a mess and he'd have to hand things off to somebody else to get the deal done.

And he did. It took more than a year to get the deal signed, but they did it.

OBSERVE UNGUARDED MOMENTS

While you have to get face time, formal business meetings, structured encounters, and planned negotiating sessions are often the least revealing kinds of face time because these are the moments when people are at their most guarded.

Hunting for Black Swans is also effective during unguarded moments at the fringes, whether at meals like my client had with his Coca-Cola contact, or the brief moments of relaxation before or after formal interactions.

During a typical business meeting, the first few minutes, before you actually get down to business, and the last few moments, as everyone is leaving, often tell you more about the other side than anything in between. That's why reporters have a credo to never turn off their recorders: you always get the best stuff at the beginning and the end of an interview.

Also pay close attention to your counterpart during interruptions, odd exchanges, or anything that interrupts the flow. When someone breaks ranks, people's façades crack just a little. Simply noticing whose cracks and how others respond verbally and nonverbally can reveal a gold mine.

WHEN IT DOESN'T MAKE SENSE, THERE'S CENTS TO BE MADE

Students often ask me whether Black Swans are specific kinds of information or any kind that helps. I always answer that they are anything that you don't know that changes things.

To drive this home, here's the story of one of my MBA students who was interning for a private equity real estate firm in Washington. Faced with actions from his counterpart that didn't pass the sense test, he innocently turned up one of the greatest Black Swans I've seen in years by using a label.

My student had been performing due diligence on potential targets when a principal at the firm asked him to look into a mixed-use property in the heart of Charleston, South Carolina. He had no experience in the Charleston market, so he called the broker selling the property and requested the marketing package.

After discussing the deal and the market, my student and his boss decided that the asking price of $4.3 million was about $450,000 too high. At that point, my student called the broker again to discuss pricing and next steps.

After initial pleasantries, the broker asked my student what he thought of the property.

"It looks like an interesting property," he said. "Unfortunately, we don't know the market fundamentals. We like downtown and King Street in particular, but we have a lot of questions."

The broker then told him that he had been in the market for more than fifteen years, so he was well informed. At this point, my student pivoted to **calibrated "How" and "What" questions** in order to gather information and judge the broker's skills.

"Great," my student said. "First and foremost, how has Charleston been affected by the economic downturn?"

The broker replied with a detailed answer, citing specific examples of market improvement. In the process, he showed my student that he was very knowledgeable.

"It sounds like I'm in good hands!" he said, **using a label to build empathy**. "Next question: What sort of cap rate can be expected in this type of building?"

Through the ensuing back-and-forth, my student learned that owners could expect rates of 6 to 7 percent because buildings like this were popular with students at the local university, a growing school where 60 percent of the student body lived off campus.

He also learned that it would be prohibitively expensive—if not physically impossible—to buy land nearby and build a similar building. In the last five years no one had built on the street because of historic preservation rules. Even if they could buy land, the broker said a similar building would cost $2.5 million just in construction.

"The building is in great shape, especially compared to the other options available to students," the broker said.

"It seems like this building functions more as a glorified dormitory than a classic multifamily building," my student said, **using a label to extract more information**.

And he got it.

"Fortunately and unfortunately, yes," the broker said. "The occupancy has historically been one hundred percent and it is a cash cow, but the students act like college students . . ."

A lightbulb went on in my student's head: there was something strange afoot. If it were such a cash cow, **why would someone sell a 100 percent occupied building located next to a growing campus in an affluent city?** That was irrational by any measure. A little befuddled but still in the negotiation mindset, my student constructed a label. Inadvertently he **mislabeled the situation**, triggering the broker to correct him and reveal a Black Swan.

"If he or she is selling such a cash cow, it seems like the seller must have doubts about future market fundamentals," he said.

"Well," he said, "the seller has some tougher properties in Atlanta and Savannah, so he has to get out of this property to pay back the other mortgages."

Bingo! With that, my student had unearthed a fantastic **Black Swan**. The seller was **suffering constraints** that, until that moment, had been unknown.

My student put the broker on mute as he described other properties and used the moment to discuss pricing with his boss. **He quickly gave him the green light to make a lowball offer—an extreme anchor—to try to yank the broker to his minimum.**

After quizzing the broker if the seller would be willing to close quickly, and getting a "yes," my student set his anchor.

"I think I have heard enough," he said. "We are willing to offer $3.4 million."

"Okay," the broker answered. "That is well below the asking price. However, I can bring the offer to the seller and see what he thinks."

Later that day, the broker came back with a counteroffer. The seller had told him that the number was too low, but he was willing to take $3.7 million. My student could barely keep from falling off his chair; the counteroffer was lower than his goal. But rather than jump at the amount—and risk leaving value on the table with a **wimp-win deal**—my student pushed further. **He said "No" without using the word.**

"That is closer to what we believe the value to be," he said, "but we cannot in good conscience pay more than $3.55 million."

(Later, my student told me—and I agreed—that he should have used a **label or calibrated question** here to push the broker to bid against himself. But he was so surprised by how far the price had dropped that he stumbled into old-school haggling.)

"I am only authorized to go down to $3.6 million," the broker answered, clearly showing that he'd never taken a negotiation class that taught **the Ackerman model and how to pivot to terms to avoid the haggle.**

My student's boss signaled to him that $3.6 million worked and he agreed to the price.

I've teased several of the techniques my student used to effectively negotiate a great deal for his firm, from **the use of labels and calibrated questions to the probing of constraints to unearth a beautiful Black Swan.** It also bears noting that my student did tons of work beforehand and had prepared labels and questions so that he was ready to jump on the Black Swan when the broker offered it.

Once he knew that the seller was trying to get money out of this building to pay off mortgages on the underperforming ones, he knew that timing was important.

Of course, there's always room for improvement. Afterward my student told me he wished he hadn't lowballed the offer so quickly and instead used the opportunity to discuss the other properties. He might have found more investment opportunities within the seller's portfolio.

In addition, he could have potentially built more **empathy** and teased out more unknown unknowns with labels or calibrated questions like "What markets are you finding difficult right now?" Maybe even gotten **face time with the seller directly**.

Still, well done!

OVERCOMING FEAR AND LEARNING TO GET WHAT YOU WANT OUT OF LIFE

People generally fear conflict, so they avoid useful arguments out of fear that the tone will escalate into personal attacks they cannot handle. People in close relationships often avoid making their own interests known and instead compromise across the board to avoid being perceived as greedy or self-interested. They fold, they grow bitter, and they grow apart. We've all heard of marriages that ended in divorce and the couple never fought.

Families are just an extreme version of all parts of humanity, from government to business. Except for a few naturals, everyone hates negotiation at first. Your hands sweat, your fight-or-flight kicks in (with a strong emphasis on *flight*), and your thoughts trip drunkenly over themselves.

The natural first impulse for most of us is to chicken out, throw in the towel, run. The mere idea of tossing out an extreme anchor is traumatic. That's why wimp-win deals are the norm in the kitchen and in the boardroom.

But stop and think about that. Are we *really* afraid of the guy across the table? I can promise you that, with very few exceptions, he's not going to reach across and slug you.

No, our sweaty palms are just an expression of physiological fear, a few trigger-happy neurons firing because of something more base: our innate human desire to get along with other members of the tribe. It's not the guy across the table who scares us: it's conflict itself.

If this book accomplishes only one thing, I hope it gets you over that fear of conflict and encourages you to navigate it with empathy. If you're going to be great at anything—a great negotiator, a great manager, a great husband, a great wife—you're going to have to do that. You're going to have to ignore that little genie who's telling you to give up, to just get along—as well as that other genie who's telling you to lash out and yell.

You're going to have to embrace regular, thoughtful conflict as the basis of effective negotiation—and of life. Please remember that our emphasis throughout the book is that the adversary is the situation and that the person that you appear to be in conflict with is actually your partner.

More than a little research has shown that genuine, honest conflict between people over their goals actually helps energize the problem-solving process in a collaborative way. Skilled negotiators have a talent for using conflict to keep the negotiation going without stumbling into a personal battle.

Remember, pushing hard for what you believe is not selfish. It is not bullying. It is not just helping you. Your amygdala, the part of the brain that processes fear, will try to convince you to give up, to flee, because the other guy is right, or you're being cruel.

But if you are an honest, decent person looking for a reasonable outcome, you can ignore the amygdala.

With the style of negotiation taught in the book—an information-obsessed, empathic search for the best possible deal—you are trying to uncover value, period. Not to strong-arm or to humiliate.

When you ask calibrated questions, yes, you are leading your counterpart to your goals. But you are also leading them to examine and articulate what they want and why and how they can achieve it. You are demanding creativity of them, and therefore pushing them toward a collaborative solution.

When I bought my red 4Runner, no doubt I disappointed the salesman by giving him a smaller payday than he would have liked. But I helped him reach his quota, and no doubt I paid more for the truck than the car lot had paid Toyota. If all I'd wanted was to "win," to humiliate, I would have stolen the thing.

And so I'm going to leave you with one request: Whether it's in the office or around the family dinner table, don't avoid honest, clear conflict. It will get you the best car price, the higher salary, and the largest donation. It will also save your marriage, your friendship, and your family.

One can only be an exceptional negotiator, and a great person, by both listening and speaking clearly and empathetically; by treating counterparts—and oneself—with dignity and respect; and most of all by being honest about what one wants and what one can—and cannot—do. Every negotiation, every conversation, every moment of life, is a series of small conflicts that, managed well, can rise to creative beauty.

Embrace them.

KEY LESSONS

What we don't know can kill us or our deals. But uncovering it can totally change the course of a negotiation and bring us unexpected success.

Finding the Black Swans—those powerful *unknown unknowns*—is intrinsically difficult, however, for the simple reason that we don't know the questions to ask. Because we don't know what the treasure is, we don't know where to dig.

Here are some of the best techniques for flushing out the Black Swans—and exploiting them. Remember, your counterpart might not even know how important the information is, or even that they shouldn't reveal it. So keep pushing, probing, and gathering information.

- Let what you know—your *known knowns*—guide you but not blind you. Every case is new, so remain flexible and adaptable. Remember the Griffin bank crisis: no hostage-taker had killed a hostage on deadline, until he did.

- Black Swans are leverage multipliers. Remember the three types of leverage: positive (the ability to give someone what they want); negative (the ability to hurt someone); and normative (using your counterpart's norms to bring them around).

- Work to understand the other side's "religion." Digging into worldviews inherently implies moving beyond the negotiating table and into the life, emotional and otherwise, of your counterpart. That's where Black Swans live.

- Review everything you hear from your counterpart. You will not hear everything the first time, so double-check. Compare notes with team members. Use backup listeners whose job is to listen between the lines. They will hear things you miss.

- Exploit the similarity principle. People are more apt to concede to someone they share a cultural similarity with, so dig for what makes them tick and show that you share common ground.

- When someone seems irrational or crazy, they most likely aren't. Faced with this situation, search for constraints, hidden desires, and bad information.

- Get face time with your counterpart. Ten minutes of face time often reveals more than days of research. Pay special attention to your counterpart's verbal and nonverbal communication at unguarded moments—at the beginning and the end of the session or when someone says something out of line.

ACKNOWLEDHEMENTS

This book would not have been possible without my son Brandon's help. Brandon has been involved in helping me shape and create these ideas since I first began teaching at Georgetown University. He was initially just there to video-record the classes but he also provided me feedback on how it was going and what was working. To be fair, he actually has been negotiating with me since he was two years old. I think I've known that ever since I found out he was using empathy to get out of trouble with his vice-principal in high school. In my first meeting with my brilliant cowriter, Tahl Raz, Brandon was there to keep the information flow going as Tahl soaked it up. In the first progress conference call with my amazing publisher, Hollis Heimbouch, Hollis asked about Brandon's role and Tahl said having Brandon around was like having another Chris in the room. Brandon has been indispensable.

Tahl Raz is a flat-out genius. Anyone who writes a business book without him hasn't gotten as far as they could have. It's that simple. I can't believe how smart he is or how quickly he gets it. He is a true business-writing artist. He's a great person as well.

Steve Ross, my agent, is a man of integrity and was perfect for this book. He has great industry knowledge and made this book happen. I am grateful to know him.

Hollis Heimbouch rocks! I am thrilled that she led the HarperCollins team and believed enough in this book to buy it. Thank you, Hollis.

Thank you, Maya Stevenson, for coming onto the Black Swan team and holding us together. We are going farther because of you.

Sheila Heen and John Richardson are two amazing people. They are the ones who really paved the way to show that these hostage negotiation ideas belong in the business world. Sheila was my teacher at Harvard Law School. She inspired me with how she taught and who she is. She asked me to teach alongside her two years later. John asked me to teach International Business Negotiation at Harvard alongside him a year after that. He guided me through that process, which led to the opportunity to become an adjunct at Georgetown. When nothing was happening for me, both John and Sheila were there. Without them I don't know where I'd be. Thank you both.

Gary Noesner was my mentor at the FBI. He inspired and remade the hostage negotiation world (with the help of his team at the Crisis Negotiation Unit—CNU). He supported me in whatever I wanted to do. He made me the FBI's lead international kidnapping negotiator. I could call Gary at five a.m. and tell him I was getting on a plane in three hours to go to a kidnapping and he would say, "Go." His support never wavered. At CNU he pulled together the most talented collection of hostage negotiators ever assembled. CNU hit its zenith when we were there. None of us knew how lucky we were. John Flood, Vince Dalfonzo, Chuck Regini, Winnie Miller, Manny Suarez, Dennis Braiden, Neil Purtell, and Steve Romano were all rock stars. I learned from you all. I can't believe what Chuck put up with from me as my partner. Dennis was a mentor and great friend. I constantly clashed with Vince and grew because of his talent.

All those who were on the FBI Critical Incident Negotiation Team during that time taught me as well. Thank you.

Tommy Corrigan and John Liguori were my brothers when I was in New York City. The three of us did extraordinary things together. I am inspired by the memory of Tommy Corrigan to this day. I was privileged to be a member of the Joint Terrorist Task Force. We fought evil. Richie DeFilippo and Charlie Beaudoin were exceptional wingmen on the Crisis Negotiation Team. Thank you both for all you taught me.

Hugh McGowan and Bob Louden from the NYPD's Hostage Negotiation Team shared their wisdom with me. Both of you have been indispensable assets to the hostage negotiation world. Thank you.

Derek Gaunt has been a great wingman in the Washington, D.C., metropolitan area. Derek gets it. Thank you, Derek. Kathy Ellingsworth and her late husband, Bill, have been dear friends and a sounding board for years. I am grateful for your support and friendship.

Tom Strentz is the godfather of the FBI's hostage/crisis negotiation program and has been an unwavering friend. I can't believe he still takes my calls.

My students at Georgetown and USC have constantly proved that these ideas work everywhere. More than one student has stopped breathing when I looked at them and said, "I need a car in sixty seconds or she dies." Thanks for coming along for the ride. Georgetown and USC have both been phenomenal places to teach. Both are truly dedicated to higher learning, the highest academic standards, and the success of their students.

The hostages and their families who allowed me in during their darkest hours to try to help are all blessed people. I am grateful to still be in touch with some of you today. What wisdom there is in the universe that decided your paths were necessary, I don't understand. I was blessed by your grace. (I need all the help I can get.)

PREPARE A NEGOTIATION ONE SHEET

Negotiation is a psychological investigation. You can gain a measure of confidence going into such an investigation with a simple preparatory exercise we advise all our clients to do. Basically, it's a list of the primary tools you anticipate using, such as labels and calibrated questions, customized to the particular negotiation.

When the pressure is on, you don't rise to the occasion—you fall to your highest level of preparation.

One note of caution before going into greater depth on this exercise: some negotiation experts fetishize preparation to such a degree that they advise people to create the equivalent of preordained scripts for exactly how the negotiation will unfold and the exact form and substance the agreement will take on. By now, after reading this far, you'll understand why that's a fool's errand. Not only will such an approach make you less agile and creative at the table, it will make you more susceptible to those who are.

Based on my company's experiences, I believe that good initial preparation for each negotiation yields at least a 7:1 rate of return on time saved renegotiating deals or clarifying implementation.

In the entertainment industry, they have a single document that summarizes a product for publicity and sales that they call a "one sheet." Along the same lines, we want to produce a negotiation "one sheet" that summarizes the tools we are going to use.

It will have five short sections

SECTION I: THE GOAL

Think through best/worst-case scenarios but only write down a specific goal that represents the best case.

Typically, negotiation experts will tell you to prepare by making a list: your bottom line; what you really want; how you're going to try to get there; and counters to your counterpart's arguments.

But this typical preparation fails in many ways. It's unimaginative and leads to the predictable bargaining dynamic of offer/counteroffer/ meet in the middle. In other words, it gets results, but they're often mediocre.

The centerpiece of the traditional preparation dynamic—and its greatest Achilles' heel—is something called the BATNA.

Roger Fisher and William Ury coined the term in their 1981 best-seller, *Getting to Yes*, and it stands for Best Alternative To a Negotiated Agreement. Basically, it's the best possible option you have if negotiations fail. Your last resort. Say you're on a car lot trying to sell your old BMW 3-series. If you already have another dealer who's given you a written offer for $10,000, that's your BATNA.

The problem is that BATNA tricks negotiators into aiming low. Researchers have found that humans have a limited capacity for keeping focus in complex, stressful situations like negotiations. And so, once a negotiation is under way, we tend to gravitate toward the focus point that has the most psychological significance for us.

In that context, obsessing over a BATNA turns it into your target, and thereby sets the upper limit of what you will ask for. After you've spent hours on a BATNA, you mentally concede everything beyond it.

God knows aiming low is seductive. Self-esteem is a huge factor in negotiation, and many people set modest goals to protect it. It's easier to claim victory when you aim low. That's why some negotiation experts say that many people who think they have "win-win" goals really have a "wimp-win" mentality. The "wimp-win" negotiator focuses on his or her bottom line, and that's where they end up.

So if BATNA isn't your centerpiece, what should be?

I tell my clients that as part of their preparation they should think about the outcome extremes: best *and* worst. If you've got both ends covered, you'll be ready for anything. So know what you cannot accept and have an idea about the best-case outcome, but keep in mind that since there's information yet to be acquired from the other side, it's quite possible that best case might be even better than you know.

Remember, never be so sure of what you want that you wouldn't take something better. Once you've got flexibility in the forefront of your mind you come into a negotiation with a winning mindset.

Let's say you're selling old speakers because you need $100 to put toward a new set. If you concentrate on the $100 minimum, you'll relax when you hear that number and that's what you'll get. But if you know that they are for sale in used audio stores for $140, you could set a high-end goal of $150, while remaining open to better things.

Now, while I counsel thinking about a best/worst range to give my clients the security of some structure, when it comes to what actually goes on your one sheet, my advice is to just stick with the high-end goal, as it will motivate and focus your psychological powers, priming you to think you are facing a "loss" for any term that falls short. Decades of goal-setting research is clear that people who set specific, challenging, but realistic goals end up getting better deals than those who don't set goals or simply strive to do their best.

Bottom line: People who expect more (and articulate it) get more.

Here are the four steps for setting your goal:

- Set an optimistic but reasonable goal and define it clearly.

- Write it down.

- Discuss your goal with a colleague (this makes it harder to wimp out).

- Carry the written goal into the negotiation.

SECTION II: SUMMARY

Summarize and write out in just a couple of sentences the known facts that have led up to the negotiation.

You're going to have to have something to talk about beyond a self-serving assessment of what you want. And you had better be ready to respond with tactical empathy to your counterpart's arguments; unless they're incompetent, the other party will come prepared to argue an interpretation of the facts that favors them.

Get on the same page at the outset.

You have to clearly describe the lay of the land before you can think about acting in its confines. Why are you there? What do you want? What do they want? Why?

You must be able to summarize a situation in a way that your counterpart will respond with a "That's right." If they don't, you haven't done it right.

SECTION III: LABELS/ACCUSATION AUDIT

Prepare three to five labels to perform an accusation audit.

Anticipate how your counterpart feels about these facts you've just summarized. Make a concise list of any accusations they might make—no matter how unfair or ridiculous they might be. Then turn each accusation into a list of no more than five labels and spend a little time role-playing it.

There are fill-in-the-blank labels that can be used in nearly every situation to extract information from your counterpart, or defuse an accusation:

It seems like _____ is valuable to you.

It seems like you don't like _____.

It seems like you value _____.

It seems like _____ makes it easier.

It seems like you're reluctant to _____.

As an example, if you're trying to renegotiate an apartment lease to allow subletters and you know the landlord is opposed to them, your prepared labels would be on the lines of "It seems as though you're not a fan of subletters" or "It seems like you want stability with your tenants."

SECTION IV: CALIBRATED QUESTIONS

Prepare three to five calibrated questions to reveal value to you and your counterpart and identify and overcome potential deal killers.

Effective negotiators look past their counterparts' stated positions (*what* the party demands) and delve into their underlying motivations (*what* is making them want what they want). Motivations are what they are worried about and what they hope for, even lust for.

Figuring out what the other party is worried about sounds simple, but our basic human expectations about negotiation often get in the way. Most of us tend to assume that the needs of the other side conflict with our own. We tend to limit our field of vision to our issues and problems, and forget that the other side has its own unique issues based on its own unique worldview. Great negotiators get past these blinders by being relentlessly curious about what is *really* motivating the other side.

Harry Potter author J. K. Rowling has a great quote that sums up this concept: "You must accept the reality of other people. You think that reality is up for negotiation, that we think it's whatever you say it is. You must accept that we are as real as you are; you must accept that you are not God."

There will be a small group of "What" and "How" questions that you will find yourself using in nearly every situation. Here are a few of them:

What are we trying to accomplish?

How is that worthwhile?

What's the core issue here?

How does that affect things?

What's the biggest challenge you face?

How does this fit into what the objective is?

QUESTIONS TO IDENTIFY BEHIND-THE-TABLE DEAL KILLERS

When implementation happens by committee, the support of that committee is key. You'll want to tailor your calibrated questions to identify and unearth the motivations of those behind the table, including:

How does this affect the rest of your team?

How on board are the people not on this call?

What do your colleagues see as their main challenges in this area?

QUESTIONS TO IDENTIFY AND DIFFUSE DEAL-KILLING ISSUES

Internal negotiating influence often sits with the people who are most comfortable with things as they are. Change may make them look as if they haven't been doing their job. Your dilemma in such a negotiation is how to make them look good in the face of that change.

You'll be tempted to concentrate on money, but put that aside for now. A surprisingly high percentage of negotiations hinge on something outside dollars and cents. Often they have more to do with self-esteem, status, autonomy, and other nonfinancial needs.

Think about their perceived losses. Never forget that a loss stings at least twice as much as an equivalent gain.

For example, the guy across the table may be hesitating to install the new accounting system he needs (and you are selling) because he doesn't want to screw anything up before his annual review in four months' time. Instead of lowering your price, you can offer to help impress his boss, and do it safely, by promising to finish the installation in ninety days, guaranteed.

QUESTIONS TO USE TO UNEARTH THE DEAL-KILLING ISSUES

What are we up against here?

   What is the biggest challenge you face?

   How does making a deal with us affect things?

   What happens if you do nothing?

   What does doing nothing cost you?

   How does making this deal resonate with what your company prides itself on?

It's often very effective to ask these in groups of two or three as they are similar enough that they help your counterpart think about the same thing from different angles.

Every situation is unique, of course, but choosing the right mix of these questions will lead your counterpart to reveal information about what they want and need—and simultaneously push them to see things from your point of view.

Be ready to execute follow-up labels to their answers to your calibrated questions.

Having labels prepared will allow you to quickly turn your

counterpart's responses back to them, which will keep them feeding you new and expanding information. Again, these are fill-in-the-blank labels that you can use quickly without tons of thought:

It seems like _____ *is important.*

It seems you feel like my company is in a unique position to _____.

It seems like you are worried that _____.

SECTION V: NONCASH OFFERS

Prepare a list of noncash items possessed by your counterpart that would be valuable.

Ask yourself: "What could they give that would almost get us to do it for free?" Think of the anecdote I told a few chapters ago about my work for the lawyers' association: My counterpart's interest was to pay me as little cash as possible in order to look good in front of his board. We came upon the idea that they pay in part by publishing a cover story about me in their magazine. That was low-cost for them and it advanced my interests considerably.

For more information on my company, The Black Swan Group, any additional information or guidance we can give you on negotiation, or for contacting me about speaking to your company, please visit our website at www.blackswanltd.com.

NOTES

CHAPTER 1: THE NEW RULES

1. Robert Mnookin, *Bargaining with the Devil: When to Negotiate, When to Fight* (New York: Simon & Schuster, 2010).

2. Roger Fisher and William Ury, *Getting to Yes: Negotiating Agreement Without Giving In* (Boston: Houghton Mifflin, 1981).

3. Daniel Kahneman, *Thinking, Fast and Slow* (New York: Farrar, Straus & Giroux, 2011).

4. Philip B. Heymann and United States Department of Justice, *Lessons of Waco: Proposed Changes in Federal Law Enforcement* (Washington, DC: U.S. Department of Justice, 1993).

CHAPTER 2: BE A MIRROR

1. George A. Miller, "The Magical Number Seven, Plus or Minus Two: Some Limits on Our Capacity for Processing Information," *Psychological Review* 63, no. 2 (1956): 81–97.

CHAPTER 3: DON'T FEEL THEIR PAIN, LABEL IT

1. Greg J. Stephens, Lauren J. Silbert, and Uri Hasson, "Speaker–Listener Neural Coupling Underlies Successful Communication,"

Proceedings of the National Academy of Sciences of the USA 107, no. 32 (August 10, 2010): 14425–30.

2. Matthew D. Lieberman et al., "Putting Feelings into Words: Affect Labeling Disrupts Amygdala Activity in Response to Affective Stimuli," *Psychological Science* 18, no. 5 (May 2007): 421–28.

CHAPTER 4: BEWARE "YES"—MASTER "NO"

1. Jim Camp, *Start with NO: The Negotiating Tools That the Pros Don't Want You to Know* (New York: Crown Business, 2002).

CHAPTER 6: BEND THEIR REALITY

1. Herb Cohen, *You Can Negotiate Anything* (Secaucus, NJ: Lyle Stuart, 1980).

2. Antonio R. Damasio, *Descartes' Error: Emotion, Reason, and the Human Brain* (New York: Quill, 2000).

3. Jeffrey J. Fox, *How to Become a Rainmaker: The People Who Get and Keep Customers* (New York: Hyperion, 2000).

4. Daniel Ames and Malia Mason, "Tandem Anchoring: Informational and Politeness Effects of Range Offers in Social Exchange," *Journal of Personality and Social Psychology* 108, no. 2 (February 2015): 254–74.

CHAPTER 7: CREATE THE ILLUSION OF CONTROL

1. Kevin Dutton, *Split-Second Persuasion: The Ancient Art and New Science of Changing Minds* (Boston: Houghton Mifflin Harcourt, 2011).

2. Dhruv Khullar, "Teaching Doctors the Art of Negotiation," *New York Times*, January 23, 2014, http://well.blogs.nytimes.com /2014/01/23/teaching-doctors-the-art-of-negotiation/, accessed September 4, 2015.

CHAPTER 8: GUARANTEE EXECUTION

1. Albert Mehrabian, *Silent Messages: Implicit Communication of Emotions and Attitudes*, 2nd ed. (Belmont, CA: Wadsworth, 1981), and Albert Mehrabian, *Nonverbal Communication* (Chicago: Aldine-Atherton, 1972).

2. Lyn M. Van Swol, Michael T. Braun, and Deepak Malhotra, "Evidence for the Pinocchio Effect: Linguistic Differences Between Lies, Deception by Omissions, and Truths," *Discourse Processes* 49, no. 2 (2012): 79–106.

CHAPTER 9: BARGAIN HARD

1. Gerald R. Williams, *Legal Negotiations and Settlement* (St. Paul, MN: West, 1983).

2. Marwan Sinaceur and Larissa Tiedens, "Get Mad and Get More than Even: The Benefits of Anger Expressions in Negotiations," *Journal of Experimental Social Psychology* 42, no. 3 (2006): 314–22.

3. Daniel R. Ames and Abbie Wazlawek, "Pushing in the Dark: Causes and Consequences of Limited Self-Awareness for Interpersonal Assertiveness," *Personality and Social Psychology Bulletin* 40, no. 6 (2014): 1–16.

CHAPTER 10: FIND THE BLACK SWAN

1. Nassim Nicholas Taleb, *Fooled by Randomness: The Hidden Role of Chance in Life and in the Markets* (New York: Random House, 2001).

2. Nassim Nicholas Taleb, *The Black Swan: The Impact of the Highly Improbable* (New York: Random House, 2007).

3. Ellen J. Langer, Arthur Blank, and Benzion Chanowitz, "The Mindlessness of Ostensibly Thoughtful Action: The Role of 'Placebic' Information in Interpersonal Interaction," *Journal of Personality and Social Psychology* 36, no. 6 (1978): 635–42.

4. Deepak Malhotra and Max H. Bazerman, *Negotiation Genius: How to Overcome Obstacles and Achieve Brilliant Results at the Bargaining Table and Beyond* (New York: Bantam Books, 2007).

INDEX